Birds of Eastern North America

Birds

of *Eastern* North America

A PHOTOGRAPHIC GUIDE

PAUL STERRY & BRIAN E. SMALL

Princeton University Press

Princeton and Oxford

Published by Princeton University Press
41 William Street, Princeton, New Jersey 08540

Requests for permission to reproduce material from this work should be sent to Permissions, Princeton University Press

In the United Kingdom: Princeton University Press, 6 Oxford Street, Woodstock, Oxfordshire OX20 1TW

Maps modified from Birds of North America Online

Sterry, Paul.
    Birds of Eastern North America : a photographic guide / Paul Sterry and Brian E. Small. — 1st ed.
        p. cm.
    Includes bibliographical references and index.
    ISBN 978-0-691-13425-3 (cloth : alk. paper)—ISBN 978-0-691-13426-0 (pbk. : alk. paper) 1. Birds—East (U.S.)—Identification. 2. Birds—Canada, Eastern—Identification. 3. Birds—East (U.S.)—Pictorial works. 4. Birds—Canada, Eastern—Pictorial works. I. Small, Brian E., 1959- II. Title.
    QL683.E27S74 2009
    598.0974—dc22   2009001494

British Library Cataloging-in-Publication Data is available

This book has been composed in ITC Officina Sans and Serif

Printed on acid-free paper

nathist.princeton.edu

Photograph page 1: Scarlet Tanager
Photograph previous page: Eastern Bluebird
Photographs opposite: Ovenbird (top), Eastern Bluebird (bottom left), Ross's Goose (bottom middle), Northern Cardinal (bottom right)

Edited and designed by D & N Publishing, Baydon, Wiltshire, UK

Printed in China by C&C Offset Printing Co.

10 9 8 7 6 5 4 3 2 1

CONTENTS

INTRODUCTION TO NORTH AMERICAN BIRDS

North America is a vast continent that embraces a huge range of climate types and habitats, from Arctic tundra and vast boreal forests in the far north, through extensive stands of temperate, deciduous forests, open grassland and wetlands galore, and superb and varied coastline, to deserts and subtropical woodland in the south. All this has resulted in the region supporting such an amazing diversity of birdlife: over 600 species are seen regularly in the region, and over 900 have been recorded in total. Man too has left his mark on the North American landscape and the history of land-use has benefited some species but been to the cost of many others.

Given the rewards on offer, it is little wonder then that birding is so popular as a hobby. The enthusiastic passion for birds we see today is founded on a heritage of detailed and dedicated ornithological study dating back two centuries or more. *Birds of Eastern North America* builds on this cumulative wealth of knowledge, providing an instructive tool for the identification of almost any bird you are likely to encounter in our region. Furthermore, the inclusion of pertinent background information helps the reader put each species in ornithological perspective and to understand the factors influencing the status—and, in many cases, the *plight*—of North American birds today.

THE REGION COVERED BY THIS BOOK

The region covered by this book comprises the whole of the eastern half of mainland North America and the Arctic and sub-Arctic islands within the territories of the U.S. and Canada. Mexico is not covered specifically in this book. However, reference is made to the Mexican distribution of a few species whose range straddles the border, and reference is also made to Mexico and other Central and South American countries in the context of wintering ranges of certain migratory North American breeding birds. The seas that fringe the North American continent are also included in the geographical extent of this book because of their obvious significance to many of our seabirds, some of which favor off-

shore waters and spend much of their lives out of sight of land. They are just as much a part of our ornithological heritage as terrestrial species and, with the rise in popularity of pelagic birding trips, they are increasingly accessible to birders.

THE CHOICE OF SPECIES

This book is intended to cater to the needs of the keen birder—the sort of person whose enthusiasm is built on several years of experience—while not neglecting the needs of the beginner. All our resident species are included here, as well as seasonal visitors to the region—those that are with us in spring and summer, as well as birds that visit us during the winter months. In addition, species that occur regularly as passage migrants—birds that pass through on migration in spring and fall (mainly seabirds)—are also included. As a reflection of their importance to birding in our region, the bulk of the book is devoted to all these common, or relatively frequently occurring, species.

Accompanying the rise in popularity of birding in general, there has been an increased interest in, and knowledge of, vagrants to the region and of geographically localized rarities. To cater to this, a generous selection of out of the ordinary species is included in the book; these are featured at the back, partly as a reflection of their lesser importance in the scheme of things overall, but also to reduce the likelihood of optimistic misidentification of the more common species.

Male Blue Grosbeak singing: vocalization can be extremely important in bird identification.

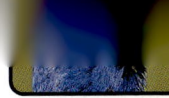

HOW TO USE THIS BOOK

This book has been designed so that the text and photographs for each species are on facing pages. A system of labeling states the identity and, if appropriate, the plumage and sex, of each photograph. The text has been written to complement the information conveyed by the photographs.

By and large, the order in which the species appear in the main section of the book roughly follows the standard systematic classification of birds, which is adopted by most contemporary field guides. However, in a few instances the standard running order has been tinkered with to allow, for example, confusingly similar species to appear on the same page, and so that, where possible, members of the same group of birds can appear side-by-side on the same page.

SPECIES DESCRIPTIONS

At the start of each species description the most commonly used and current American name is given. This is followed by the scientific name of the bird in question, which comprises the species' genus name first, followed by its specific name. In a few instances, reference is made, either in the species heading or the main body of the text, to a further subdivision—subspecies— where this is pertinent. There then follows some measure of the species' size. In most instances, the length ("L" in inches) is given, but for birds that are more commonly seen in flight, such as birds of prey, wingspan ("W" in inches) is given instead.

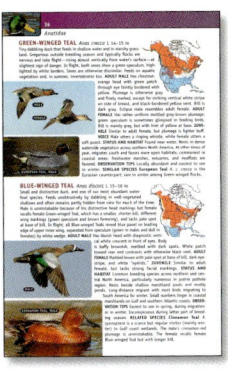

The text has been written in as concise a manner as possible. To avoid potential ambiguities in species descriptions, for example with regards to which age or sex is being described, the plumage in question appears in bold at the start of the relevant passage of text.

VOICE

Information is then given about the voice of the bird; in most cases this involves a phonetic description of the call and, with the majority of songbirds, the song itself is also portrayed.

STATUS AND HABITAT

Details about the status of each species in the region is then given. This includes an indication of whether it is common or otherwise, and whether it is a year-round resident, or a seasonal visitor or passage migrant. A rough indication of population numbers is given in a few instances. Most birds are extremely habitat-specific and so information is provided about their preferences. Not only does this help narrow down the field for observers trying to identify a mystery bird, but it can also be used as a pointer if you want to actively seek out a particular species.

OBSERVATION TIPS

For each species, information is provided that will help birders pinpoint where to see the bird in question, or at least improve the chances of discovery or observation. In some cases, tips are provided that will help distinguish the species from any superficially similar relatives.

MAPS

The maps provide invaluable information about the distribution and occurrence of each species in the region. Three colors have been employed to assist the reader in getting the maximum information from the maps: ■ represents the range where a species is present year-round; ■ represents the range where a species is present only in summer, typically its breeding season; ■ represents the range where a species is present only in winter. The maps represent the current ranges of birds in the region in general terms. Please bear in mind that, given the size of the maps, small and isolated populations will not necessarily be featured. Furthermore, the ranges of some species changes from year to year; this is particularly true of certain winter visitors and passage migrants.

PHOTOGRAPHS

Great care has gone into the selection of photographs for this book and in many cases the images have been taken specifically for this project. Preference has been given to photographs that serve both to illustrate key identification features and to emphasize the beauty of the bird in question. Wherever possible, the rigid constraints of most previous photographic guides to birds have been avoided and contemporary approaches to design have been employed.

For each species, photographic emphasis has been given to the plumage, or plumages, most likely to be encountered in the region. However, by using inset photographs, on both the right-hand and left-hand pages, as comprehensive a range of additional plumages and poses as possible has been included.

TOPOGRAPHY

axillaries

underwing coverts

undertail coverts

tail

tertials

secondaries

tarsus

primaries

crown

eye

lore

supercilium

upper mandible (bill)

ear coverts

lower mandible (bill)

mantle

throat

breast

median coverts

greater coverts

tertials

flank

rump

secondaries

primaries

belly

tarsus

undertail coverts

tail

GLOSSARY

Axillaries Feathers on the part of the underwing that corresponds roughly to what we might call the "armpit."

Carpal The part of the wing that corresponds to the "wrist"; this area of feathering is contrastingly dark in several raptor species.

Cere Bare skin at the base of the bill and around the nostrils.

Eclipse The femalelike plumage acquired by many male ducks during their summer molt.

Eyestripe A stripe through the eye, from the base of the bill to the ear coverts.

1st-fall A bird in its first fall, whose plumage may be juvenile or 1st-winter, depending on when molt occurs.

1st-winter The plumage acquired after a bird's juvenile feathers have been molted.

Flight feathers The long feathers (primaries, secondaries, and tertials) on the trailing half of the wing.

Immature A young bird whose plumage is not adult. Depending on the species, this stage may last months or years.

Juvenile A newly fledged bird in its first set of feathers.

Length The distance from the tip of the bill to the tip of the center of the tail.

Leucistic Atypically pale appearance of the plumage, or parts of the plumage, due to a lack of feather pigmentation.

Lore Area of feathering between the eye and the base of the upper mandible.

Malar stripe Narrow stripe of feathers that borders the throat.

Mantle Area of feathers on the upper back.

Molt The process of feather replacement in the cycle of plumage renewal.

Mustachial stripe A line of feathers running from the base of the lower mandible to the cheeks.

Orbital ring Ring of bare skin surrounding the eye.

Pelagic Favoring the open sea.

Primaries The outermost flight feathers.

Secondaries The middle flight feathers.

Species (sp.) A group of genetically similar individuals, members of which can reproduce with one another and produce viable offspring; fertile offspring cannot be produced when members of two separate species interbreed.

Speculum A glossy patch seen on the upper secondaries of some duck species.

Submustachial stripe The line of feathers (typically contrastingly pale) between the malar and moustachial stripes.

Subspecies (ssp.) A population of individuals of a given species that possess distinct plumage differences from other populations; these are often geographically separated.

Supercilium A typically pale stripe of feathers that runs much of the length of the head above the eye.

Tarsus What most people refer to as a bird's "leg," although strictly speaking it is anatomically part of the foot.

Tertials The innermost flight feathers

Tibia The visible upper part of a bird's leg.

Vagrant A bird that appears accidentally outside the species' typical range, be that breeding, nonbreeding, or on migration.

Wing bar A striking bar on the wings (typically either white or dark), formed by pale or dark margins to the wing covert feathers.

Wing coverts The feathers that cloak the leading half (as seen in flight) of both surfaces of the wings.

Wingspan The distance from one wingtip to the other.

PLUMAGE

Birds are unique in many respects, but perhaps their most visible characteristic is the layer of feathers that covers their bodies. These serve a variety of functions in the day-to-day lives of birds, and feathers on different parts of the body have evolved for a range of purposes. Those that cover the bulk of the body provide superb insulation against the cold and, to varying degrees, waterproofing too. And of course there are the feathers on the wing that enable flight in all its forms to take place. From the birder's point of view, feathers are there to be marveled at but, when interpreted correctly, they can also provide a wealth of information about the bird in question. The sex of an individual can often be told at a glance and, in addition, its age and whether or not it is in breeding or nonbreeding plumage can also be discerned in many cases. Such information is interesting in its own right but more importantly it offers clues to birders with regards to identification.

From the bird's point of view, the colors and plumage patterns are fundamentally important: during the breeding season, social responses are often dictated by appearance while at the other extreme, for birds with camouflaged plumage, the ability to blend in with the surroundings can mean the difference between life and death.

Feathers do not grow continually like mammalian hair, and once they are fully formed they are essentially dead. As a result of the wear and tear of everyday life, the feathers become abraded and over a period of time the patterns and colors fade. And it is not just a bird's appearance that can change due to wear: flight feathers can become worn and damaged to the point that the ability to fly is impaired. To combat this gradual deterioration, birds molt and replace their feathers on a regular basis.

In most cases, molting occurs at specific times of the year and takes place over a comparatively brief space of time. For most birds, the main molt occurs in late summer, after the breeding season has finished; many migratory birds that breed in the region molt before they embark on their journeys in fall. Some birds, notably many passerines, have very distinct breeding and nonbreeding (or summer and winter) plumages. For some, the transformation is achieved by having a second, partial molt, in the spring, but with certain groups, such as buntings and finches, comparatively dowdy plumage seen in fall and winter gives way to the bright colors of spring and early summer by abrasion of the pale tips to feathers on many parts of the body.

The ability to fly is a function that all North American birds need to retain at all costs. And so the replacement of flight feathers presents a challenge, which is addressed in a variety ways by different groups of birds. Waterfowl, for example, molt all their flight feathers in one go, typically in summer. Being completely flightless for a month or more makes them vulnerable and most species undertake the process in the comparatively safe havens of inaccessible marshes or the open sea. Raptors on the other hand, which spend a far greater proportion of the lives in the air, replace their flight feathers one by one, over an extended period. As a result, they retain the ability to fly, regardless of the time of year.

Male (*left*) and female (*right*) Scarlet Tanagers are visibly different from each other. Not all North American species show such a striking difference between the sexes.

HABITATS FOR BIRDS

A combination of geology, geography, and historical land-use has conspired to create a wealth of different habitats in North America. Although a few bird species are rather catholic in their choice of habitat, birders soon come to realize that the majority have much more specific needs. Their behavior, feeding and nesting requirements, and indeed structure, have evolved to suit special niches in particular habitats. However, although a species may be habitat-specific, it does not follow that it will be found in all examples of this habitat throughout the region. Climatic factors can have a profound effect on a species' range, influencing, for example, the ability of a bird to feed, or more profoundly, to survive extreme weather.

For some birders, studying the distinctions between our different habitats may seem like a rather esoteric pursuit, and one that lacks relevance to their everyday activities. However, it really is worth spending time familiarizing yourself with their basic characters and differences for more practical reasons. Developing an understanding of the habitat in which a bird lives helps us to appreciate more fully the life of the bird in question in the context of the environment as a whole. From a more practical point of view, an awareness of a given species' preferred habitat means you will save yourself a lot of time and effort when it comes to pinning down localized species. Habitat preferences are also a useful clue to the identity of many birds. The following pages detail our most characteristic and distinctive habitats.

THE COAST

North America's coastline is varied and stunningly beautiful in places. Although development mars some stretches of shoreline, much remains unspoiled and harbors some of our most charismatic birds. The rich intertidal zone, bathed twice daily by an advancing and retreating tide, and the offshore waters too, are fundamental to the diversity and abundance of birdlife around our coasts. Our coastline is extremely varied, but in all its forms, whether dramatic cliffs or expansive estuaries and salt marshes, it contains a wonderful selection of birds.

Cliffs

For breathtaking scenery and a sense of untamed nature, coastal cliffs offer unrivaled opportunities for the birder. Man has had minimal impact on these areas and during the spring and summer months a few select locations in the northern parts of the continent are thronged with breeding seabirds. Inaccessible but stable ledges support colonies of murres and Kittiwakes, while Atlantic Puffins favor grassy slopes in which they can excavate burrows. Gulls of various species are another common feature of seabird cliffs.

Atlantic Puffin

ABOVE: **Purple Sandpiper;** BELOW: **Sanderling**

Rocky Shores

For the keen student of marine life, the intertidal zone on a rocky shore is an unbelievably rewarding place to visit. However, despite the fact that rock pools and gullies team with life, the variety of birdlife is comparatively limited. During spring and summer, you can expect to find American Oyster-catchers nesting above the high-tide line. Outside the breeding season, Ruddy Turnstones are wide-spread and Purple Sandpipers join them in the northern stretches of coastline.

Sandy Shores and Dunes

Popular places for spending vacations, sandy shores are also of interest to the birder. Beneath the surface of the sand lives an abundance of marine worms, crustaceans, and mollusks whose presence would go largely undetected were it not for the feeding activities of birds and the profusion of dead shells found along the strandline. Outside the breeding season, look for Sanderlings as they follow the line of breaking waves in search of small invertebrates; gulls of various species are seldom far away. Offshore, fish and crustaceans provide a rich supply of food for those bird species that are sufficiently well adapted to catch them. During the summer months, terns can be seen plunge-diving here while during the winter months grebes, loons, and sea ducks exploit this resource. On the landward side of the beach, colonizing plants establish stable dune systems where birds such as plovers and terns can nest. Sadly, however, human disturbance effectively excludes these species from many suitable areas.

Estuaries and Salt Marshes

To the unenlightened eye, an estuary may seem like a vast expanse of mudflats, studded with a mosaic of bedraggled-looking vegetation and very little else. For the birder, however, this is one of the most exhilarating of all habitats to visit. Incredible numbers of marine worms and tiny mollusks thrive in the oozing mud, their numbers supported by the vast amount of organic matter deposited when river meets sea. Benefiting from all this biological richness are the shorebirds and waterfowl that feed on our estuaries in huge numbers from fall to spring.

Shorebirds are perhaps the most characteristic group to exploit this resource, each species having a bill length and feeding strategy adapted to suit a particular food source; this helps avoid undue competition between different species. Dunlins, for example, tend to feed on small surface-living animals while godwits use their long bills to probe deep for more substantial prey. Waterfowl too occur in huge numbers on many estuaries, feeding either on minute animals filtered from the mud or on plant material, depending on the species involved. Many or our larger estuaries are globally important refuges for many bird species.

Dunlin

Atlantic coast salt marsh, estuary, and mudflats

Mangroves

Mangrove trees are specially adapted to a colonizing life on coastal fringes. The wooded swampy habitats that they create are extremely productive and their network of roots trap silt and organic debris, and provide a sheltered environment for many creatures, and a nursery for young fish. In turn, fish-eating birds, such as herons and egrets, reap the rewards. Mangroves thrive only in tropical climates and consequently, in North America, are restricted to Florida and the southeast.

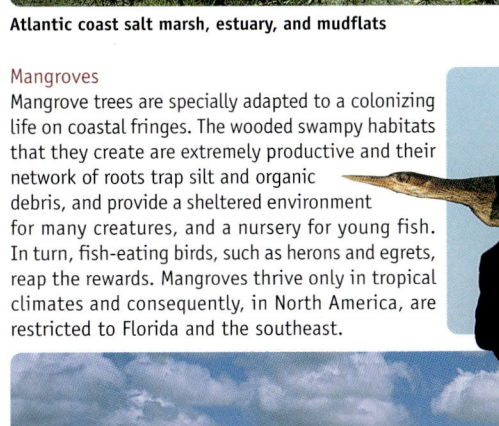

ABOVE: **Colonizing mangroves on the Florida coast;** INSET: **Anhinga**

Spotted Sandpiper

FRESHWATER

For the birder, freshwater habitats have the same magnetic appeal as do coastal habitats. North America has a wealth of examples, from small ponds and streams to large lakes and river systems; few people have to travel far to visit one or more of these habitats.

Rivers and Streams

Flowing water has a charm all of its own and a trip to a river and stream will invariably yield sightings of interesting birds. If the margins are cloaked with vegetation, a rich variety of invertebrate life will be found there, matched, beneath the surface of the water (assuming it is clean and unpolluted), by a wealth of invertebrate and fish life, sheltering among the drifts of submerged aquatic plants. In turn, this abundance of freshwater life supports a splendid array of birds, some species of which are found nowhere else.

Birdlife abounds on many rivers and streams, larger ones supporting populations of ducks and egrets in spring and summer. Martins and swallows feed overhead on flying insects in the summer months while Spotted Sandpipers forage along the margins of boulder-strewn watercourses during the breeding season.

Lakes and Ponds

Bodies of standing water typically harbor a strikingly different range of plants and animals from those found in flowing water. Many seemingly natural sites are man-made, or at least man-influenced, but with maturity they can be surprisingly rich. By midsummer a rich growth of aquatic plants dominates many of our smaller ponds as well as the margins of lakes. Where they are left to their own devices, the margins are soon encroached by stands of emergent plants, and species such as the Common Reed sometimes form extensive beds around larger lakes. Evidence of the abundance of invertebrate life beneath the surface is provided by the emergence, from aquatic immature stages, of adult dragonflies and caddis flies.

American Coots and Moorhens are common on lowland lakes and ponds. If the water body in question is large enough to support a significant fish population, and relatively undisturbed, then loons and grebes may nest in the summer months. In fall and winter, areas of open water become refuges for large flocks of waterbirds, ducks in particular.

ABOVE: **A classic freshwater pond fringed with emergent vegetation;** INSET: **American Coot**

Marshes and Bogs

The encroachment of vegetation into areas of open water leads to the creation of marshes. The term "marsh" is a rather imprecise one in ecological terms and covers wetlands found on a range of soil types. But on particularly acid soils the wetlands that form are called "bogs," and cotton grasses and *Sphagnum* mosses are typical plants. Nesting shorebirds and ducks favor these habitats during the breeding season, as do rails and specialized sparrow and wood-warbler species.

The Everglades

Comprising such an extensive mixture of wetland habitats (rivers, streams, lakes, ponds, and marshes), and with such a subtropical feel, the Everglades deserves a mention in its own right. Located on the southern tip of Florida, and fringed in places by mangrove swamps (*see* below), it is little bit of the Caribbean on mainland North American soil. Home to an impressive array of wetland birds, it is critically important for species such as Anhinga and Wood Stork, and a major breeding and wintering center for many other aquatic species. Adding further to its appeal to birders is the fact that many of the species that occur there are almost indifferent to people, allowing superb views to be obtained.

ABOVE: **Sora**

ABOVE: **The vast Everglades wetlands;** INSET: **Snail Kite**

WOODS AND FORESTS

The vast tracts of virgin forest that once cloaked much of the eastern seaboard of North America prior to the arrival of European settlers are long since gone, felled and cleared over the centuries. However, regrowth has ensured that huge areas of wooded habitat can be found today and birders will find they support a wealth of birdlife.

Deciduous Forests

Woodlands of deciduous trees are found throughout most of the region. As their name suggests, deciduous trees shed their leaves in winter and grow a new set the following spring. The seasonality seen in deciduous woodland is among the most marked and easily observed of any habitat in the region and it is reflected in the seasonal occurrence and abundance in the birdlife harbored there. Almost all woodland in the region has been, and still is, influenced in some way by man.

Most of our deciduous woodlands are home to thriving populations of birds, with both residents and summer visitors breeding there. Most of our migrant visitors include insects and other invertebrates in their diet and the fact that this resource is in short supply in winter is the main reason why they are only with us during the summer months. Many residents also include insects in their diet during the breeding season, but turn to seeds and nuts during the winter months; a few specialized birds manage to find enough invertebrates to keep them going throughout the year. Residents include species of woodpecker and chickadee, while many species of flycatcher, vireo, and wood-warbler are well represented only during the summer months.

Coniferous Forests

Unlike deciduous trees, conifers are, with the exception of a few species, evergreen and keep their leaves throughout the year. Instead of having broad, often rounded leaves, they have narrow ones that are called needles. Their flowers and seeds are borne in structures known as cones, and the shape of the trees themselves is often conical in outline. Crossbills and certain nuthatch species are characteristic of mature conifer forests and several wood-warbler species are also restricted to conifers, and often associated with specific tree species. Conifer forests are often associated with upland areas in temperate regions of North America. But they are at their most extensive across the sub-Arctic, where they are major components of the boreal forests (Taiga) that cloak these latitudes.

TOP: **Boreal "Taiga" forest;** ABOVE: **Blackpoll Warbler**

PRAIRIES, GRASSLAND, FARMLAND, AND SCRUB

Little remains of the original prairies—North America's natural grasslands, dominated by wildflowers and native grasses—that once covered much of the interior. And gone with them are many populations of bird species that depend exclusively on this habitat. Fortunately, however, a few pockets of prairies still remain, typically protected to varying degrees by law, and these areas are where birders should visit in search of grouse and sparrow species that favor them exclusively. Much of the grassland that we see today is secondary habitat, colonizing and encouraged in historical terms in the wake of forest clearance, or planted subsequently. Despite its man-made or man-influenced origins, grassland can still be good for birds. Arable farmland may fall loosely under the category of grassland—crop species such as wheat, barley, and oats are grasses after all—but their interest to the birder tends to be minimal in many areas.

Yellow Warbler, typical of secondary scrub habitats

Formerly, populations of insects and other invertebrates would have fed hungry broods in spring and summer while weed seeds and spilt grain would have supported huge flocks of buntings and finches in fall and winter. Nowadays, however, the use of ever-more efficient insecticides and molluscicides ensures that there are precious few invertebrates for birds to feed on during the summer months. Modern herbicides ensure that "weeds" are kept to a minimum and decades of chemical use has resulted in the soil's seed bank being depleted dramatically. And the arable crops themselves are harvested extremely efficiently these days, with little left to waste.

Scrub is a transition habitat where shrubby plants, many of them associated with woodland margins, take over neglected areas of farmland and grassland. The habitat is often ignored in ecological terms but is extremely important for many birds, insects providing food in the summer months and berries and fruits in fall. Good, thick cover of impenetrable scrub provides excellent cover for nesting songbirds.

ABOVE: **Natural prairie grassland, home to specialist bird species**
INSET: **Eastern Meadowlark, a species that favors a range of grassland habitats**

ABOVE: Verdin; BELOW: Swainson's Thrushes are typical breeding birds of high elevation forests in the south of the species' range.

DESERTS

In North America, desert habitats are confined to the southwest, and in terms of scenery and wildlife they are truly amazing. A desert habitat is typically defined as an area that receives less than 10 inches of rain per year, and the best examples are found outside the range of this book in states such as California, Arizona, and New Mexico. However, arid habitats, approaching deserts in terms of their structure and birdlife, are found in the drier parts of Texas, within the range of this book.

UPLANDS

The uplands of eastern North America may lack the grandeur of the Rockies and other western ranges, but they do nevertheless have a rugged appeal to lovers of the great outdoors. Only the highest peaks are above the treeline and consequently species of wood-warbler, woodpecker, and thrushes are among the more typical species encountered; these are adapted to live in forested habitats but are not exclusively found in upland woodlands. There are few specialized birds associated with eastern North America's upland ranges.

TUNDRA

Northern latitudes, within the Arctic circle, are too hostile in environmental terms for trees to grow and the vegetation typically comprises low-growing shrubs, mosses, and lichens. Collectively this habitat is referred to as "tundra" and in many areas the ground itself is frozen solid for much of the year. Snow blankets the landscape in winter and, unsurprisingly, only a small number of extremely hardy, resident species are found at this time of year. But come the spring and the landscape is transformed. Insect life abounds and in turn large numbers of migratory waders and waterfowl make an appearance, nesting and feeding their young on this brief seasonal bounty.

ABOVE: Tundra; INSET: Snow Bunting

THE URBAN ENVIRONMENT

For many North Americans who live in towns and cities, the urban environment is the one with which they are most familiar. It is encountered on a day-to-day basis with trips to the countryside relegated to weekend visits or vacations. It would be a mistake, however, to assume that the urban environment is without its wildlife interest. Many of our birds are extremely adaptable and have successfully colonized this seemingly unpromising habitat. In part this is because many features associated with our buildings and gardens mimic special niches in natural habitats. Mature gardens with hedges and shrubs, for example, recall woodland margins while buildings resemble man-made cliffs with their roof spaces doubling as artificial caves.

Visit any mature city park and you will find an array of birds more usually associated with woodland or open country. These include American Robins, Blue Jays, and even woodpeckers and chickadees in particularly leafy suburbs; European Starlings are less welcome urban residents in many areas, partly because of their sheer numbers but also for the impact they have on native bird species. A number of these park dwellers also find town gardens much to their liking—the more informal the garden the more species it is likely to attract. As a reflection of the comparatively healthy numbers of songbirds in urban and suburban districts, the Sharp-shinned Hawk population is also thriving in many towns.

RIGHT: **Bohemian Waxwings visit parks and gardens in winter to feed on berries.**
BELOW: **A typical suburban garden that is good for birds**

IDENTIFYING BIRDS

Some birds are so characteristic in appearance that, even if you have never seen one before, you will have no difficulty in identifying it correctly. In this respect, think of species like the Atlantic Puffin or Northern Cardinal. However, what about a nondescript shorebird in winter plumage, or a silent wood-warbler, or a juvenile sparrow? How should you go about making a correct identification in these cases, where plenty of alternative choices are available?

The first thing you should do is to make notes at the time of your observation; it is amazing what tricks the memory can play if you write things down later. Then you can refer to this book at your leisure. All the key information you need for a correct identification is contained within the species descriptions in *Birds of Eastern North America*.

Firstly, try to gauge the size of the bird in question, bearing in mind that, at a distance, absolute size is always difficult to determine: better to try and assess the size *relative* to a nearby species whose identity is known with certainty. Next, look at the shape of the bird and its proportions. For example does it have rounded or pointed wings in flight? Are its legs long and shorebird-like? What shape is the bill, and is the tail long or short?

If time permits, try to study and describe accurately the colors and patterns on the body of the bird. Bear in mind though that appearances can be deceptive: the angle of the light, for example, can have a profound influence on a bird's appearance and it is worth remembering that variations in plumage do occur, even in birds of the same species, age, and sex. You may only get a frustratingly brief, or a partial, view of a bird and consequently it can be difficult to assess all the potential characters that might be needed for identification. However, with each group of birds, there tends to one part of the body where sufficient key identification features are present to enable distinction between similar species. It might be the pattern of stripes on the head of a sparrow, for example, the presence or absence of wing bars on a warbler, or the shape and extent of white on the rump of a flying shorebird. If you can determine which are the key areas to concentrate on for a particular bird (assuming you see it well enough to decide, for example, that it is a sparrow and not a finch) you will improve greatly your chances of making a correct identification.

Most birds found in North America are extremely habitat specific and consequently *where* you see a mystery bird can have a profound bearing on your ability to identify it. The same is true for resident species, for migrants and displaced vagrants. Many birds are vocal enough for their calls and songs to be used accurately in identification. Learning them with any degree of confidence is a matter of experience, but you can speed up the process by listening to recordings.

A range of different features, including plumage, call, and time of year, needed to be considered before coming to the conclusion that this bird was a winter adult Short-billed Dowitcher.

MIGRATION AND MOVEMENTS

In common with other parts of the temperate Northern Hemisphere, much of North America experiences a climate that changes throughout the year. Broadly speaking, we can recognize four fairly distinct seasons—spring, summer, fall, and winter—and these have a profound influence on almost all of our birds. The seasonal responses by birds can be subtle: the diet of some species varies according to season, and hardy mountain species may be forced to descend to lower altitudes in response to bad weather. Other birds make more widespread movements, for example, birds that disperse outside the breeding season and wander nomadically in search of food within the same general area overall. Others may switch habitat altogether between the breeding and nonbreeding seasons, for example many shorebirds, which nest on Arctic tundra but spend the rest of their lives on the coast.

In migration terms, the most conspicuous exponents of this survival strategy are those species that visit us during the summer months to breed. Many of our most familiar songbirds fall into this category and the majority of wood-warbler species, for example, are only with us for a few brief months in spring and early summer. As a general rule, summer migrant visitors that breed in our region head south in the fall, many wintering in Central and South America.

Although many small birds migrate at night, and hence their migration cannot actually be witnessed, these birds have to stop off to feed during the daytime. Many concentrate along the coast—either the point of departure or the first point of arrival, depending on the direction of migration—especially if bad weather halts their progress; nocturnal migrants favor clear nights and are presumed to use the stars as navigation aids. Migration can also add a bit of spice to the life of a birder because, being influenced by the weather and hence somewhat unpredictable, you never really know what might turn up where at migration times.

Great Shearwaters, which breed south of the equator, visit the North Atlantic during the summer months, outside their breeding season.

Visit the Gulf coast in April and May and you will witness impressive visible migration, that of songbirds being particularly noticeable on some days. Almost any migratory species that breeds in eastern North America could turn up, such as this male Black-throated Green Warbler.

Anatidae

TUNDRA SWAN *Cygnus columbianus* L 50–60 in

Large wetland bird. Long neck, short legs, and all white adult plumage make identification easy although confusion with Trumpeter is possible; smaller body size and bill color useful when comparing with Mute. Feeds on vegetation; terrestrial plants are "grazed" while aquatic plants are collected by submerging the long neck. In flight, head and neck are held out-

ADULT

stretched. Sexes are similar. **ADULT** Has mostly pure white plumage but this can look dirty after feeding in murky waters. Legs are dark; bill is mainly dark, but note small yellow teardrop-shaped spot at base (absent in many individuals) and slightly concave upper profile (cf. Trumpeter). **JUVENILE** Has grayish white plumage, which gets whiter as winter progresses. Legs are dark and bill is dull pink, darkening with age. **VOICE** Utters a honking bark *kow-Hooo*. **STATUS AND HABITAT** Nests beside tundra lakes and pools. Resting migrants usually stop off on rivers and lakes. Winters on coastal marshes and grassland, usually near water (favored for roosting). **COMMENT** Eurasian ssp. *bewickii* (Bewick's Swan) turns up occasionally with Tundra flocks in winter; basal third of bill is yellow.

TRUMPETER SWAN *Cygnus buccinator* L 60–70 in

Appreciably bigger than Tundra when seen side-by-side. Has a plump body, relatively short legs, and extremely long neck. Bill is triangular in outline and looks disproportionately large for size of head (looks more in proportion in Tundra). Grazes on grassland and also feeds on aquatic plants uprooted by submerging long neck. In flight, head and neck are held outstretched. Sexes are similar. **ADULT** Has mostly pure white plumage but neck and belly are sometimes stained with mud, oxides, and algae. Legs

ADULT

are dark and bill is mainly dark, but base of lower mandible is pale. Upper profile of bill is straight (cf. Tundra) and continues slope of forehead. **JUVENILE** Has grubby pinkish white plumage. Bill is grubby pink. **VOICE** Utters a loud, nasal trumpeting *oh-HO*. **STATUS AND HABITAT** Formerly hunted close to extinction, is now rare and endangered breeder that nests beside forested lakes; mostly in Alaska, but also scattered across northern latitudes. Winters on or near wetlands. **OBSERVATION TIPS** Avoid causing disturbance in breeding season; best looked for in winter.

MUTE SWAN *Cygnus olor* L 60–70 in

Huge and unmistakable waterbird. Introduced but now a common sight in the northeast, even on ornamental and urban ponds. Bill color and shape allow separation from our smaller native species. Neck is held curved when swimming (straighter in Tundra and Trumpeter). Wings make a throbbing and humming sound in flight. Sexes are similar. **ADULT MALE** Has pure white plumage and pinkish orange bill with large, black basal knob (most obvious in spring and summer). **ADULT FEMALE**

ADULT MALE

Similar to adult male, but bill's basal knob is smaller. **JUVENILE** Has pale pinkish gray plumage and a pinkish gray bill that is black at base. **VOICE** Mostly silent, but may vocalize, and hisses when alarmed. **STATUS AND HABITAT** Introduced from Eurasia but now the most likely swan to be encountered in the northeast. Nests beside lakes and rivers and mainly a year-round resident. A real threat to native waterfowl species, which it outcompetes for food in winter. **OBSERVATION TIPS** Chesapeake Bay is a hotspot for the species.

JUVENILE

TUNDRA SWAN

ADULT

JUVENILE

TRUMPETER SWAN

ADULT

MALE

FEMALE

MUTE SWAN

JUVENILE

JUVENILE

GREATER WHITE-FRONTED GOOSE
Anser albifrons L 28–30 in

Bulky goose. Adult has diagnostic white "blaze" on forehead. Juvenile lacks this feature and could be confused with feral Graylag Goose (*see* p.322). Several subspecies are recognized, but plumage variability often makes precise identification difficult. Broadly speaking, there are two extremes: pale tundra-breeding forms and darker taiga-breeding birds; they usually occur in separate populations in winter. Sexes are similar. All white-fronts fly in V-formation on migration and in winter. Feed by grazing vegetation, particularly grasses in winter. **ADULT** Has gray-brown plumage, palest in tundra birds and darkest in taiga birds. White on forehead is more extensive in tundra birds than taiga ones. In flight, all birds show white on upper tail. All birds show variable black barring on underparts, and white vent, which extends as white line to flanks. Legs are orange and bill is pinkish orange. **JUVENILE** Similar to adult, but lacks white on forehead and dark markings on underparts. **VOICE** Utters musical barking calls, especially in flight. **STATUS AND HABITAT** Locally common. Breeds on tundra and taiga, Alaska to Greenland (and Eurasia). Winters mainly on farmland and freshwater marshes. **OBSERVATION TIPS** Easiest to observe in winter and Texas wetlands are hotspots.

SNOW GOOSE *Chen caerulescens* L 26–33 in

Distinctive Arctic tundra goose. Confusingly, occurs in two distinct light and blue (or "dark") color morphs. Blue morph was formerly considered a separate species, Blue Goose. Both morphs are distinctive and confusion is only really possible with appreciably smaller Ross's Goose, or white, domesticated form of Graylag Goose (*see* p.322). Sexes are similar. Feeds by grazing vegetation. Long-distance flights usually undertaken in V-

ADULT WHITE MORPH

formation. **ADULT WHITE MORPH** Has mainly white plumage, with black primaries. Bill and legs are pink. **JUVENILE WHITE MORPH** Has whitish plumage, except for buff-brown back and dark primaries. Bill and legs are dark. **ADULT BLUE MORPH** Has mainly dark gray-brown plumage, except for white head and neck, white vent, and pale wing coverts. Bill and legs are pink. **JUVENILE BLUE MORPH** Dark buffy brown, except for white vent. Bill and legs are dark. **VOICE** Utters a barking, honking *whook*. **STATUS AND HABITAT** Locally abundant. Nests on tundra and winters on farmland and wetlands. **OBSERVATION TIPS** Easiest to observe at regular wintering grounds, mainly Texas, Mississippi, and Atlantic wetlands.

ADULT WHITE MORPH

ROSS'S GOOSE
Chen rossii L 22–24 in

Small Arctic goose. Superficially similar to Snow Goose with which it is often observed, but appreciably smaller, with a more dainty bill. Occurs in two color forms: white morph is by far the commoner; blue morph is rare. Sexes are similar. Feeds by grazing vegetation. In flight, wingbeats are noticeably more rapid than in other, larger geese. **ADULT WHITE MORPH** Has white plumage, except for black primaries. Bill and legs are pink. **JUVENILE WHITE MORPH** Similar to adult, but with slightly dirty looking plumage. **ADULT BLUE MORPH** Mainly dark blue-gray, except for white on face, underparts, and vent. Bill and legs are pink. **JUVENILE BLUE MORPH** Similar to adult. **VOICE** Utters a soft, squeaking *keek-keek*. **STATUS AND HABITAT** Locally common. Nests on tundra and winters on farmland and wetlands. **OBSERVATION TIPS** Easiest to see in winter; Texas coastal wetlands are hotspots.

ADULT BLUE MORPH

GREATER WHITE-FRONTED GOOSE

ADULT

ADULT

ADULT WHITE MORPH

ADULT BLUE MORPH

SNOW GOOSE

JUVENILE BLUE MORPH

ADULT WHITE MORPH

ADULT BLUE MORPH

ROSS'S GOOSE

Anatidae

CACKLING GOOSE *Branta hutchinsii* L 25–27 in

Recent addition to North American list—split from Canada Goose species complex. Four subspecies are recognized; plumages are all broadly comparable to Canada Goose. However, all subspecies of Cackling are small, compact birds with almost ducklike proportions; note proportionately short neck and dainty bill. Cackling also shows proportionately longer, more pointed wings in flight. Sexes are similar. Feeds by grazing vegetation. **ADULT** Has black head and neck, white cheek and white vent. Body plumage varies according to subspecies: ranges from gray-brown in *hutchinsii* ("Richardson's") to dark reddish brown in *taverneri*. **JUVENILE** Similar to adult. **VOICE** Honking *hronk*, higher pitched than Canada. **STATUS AND HABITAT** Locally common. Nests on tundra, mainly Alaska to Hudson Bay. Winters on marshes and farmland. **OBSERVATION TIPS** Visit Texas wetlands in winter, where "Richardson's" is the most likely subspecies to be encountered.

CANADA GOOSE *Branta canadensis* L 36–46 in

Our most familiar goose. Several subspecies, separable by size and proportions, are recognized; detailed discussion of these is beyond this book's scope and only extremes are dealt with here. Confusingly, intermediates occur between Canada Goose ssp. and Cackling Goose (formerly part of Canada Goose species complex), which has recently been assigned species status. Large Canada Geese are unmistakable, but smallest subspecies are similar in size to largest subspecies of Cackling Goose! Neck length is a good

ADULTS

feature for separation: proportionately longer in all Canada Goose races than in Cackling Goose. **ADULT** Has black head and neck, and white cheek. Bill and legs are black. Typical birds have gray-brown body plumage, except for white vent and pale breast. Arctic and boreal nesters are typically smaller than subspecies that breed further south. **JUVENILE** Similar to adult. **VOICE** Familiar honking *hronk*. **STATUS AND HABITAT** Abundant. Mostly a migrant breeding visitor to Canada, moving south in winter; present year-round in much of U.S. Favors freshwater marshes, pasture, and farmland. **OBSERVATION TIPS** Easy to observe. Leave subspecies assignment to the experts.

BRANT *Branta bernicla* L 24–26 in

Small coastal goose. Three subspecies are recognized, separable by belly markings; they have reasonably distinct breeding and wintering grounds: *nigricans* (Black Brant) breeds in Siberia and northwestern North American Arctic and winters on Pacific coast of North America; *hrota* (Pale-bellied Brant) breeds in Greenland and eastern North American Arctic, and winters either on our Atlantic coast or in Europe; *bernicla* (Dark-bellied Brant) breeds in Russian Arctic and winters in Europe. Intermediate "Gray-bellied Brant" breeds in Canada and winters on WA coast. All birds feed on marine eelgrass and Sea Lettuce, sometimes also on coastal grassland. **ADULT** Has black head and neck with white "collar," dark gray upperparts, and white vent. Breast and belly are uniformly dark gray in *nigricans*; dark below, but paler on flanks in *bernicla* and Gray-bellied; uniformly pale gray in *hrota*. **JUVENILE** Similar to respective parents, but white collar is absent until late winter, and back feathers show pale edges. **VOICE** A nasal, honking *kruut*. **STATUS AND HABITAT** Breeds on tundra, winters in estuaries. Locally common. **OBSERVATION TIPS** Pale-bellied Brants winter on Atlantic seaboard.

ADULT

ADULT

CACKLING GOOSE

CANADA GOOSE

ADULT

ADULT

ADULTS

PALE-BELLIED BRANT

BRANT

ADULT

BLACK BRANT

ADULT

Anatidae

BLACK-BELLIED WHISTLING-DUCK
Dendrocygna autumnalis L 19–22 in
Colorful long-necked, long-legged duck with an upright posture; nervous and wary. Often perches on branches or rocks, and nests in tree holes. In flight, note the relatively long wings. Highly gregarious outside breeding season. Feeds on aquatic plants, grasses, and cereals as well as freshwater invertebrates; typically feeds at night. Sexes are similar. **ADULT** Has an orange-brown back, breast, and lower neck. Upper neck and head are gray, except for rufous crown. Belly is black and note the pale wing panel; in flight wings look contrastingly black and white. Legs are pink and bill is bright red. **JUVENILE** Similar to adult, but plumage colors are duller and belly is grayish. Bill and legs are gray. **VOICE** Utters a whistling *pe-choo*. **STATUS AND HABITAT** Favors freshwater wetlands and adjacent farmland and grassland. Widespread in Central and South America but range extends to Florida and south Texas. Present year-round, although Texas range is more extensive in summer. **OBSERVATION TIPS** Easy to see in southern Texas, especially in winter; hotspots include the Santa Ana and Arkansas National Wildlife Refuges.

ADULTS

FULVOUS WHISTLING-DUCK
Dendrocygna bicolor L 18–20 in
Has similar habits and posture to Black-bellied, but plumage is much more fulvous brown overall with contrasting dark wings; white rump and contrasting black tail are also striking in flight. Usually feeds at night. Sexes are similar. **ADULT** Orange-brown overall, darkest on crown, back of neck, and back. Bill and legs are blue-gray and wings appear uniformly dark in flight. **JUVENILE** Similar to adult. **VOICE** Has a squeaky whistling call. **STATUS AND HABITAT** A mostly tropical species whose range extends to southern Texas and Florida. Favors grassy marshes and rice fields. **OBSERVATION TIPS** Lake Okeechobee marshes in Florida are good; common on Texas coastal wetlands in summer.

WOOD DUCK *Aix sponsa* L 17–19 in
Attractive dabbling duck. Males are instantly recognizable; even duller females are well marked. Flies on rapid wingbeats and maneuvers capably through forested terrain. Seen in small flocks outside breeding season. Nests in tree holes and artificial nest boxes. Often perches on branches. Feeds on acorns, fruits, and invertebrates. Sexes are dissimilar. **ADULT MALE** Has shiny green-blue crown and mane, adorned with white lines. Chin and throat are white, extending onto face as white lines. Breast is maroon, flanks are buff, and back is greenish; these three areas are separated by white lines. Note red eye and red at base of bill. **ADULT FEMALE** Mainly brownish, darkest on back and head. Breast and flanks are marked with fine pale streak-like spots. Note the white spectacle around the eye and white on throat and margin of gray bill. **JUVENILE** Resembles adult female, but plumage is duller and patterns less striking. **VOICE** Mostly silent, but females utter a squealing *oo-Eeek*. **STATUS AND HABITAT** Favors forested flooded valleys and swamps; requires areas that are flooded during breeding season. Overhunting and habitat destruction brought virtual extinction by end of 19th century. Hunting restrictions and conservation measures allowed recovery: population now around 1,000,000 birds.

MALE

ADULT

JUVENILE

BLACK-BELLIED WHISTLING-DUCK

ADULT

FULVOUS WHISTLING-DUCK

WOOD DUCK

FEMALE

MALE

Anatidae

MALLARD *Anas platyrhynchos* L 22–24 in

Our most familiar dabbling duck. Feeds on aquatic vegetation, and some invertebrates. In flight, both sexes show white-bordered blue speculum. Sexes are dissimilar. **ADULT MALE** Has yellow bill and green, shiny head and upper neck, separated from chestnut breast by white collar. Underparts are gray-brown, except for black vent and white tail. Back is gray-brown, grading to reddish brown. Legs and feet are orange. In eclipse plumage, male resembles adult female, but note yellow bill color and well-defined reddish brown breast. **ADULT FEMALE** Has orange-brown bill and mottled brown plumage. Legs and

feet are dull orange-yellow. **JUVENILE** Similar to adult female. **VOICE** Male utters a range of whistles and nasal calls. Female utters familiar quacking calls. **STATUS AND HABITAT** Found in almost every habitat where water is present, with the exception of the highest mountains and northernmost tundra. Commonest on lowland lakes, rivers, and marshes, but also thrives on ornamental lakes in urban areas, where it often becomes tame and inter-breeds with "farmyard" ducks. Most Canadian birds move south, or to the coast, in winter. **OBSERVATION TIPS** Ubiquitous and hard to miss.

AMERICAN BLACK DUCK
Anas rubripes L 22–24 in

Eastern specialty that recalls female and eclipse male Mallard. Distinguished from both by dark (not whitish) tail feathers, purple (not blue) speculum that has only limited white edging, and darker body plumage overall. Lacks reddish breast seen in eclipse male Mallard and American Black Duck × Mallard hybrids. Sexes are separable. **ADULT MALE** Has mostly blackish brown body plumage with clear separation from buffish brown-gray neck, head, and face; crown is darker. Bill is greenish yellow and feet and legs are orange. Plumage is similar in eclipse but slightly paler. **ADULT FEMALE** Similar to male but body plumage is paler overall. Bill is dull greenish gray and legs and feet are orange. **JUVENILE** Similar to adult female. **VOICE** Similar to Mallard. **STATUS AND HABITAT** Fairly common in east. Breeds in ponds, marshes, and other wetlands and present year-round in center of range. Northern birds move south in winter and outside breeding season greatest numbers are found on coastal salt marshes. **OBSERVATION TIPS** Fairly easy to see in suitable habitats.

MOTTLED DUCK *Anas fulvigula* L 21–23 in

Gulf coast specialty that recalls a female Mallard or pale version of American Black Duck and is intermediate in many ways between them. Separated from both by its tawny brown body plumage (paler and warmer than American Black but darker than Mallard); greenish speculum (purple in American Black and blue in Mallard); and brown tail (blackish brown in American Black and whitish in Mallard). Usually seen in pairs. Sexes are separable. **ADULT MALE** Has tawny brown body plumage with clear separation from

buffy brown neck and head; crown and eyestripe are brown, bill is yellow, and legs are orange. In eclipse, plumage is similar but paler. **ADULT FEMALE** Similar to adult male, but paler with more olive-orange bill. **JUVENILE** Similar to adult female. **VOICE** Utters soft, Mallard-like quacking calls. **STATUS AND HABITAT** Locally fairly common on Gulf coast and in Florida where it is present year-round on salt marshes, coastal wetlands, and agricultural land. **OBSERVATION TIPS** Fairly easy to see in suitable habitats along Gulf coast.

FEMALE

MALLARD

MALE

FEMALE

AMERICAN BLACK DUCK

MALE

MOTTLED DUCK

MALE

Anatidae

GADWALL *Anas strepera* L 19–21 in

Familiar and rather understated dabbling duck. At a distance, male's plumage looks gray and brown but close range view reveals beautifully intricate, vermiculate patterns. In flight, both sexes show white in speculum, highlighted by black border; extent of white is greatest in male, which also shows chestnut on inner wing. Sexes are dissimilar in other respects. **ADULT MALE** Has a buffy gray head and neck, with clear separation from darker gray, finely patterned breast and flanks. Center of belly is white and vent is black; latter is a useful identification feature even at a distance. Has a dark bill and yellow legs. In eclipse plumage, male resembles

MALE

FEMALE

an adult female. **ADULT FEMALE** Has mottled brown plumage with a grayish head. White speculum can sometimes be glimpsed in feeding birds. Bill is yellowish. **JUVENILE** Resembles adult female. **VOICE** Male utters a croaking call and female utters a Mallard-like *quack*. **STATUS AND HABITAT** Invariably associated with freshwater habitats, favoring shallow ponds and marshes where birds can dabble (and if necessary upend) for water plants. Breeds extensively across central North America, particularly in prairie pools; in region covered by this book, winter concentrations are on freshwater wetlands near Atlantic and Gulf coasts. **OBSERVATION TIPS** Easiest to find in winter.

AMERICAN WIGEON *Anas americana* L 18–21 in

Medium-sized dabbling duck. Adult male breeding plumage is distinctive, but separation of other plumages from Eurasian Wigeon is a challenge. American's white axillaries ("armpits") are useful field mark at all times (gray in Eurasian). Forms sizeable flocks outside breeding season. Feeds on aquatic plants and also grazes grassland. **ADULT MALE** Has a striking head pattern with green stripe stretching back from eye, creamy white forehead and crown, and speckled gray face and neck. Body plumage is otherwise mainly pinkish buff, except for bold black and white vent. In flight, note striking white patch on upper surface of inner wing. **ADULT FEMALE** Has speckled gray head and neck (good for separation from female Eurasian) and otherwise orange-brown, finely marked body plumage, except for white belly. Bill and legs are gray. **JUVENILE** Similar to adult female. **VOICE** Male utters a distinctive three-noted whistle, *whi-whee-whew*. **STATUS AND HABITAT** Abundant. Nests beside tundra pools and northern marshes. Migrates south for winter, favoring open wetlands and adjacent grassland, and estuaries; in region covered by this book, greatest winter concentrations are near coasts. **OBSERVATION TIPS** Easiest to observe in winter. **SIMILAR SPECIES Eurasian Wigeon** *A. penelope* (19–21 in) Male is colorful and distinctive and utters an evocative *wheee-oo* whistling

EURASIAN WIGEON

MALE

call. Has mostly orange-red head and yellow forehead. Breast is pinkish, while rest of plumage is mainly gray and finely marked, except for white belly and striking black and white vent. In flight, note striking white patch on wing. Bill is pale gray and dark-tipped. Eclipse male recalls adult female. Adult female is very similar to female American Wigeon: mainly reddish brown, darkest on head and back, but with white belly and vent; lacks male's white wing patch. Bill is gray and dark-tipped. Winter visitor, a few hundred recorded each year, mainly from coastal habitats from New England to Chesapeake Bay. Associates and occasionally hybridizes with American Wigeon.

MALE

GADWALL

FEMALE

MALE

MALE

AMERICAN WIGEON

FEMALE

Anatidae

NORTHERN PINTAIL *Anas acuta* L 21–26 in

An elegant duck that feeds on aquatic plants by dabbling and upending; also feeds on land. Male is unmistakable and even the rather drab female has a distinctive, elongated appearance with pointed rear end. Unobtrusive during breeding season, but feeds in open areas in flocks at other times. Looks long-winged in flight; male's gray wings and green speculum (with white trailing edge) are striking; female's white trailing edge on inner wing is obvious. Sexes are dissimilar in other respects. **ADULT MALE** Has chocolate brown head and nape, with white breast extending as stripe up side of head. Plumage is otherwise gray and finely marked, but note cream and black vent, and long, pointed tail, often held at an angle. Eclipse male resembles adult

ADULTS

female, but retains pattern and colors on wings. **ADULT FEMALE** Has mottled buffy brown plumage. **JUVENILE** Similar to adult female, but complex feather markings are less well developed. **VOICE** Male utters a whistling call; female's call is grating and harsh. **STATUS AND HABITAT** Several million occur in North America as a whole but species is commonest in west, outside the range of this book. Still common in east although numbers are declining due to changes in agricultural land-use during breeding season. Favors marshy edge habitat and adjacent farmland for nesting. In winter, flocks are found on wetlands and adjacent arable fields, marshes, and estuaries. **OBSERVATION TIPS** Easiest to observe in winter and greatest concentrations within range covered by this book are in coastal areas. Often upends in water to feed, revealing striking vent colors and elongated tail.

NORTHERN SHOVELER *Anas clypeata* L 17–20 in

Unmistakable duck, even when seen in silhouette, due to its long, flattened bill. Unobtrusive for much of the time, favoring water margins with dense vegetation and moving quietly through open shallows, filtering food with bill. Often occurs in small flocks outside the breeding season, which typically are nervous and flighty. In flight, male shows blue forewing panel and white-bordered green speculum; female's wing pattern is similar, but blue is replaced by gray. Sexes are dissimilar in other respects. **ADULT MALE** Has shiny green head (looks dark in poor light), white breast and chestnut on flanks and belly. Vent is black and white and back is mainly

MALE

dark. Note the bright yellow eye and dark gray bill. Eclipse male resembles adult female, although body is more rufous, head is grayer, and bill is dark. **ADULT FEMALE** Has mottled buffy brown plumage and yellowish bill. **JUVENILE** Similar to adult female. **VOICE** Male utters a sharp *tuk-tuk*; female utters a soft *quack*. **STATUS AND HABITAT** Widespread and fairly common. Nests beside shallow pools and marshes, mainly at northern latitudes. Favors estuaries, freshwater marshes, and lakes in winter. **OBSERVATION TIPS** Easiest to find in winter and, within range covered by this book, greatest concentrations are found on coastal wetlands.

MALE

NORTHERN PINTAIL

FEMALE

MALE

NORTHERN SHOVELER

FEMALE

GREEN-WINGED TEAL *Anas crecca* L 14–15 in

Tiny dabbling duck that feeds in shallow water and in marshy grass-land. Gregarious outside breeding season and typically flocks are nervous and take flight—rising almost vertically from water's surface—at slightest sign of danger. In flight, both sexes show a green speculum, high-lighted by white borders. Sexes are otherwise dissimilar. Feeds on aquatic vegetation and, in summer, invertebrates too. **ADULT MALE** Has chestnut-

orange head with green patch through eye faintly bordered with yellow. Plumage is otherwise gray and finely marked, except for striking vertical white stripe on side of breast, and black-bordered yellow vent. Bill is dark gray. Eclipse male resembles adult female. **ADULT FEMALE** Has rather uniform mottled gray-brown plumage; green speculum is sometimes glimpsed in feeding birds. Bill is mainly gray, but with hint of yellow at base. **JUVE-NILE** Similar to adult female, but plumage is lighter buff. **VOICE** Male utters a ringing whistle, while female utters a soft *quack*. **STATUS AND HABITAT** Found near water. Nests in dense waterside vegetation across northern North America. At other times of year, migrates south and favors more open habitats; commonest in coastal areas: freshwater marshes, estuaries, and mudflats are favored. **OBSERVATION TIPS** Locally abundant and easiest to see in winter. **SIMILAR SPECIES European Teal** *A. c. crecca* is the Eurasian counterpart; rare in winter among Green-winged flocks.

EUROPEAN TEAL, MALE

BLUE-WINGED TEAL *Anas discors* L 15–16 in

Small and distinctive duck, and one of our most abundant water-fowl species. Feeds unobtrusively by dabbling in well-vegetated shallows and often remains partly hidden from view for much of the time. Male is unmistakable because of his distinctive head markings but female recalls female Green-winged Teal, which has a smaller, shorter bill, different wing markings (green speculum and brown forewing), and lacks pale spot at base of bill. In flight, all Blue-winged Teals reveal blue panel on leading edge of upper inner wing, separated from speculum (green in males and dull in females) by white wedge. **ADULT MALE** Has bluish head with diagnostic verti-

MALE

cal white crescent in front of eyes. Body is buffy brownish, marbled with dark spots. White patch toward rear end contrasts with otherwise black vent. **ADULT FEMALE** Marbled brown with pale spot at base of bill, dark eye-stripe, and white "eyelids." **JUVENILE** Similar to adult female, but lacks strong facial markings. **STATUS AND HABITAT** Common breeding species across northern and central North America, particularly numerous in prairie pothole region. Nests beside shallow marshland pools and muddy ponds. Long-distance migrant with most birds migrating to South America for winter. Small numbers linger in coastal marshlands on Gulf and southern Atlantic coasts. **OBSERVATION TIPS** Easiest to see in spring, during migration, or in winter. Inconspicuous during latter part of breeding season. **RELATED SPECIES Cinnamon Teal** *A. cyanoptera* (L 15–17 in) is a scarce but regular visitor (mainly winter) to Gulf coast wetlands. The male's cinnamon-red plumage is unmistakable. The female recalls female Blue-winged Teal but with longer bill.

CINNAMON TEAL, MALE

FEMALE
GREEN-WINGED TEAL
MALE

FEMALE
BLUE-WINGED TEAL
MALE

Anatidae

CANVASBACK *Aythya valisineria* L 20–23 in

Robust diving duck that feeds on submerged vegetation and some invertebrates. Forms sizeable flocks (known as "rafts") outside breeding season. Similar to Redhead, but separable by key plumage differences, shape of head, and structure and markings of bill: Canvasback has a uniformly dark grayish black, long, triangular bill, the upperside of which follows and continues the slope of the flat forehead; Redhead has a rounded head and comparatively dainty bill that is pale grayish blue with subterminal white band and black tip. All birds show pale underwings in flight. **ADULT MALE** Has a reddish chestnut head, black breast and vent, and otherwise very pale gray body. Note the bright red eye, dark grayish black bill, and, in flight, whitish upper wings. **ADULT FEMALE** Has buffy brownish head and neck, and pale gray-brown body with dark-

MALE

er vent. Note the faint pale "spectacle." **JUVENILE** Similar to adult female but more uniformly buff-gray. **VOICE** Mostly silent. **STATUS AND HABITAT** Has declined in recent years but still locally common. Favors prairie potholes and marshes for nesting, and breeding range is almost entirely in west and northwest (beyond range covered by this book). Winters mainly on coasts, but may occur inland, and locally common in east at this time of year. **OBSERVATION TIPS** Buds of wild celery *Vallisneria americana* (a submerged aquatic plant of fresh and brackish waters) are important winter food and Canvasback distribution is influenced by this plant's occurrence; consequently, coastal wetlands are much favored. Chesapeake Bay is a hotspot for the species.

REDHEAD *Aythya americana* L 18–21 in

Attractive diving duck that feeds on submerged plants and some invertebrates. Superficially similar to Canvasback, but see that species' description for discussion of key differences. In particular, note the Redhead's rounded head shape and tricolored, shorter, and less sloped, bill. In flight all birds show pale underwings. Sexes are dissimilar in other respects. **ADULT MALE** Has a reddish orange head and upper neck, clearly demarcated from the black lower neck and breast. Vent is black and body is otherwise gray. In flight, gray upper wing coverts contrast with paler flight feathers. Note the bright yellowish eye. **ADULT FEMALE** Has mainly buffy

MALE

brownish plumage, with a faint pale "spectacle" and whitish throat. **JUVENILE** Similar to adult female. **VOICE** Mostly silent, but male's courtship call is a nasal catlike *mee'ow*. **STATUS AND HABITAT** Locally common and favors prairie pothole habitats for nesting in west of its range, but also small pools in northeast. Winters mainly on Gulf of Mexico, specifically Laguna Madre, Texas and Laguna Madre, Tamaulipas, Mexico. Smaller numbers winter in wetlands of southern U.S. **OBSERVATION TIPS** Relatively easy to find, within its range, at the start of the breeding season. Otherwise, visit coastal wetlands in winter. **COMMENT** An occasional nest parasite, both of other Redheads and other duck species; some females do not make their own nest and lay only in those of other individuals.

MALE

CANVASBACK

FEMALE

MALE

REDHEAD

FEMALE

Anatidae

RING-NECKED DUCK *Aythya collaris* L 15–18 in

Distinctive diving duck that feeds on submerged seeds, roots, and invertebrates. Male in particular is strikingly marked, but both sexes can be recognized by peaked crown and tricolored bill: dark gray with a subterminal white band and black tip. In flight, all birds show whitish underwings and pale gray flight feathers, contrasting with darker upper wing coverts. **ADULT MALE** Has light gray belly and flanks, the leading edge of which is pale and appears as a vertical white line in swimming birds. The plumage is otherwise mainly black, although in good light note the purple sheen to the head and neck. Note also the white border defining base of bill. **ADULT FEMALE** Has a grayish head with a white patch at base of bill, and a white "spectacle" around eye. Body plumage is brown, palest on belly and flanks. **JUVENILE** Similar to adult female, but with less well-marked bill. **VOICE** Mostly silent. **STATUS AND HABITAT** Widespread and locally common within breeding range in summer on ponds and marshes. In winter, found on freshwater lakes, and on coasts, across southern U.S. states. **OBSERVATION TIPS** Easiest to observe in winter.

MALE
FEMALE

GREATER SCAUP *Aythya marila* L 17–19 in

Bulky, robust diving duck. Feeds on submerged roots, seeds, and invertebrates. Superficially similar to slightly smaller Lesser Scaup, but size is not always a useful means of identification. Head shape is generally reliable in relaxed birds: rounded in Greater, but distinctly peaked in Lesser. In flight, more of the upper wing flight feathers appear whitish in Greater than in Lesser. At close range, black tip to otherwise dark gray bill is more extensive in Greater than Lesser (hard to judge in field). **ADULT MALE** Has green-glossed head and dark breast; both can look black in poor light. Belly and flanks are white and back is pale gray, palest toward front. Vent is black; note bright yellow eye. Eclipse plumage pattern recalls adult male, but pale elements are buff-gray. **ADULT FEMALE** Has mainly brown plumage, palest and grayest on flanks and back; white belly is seen in flight. Note striking white patch at base of bill. **JUVENILE** Similar to adult female. **VOICE** Mostly silent. **STATUS AND HABITAT** Locally common. Nests on tundra marshes and pools, winters mainly on coasts or large lakes. **OBSERVATION TIPS** Easiest to observe in winter. Coastal winter scaup flocks are likely to be Greaters.

MALE

LESSER SCAUP *Aythya affinis* L 16–17 in

Familiar diving duck. Similar to Greater Scaup counterparts (*see* that species' account for details) but peaked crown is reliable diagnostic feature as is upper wing pattern in flight—only inner flight feathers are whitish. **ADULT MALE** Has black head and neck, former appears shiny purple in good light (green in male Greater). Belly and flanks are white and back is gray, palest toward front. Vent is black; note bright yellow eye. Eclipse plumage pattern recalls adult male but pale elements are buffy. **ADULT FEMALE** Mainly brown, palest and grayer on back and flanks. White belly is seen in flight. **JUVENILE** Similar to adult female. **VOICE** Mostly silent. **STATUS AND HABITAT** Abundant, nesting beside marshes and prairie potholes, and wintering on pools and lakes further south. **OBSERVATION TIPS** Easiest to find in winter, on freshwater wetlands near Gulf coast. Inland scaup flocks are likely to be Lessers.

MALE

FEMALE

RING-NECKED DUCK

MALE

FEMALE

GREATER SCAUP

MALE

FEMALE

LESSER SCAUP

MALE

Anatidae

BLACK SCOTER *Melanitta nigra* L 18–20 in

Rather uniformly dark diving duck. Male is only duck in the region with all-black plumage and female's nearly all dark plumage is relieved only by her contrasting pale cheeks. Relatively long tail is sometimes elevated when swimming. Outside breeding season, Black Scoters are highly gregarious. In flight, all birds look mainly dark, although in good light paler flight feathers can sometimes be discerned. **ADULT MALE** Has uniformly black plumage. Otherwise dark bill has a striking bulbous yellow knob at base. First-

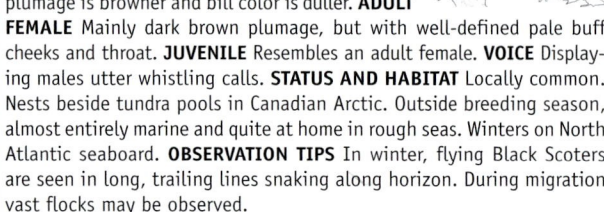

winter male is similar to adult male although plumage is browner and bill color is duller. **ADULT FEMALE** Mainly dark brown plumage, but with well-defined pale buff cheeks and throat. **JUVENILE** Resembles an adult female. **VOICE** Displaying males utter whistling calls. **STATUS AND HABITAT** Locally common. Nests beside tundra pools in Canadian Arctic. Outside breeding season, almost entirely marine and quite at home in rough seas. Winters on North Atlantic seaboard. **OBSERVATION TIPS** In winter, flying Black Scoters are seen in long, trailing lines snaking along horizon. During migration vast flocks may be observed.

WHITE-WINGED SCOTER *Melanitta fusca* L 20–22 in

Bulky duck that dives frequently and for long periods. Similar to, but larger than, Black Scoter with which it sometimes consorts in winter. Both sexes have white inner flight feathers, striking and obvious in flight but often visible, albeit only partially, in swimming birds too. White markings on head of male enable easy identification, while female's facial markings are useful features to look for. **ADULT MALE** Has mainly black plumage (dark brown on flanks), which emphasizes striking white horizontal comma-shaped patch seen below pale eye, and glimpsed patch of white on closed wings of swimming birds. Bill is mostly pinkish, but more blackish near the base. First-winter male is browner overall than adult and lacks white under eye. **ADULT**

FEMALE Mainly dark sooty brown plumage, but note pale cheek patch and pale patch at base of dark bill. **VOICE** Mostly silent, but occasionally quacks and breeding males whistle. **STATUS AND HABITAT** Locally common. Nests beside inland tundra pools in Arctic. Outside breeding season, almost exclusively coastal, favoring bays and estuaries with sandy seabeds. **OBSERVATION TIPS** Easiest to find in winter—scan a sheltered bay from an elevated vantage point and look for the diagnostic white highlights on otherwise dark-looking birds.

SURF SCOTER *Melanitta perspicillata* L 19–20 in

Hardy sea duck with a particularly large, triangular bill. Dives frequently and for long periods, feeding on marine invertebrates. In flight, all birds show uniformly dark wings. Male is distinctive, white head markings and colorful bill contrasting with otherwise black plumage. Female could be confused with females of other scoter species: head markings and bill size allow separation from Black; uniformly dark wings distinguish it from White-winged. **ADULT MALE** Has mainly black plumage, but note prominent white patches on nape and forehead. Bill is orange-yellow on top and to the tip,

with a white basal patch encompassing a large, black spot; at close range note the whitish eye. First-winter male has brownish plumage, but a hint of adult's bill pattern. **ADULT FEMALE** Mainly dark gray-brown plumage with white patch at base of bill, and one behind eye. **VOICE** Mostly silent but breeding males whistle. **STATUS AND HABITAT** Locally common. Nests beside lakes and winters on coasts. **OBSERVATION TIPS** Typically feeds close to shore, sometimes in surf.

BLACK SCOTER

FEMALE

MALE

WHITE-WINGED SCOTER

FEMALE

MALE

SURF SCOTER

FEMALE

MALE

Anatidae

HARLEQUIN DUCK *Histrionicus histrionicus* L 16–18 in

Plump-bodied diving duck. Feeds on submerged aquatic inverte-brates. Male is stunningly marked and unmistakable. Female's plumage recalls that of female scaups and scoters; note, however, smaller bill (cf. other diving ducks) and more rounded head shape (shared with male). Not especially gregarious, even outside breeding season. **ADULT MALE** Has mainly dark blue body plumage and red flanks. Head is adorned with white markings: crescent at base of bill, spot and streak behind eye. Note also the white half collar and white stripes on flanks and back. Eclipse male is sooty brown, but with hint of adult markings. **ADULT FEMALE** Brown, palest on belly, with a white spot on side of head. **JUVENILE** Similar to adult female. **VOICE** Mostly silent, but sometimes quacks or whistles. **STATUS AND HABITAT** Very common locally. During breeding season, found on fast-flowing rivers, mainly in Arctic. Outside breeding season, mostly coastal, favoring exposed rocky shores on North Atlantic seaboard. **OBSERVATION TIPS** Hike alongside a boulder-strewn northern river in spring and you should see the occasional pair. Most birds are found on coasts between August and March.

MALE

LONG-TAILED DUCK *Clangula hyemalis* L 16–22 in

Attractive diving duck associated with open seas in winter and in its element even among tempestuous waves. Dives frequently, in search of bottom-dwelling invertebrates. Gregarious outside breeding season. In flight, note dark wings and mainly white underparts. Sexes are dissimilar and plumage of both varies considerably throughout year. Only male sports a long tail. **ADULT MALE** In winter and spring looks mainly black, gray, and white, with buffy patch around eye and pink band on bill. In summer and in eclipse, has mainly brown and black plumage, with white on belly and flanks and pale buff patch around eye. **ADULT FEMALE** In winter has mainly brown and white plumage; face is white except for dark cheek patch and crown. In summer, similar, but face is mainly brown, with pale patch around eye. **JUVENILE** Similar to adult female in summer, but more brown overall. **VOICE** Male utters characteristic nasal *ow-owlee*. **STATUS AND HABITAT** Common, but declining. Found on tundra marshes and pools during breeding season. At other times, mainly coastal but also on Great Lakes. **OBSERVATION TIPS** Elevated vantage points overlooking sandy bays often provide best chances of seeing species well, other than in flight.

MALE, SUMMER MOLTING

BUFFLEHEAD *Bucephala albeola* L 13–14 in

Small, distinctive diving duck with a dainty bill. Feeds on aquatic invertebrates. Male is unmistakable and female is easy to identify when plumage and size are considered fully. In flight, all birds show white inner flight feathers and take off almost vertically from water when alarmed. **ADULT MALE** Has rather large, rounded head that looks black and white in poor light; good light reveals an iridescent purple sheen to black elements. Body plumage is otherwise white, except for black back. Eclipse and first-winter males recall adult female. **ADULT FEMALE** Dark brown back and head, except for striking white oval patch on cheek. White on wing can be glimpsed in swimming birds. Neck and underparts grayish white. **JUVENILE** Similar to adult female. **VOICE** Mostly silent. **STATUS AND HABITAT** Fairly common. Found on wooded lakes in breeding season, nesting in tree holes. In winter, on sheltered coastal bays and inland lakes.

FEMALE

FEMALE

MALE

HARLEQUIN DUCK

MALE

FEMALE, WINTER

LONG-TAILED DUCK

MALE, WINTER
DISPLAYING

BUFFLEHEAD

MALE

Anatidae

BARROW'S GOLDENEYE
Bucephala islandica L 17–19 in
Compact diving duck that feeds on aquatic invertebrates. Similar
to Common Goldeneye, but note Barrow's steeper forehead and smaller bill.
Adult male's crescent shaped (not oval) white face patch is diagnostic, and
greater extent of black on back is a useful distinguishing feature. In flight,
white on inner upper wing is less extensive than in Common Goldeneye.
ADULT MALE Has proportionately large, rounded, iridescent purple head with
very steep forehead and vertical white crescent marking just behind base of bill. Ladder of white markings can be seen on otherwise black back; black extends forward as prominent "spur" shape in swimming birds. Vent is black, but neck and underparts are otherwise white. Note the beady yellow eye.
First-winter plumage has colors of adult female, but hint of adult's facial crescent. **ADULT FEMALE**
Dark brown head separated from gray-brown body plumage by pale neck. Bill is mostly dull orange-
yellow (color confined to tip in female Common), but a bit darker in summer. **JUVENILE** Similar to
adult female, but bill and eye are dark. **VOICE** Mostly silent. **STATUS AND HABITAT** Local in east (far
more widespread in western North America). In summer, found on Arctic lakes and ponds. Most move
to sheltered coasts in winter. **OBSERVATION TIPS** Search northern coasts in winter.

COMMON GOLDENEYE
Bucephala clangula L 17–19 in
Robust diving duck. Both sexes are similar to their Barrow's coun-
terparts—*see* that species' description for differences. In flight, white on
inner upper wings is more extensive in male than female. **ADULT MALE**
Has mainly black and white plumage. Rounded, peaked head appears dark

MALE

in poor light, but iridescent green in
sunshine. Note beady yellow eye and
striking white oval patch at base of bill.
Eclipse male resembles an adult female,
but retains his more striking white wing pattern. **ADULT FEMALE**
Gray-brown body plumage separated from dark brown head by
pale neck. Note beady yellow eye. **JUVENILE** Similar to adult
female, but with dark eye. **VOICE** Displaying male utters squeaky
calls. Otherwise silent. **STATUS AND HABITAT** Common and widespread. In summer, found on wooded lakes, nesting in tree holes.
In winter, commonest on coasts, although also found on ice-free
inland lakes across region.

RUDDY DUCK *Oxyura jamaicensis* L 14–16 in
Small diving duck that feeds on aquatic invertebrates and submerged
roots and seeds. Both sexes regularly cock their spiky-looking tails.
Breeding male is unmistakable and engages in "bubbling" chest-beating
courtship displays in spring. In winter, all birds could perhaps be confused
with a small grebe, but Ruddy Duck's proportionately large bill easily dispels
confusion. **ADULT MALE** In breeding plumage, has orange-chestnut body

MALE NONBREEDING

plumage, white cheeks, black cap and
nape, and bright blue bill. Note also the
small white vent. Outside breeding sea-
son, body plumage is gray-brown and bill is more dull grayish.
ADULT FEMALE Gray-brown plumage, with paler cheeks that are
broken by dark line from base of bill; bill is dull blue-gray, similar to that seen in winter male. **VOICE** Mostly silent. **STATUS
AND HABITAT** Local breeding species in east, favoring freshwater marshes and well-vegetated lakes; nests among emergent
vegetation. In winter, found on sheltered estuaries and bays on
Atlantic and Gulf coasts, and ice-free lakes and ponds inland.

FEMALE

BARROW'S GOLDENEYE

MALE

FEMALE

COMMON GOLDENEYE

MALE

RUDDY DUCK

FEMALE

MALE, BREEDING

Anatidae

HOODED MERGANSER
Lophodytes cucullatus L 17–19 in
Small, bizarrely shaped diving duck with slender bill and large head.
Dives frequently in search of small fish and invertebrates. Male is unmistakable; size, proportions, and color in female are good means of identification.
ADULT MALE Has large crest that can be flattened or fanned, presenting a
large, gleaming white patch on otherwise dark head. Bill is dark and note
beady yellow eye. Back is mainly dark and breast is
white, marked with two black lines on sides, separating
breast from otherwise orange-brown flanks. Eclipse male
is similar to adult female, but with duller colors; retains bright eye. **ADULT
FEMALE** Orange-buff head with long, shaggy crest. Plumage is otherwise mainly
gray-brown, darkest on back; belly is white. Eye is dark. **JUVENILE** Similar to adult
female. **VOICE** Mostly silent. **STATUS AND HABITAT** In summer, found in forested
wetlands; nests in tree holes. Outside breeding season, most birds move to southeast wetlands, favoring freshwater sites. **OBSERVATION TIPS** Typically shy during
breeding season; easier to observe in winter although still has retiring habits.

COMMON MERGANSER *Mergus merganser* L 24–26 in
Large, slender-bodied, and elegant diving duck that swims with a
stately posture. Dives frequently for fish and invertebrates. In
flight, upper surface of male's inner wing is white, except for narrow black
line; in female, white is restricted to trailing edge. **ADULT MALE** Unmistakable,
with bright red-orange bill, glossy green head (looks dark in poor light), white
body, and black back. Close view reveals pink wash on white breast and underparts. Eclipse male resembles adult female, although white wing pattern is
retained. **ADULT FEMALE** Orange-red head and neck with shaggy crest and well
defined white throat. Body plumage is grayish, palest on breast. Note the reddish
orange bill. **JUVENILE** Resembles adult female,
but with duller colors. **VOICE** Male utters ringing
display calls. Otherwise silent. **STATUS AND HABI-
TAT** Widespread and common. In summer, favors
wooded lakes and rivers; nests in tree holes. Outside breeding season, moves south to ice-free
freshwater lakes across region; occasionally found
on coasts. **OBSERVATION TIPS** Ice-bound lake
margins often concentrate birds in winter.

RED-BREASTED MERGANSER
Mergus serrator L 22–24 in
Slim diving duck. Recalls Common Merganser, but smaller and both
sexes have shaggy, spiky, crest rather than a sleek head. Dives frequently in
search of fish and invertebrates. In flight, both sexes show white on upper
inner wing; extent is greatest in males, the white divided by two black lines.
ADULT MALE Has a narrow reddish bill, a green head (looks dark in poor light),
white neck, and streaked orange-red breast. Flanks are gray and back is black.
Eclipse male is similar to adult female, but retains wing pattern. **ADULT FEMALE**
Reddish bill, dirty orange head and
nape, but a paler throat; body plumage is otherwise grayish buff.
JUVENILE Resembles adult female. **VOICE** Males utter soft, grunting display calls. Otherwise silent. **STATUS AND HABITAT** Common. In summer, found on tundra and boreal forest lakes. Outside
breeding season, most birds move to coasts although some may
occur on large, ice-free freshwater lakes. **OBSERVATION TIPS** Easiest to find in winter: search estuaries and large, sheltered bays.

FEMALE

MALE

HOODED MERGANSER

FEMALE

COMMON MERGANSER

MALE

FEMALE

RED-BREASTED MERGANSER

MALE

Anatidae and Cracidae

COMMON EIDER *Somateria mollissima* L 23–25 in

Bulky sea duck that dives frequently and for long periods. Distinctive even in silhouette—large, wedge-shaped bill follows slope of forehead. Highly gregarious for most of year. In summer, several females may band together, accompanied by "creche" of youngsters. In flight, male looks black and white, while female can look uniformly dark in poor light. Except during summer molt, sexes have strikingly dissimilar plumages. Three of the four North American subspecies occur in the region covered by this book. **ADULT MALE** Has mainly black underparts and white upperparts, except for black cap, lime green nape and pinkish flush on breast. In eclipse plumage, male is mainly a mixture of brown and black, although some white feathering is always visible on back. Bill is yellow, smaller, and broader-based in Atlantic ssp. *dresseri* than "Hudson Bay" ssp. *sedentaria* or Arctic ssp. *borealis*. Note: ssp. *v-nigrum* from Pacific has orange bill but occurs outside range of this book. **ADULT FEMALE** Brown with darker barring, plumage affording superb camouflage when bird is nesting. Bill is dark gray. **JUVENILE** Similar to adult female, but typically shows a pale stripe above eye. **VOICE** Male utters a characteristic, and rather endearing, cooing *ah-Whooo*. While doing so, head is thrown back in a distinctive manner. **STATUS AND HABITAT** Mainly coastal, nesting close to seashore and usually feeding in inshore waters. Favors estuaries and rocky shores, diving for invertebrates, particularly mussels and other mollusks. Some birds are resident while northern populations move south in winter. **OBSERVATION TIPS** Easy to see on northeast rocky shores.

KING EIDER *Somateria spectabilis* L 21–23 in

Distinctive sea duck that dives regularly and for extended periods in search of marine invertebrates. Adult male in summer is unmistakable, but female could be confused with female Common Eider: note King Eider's smaller size, more dainty bill and smaller head, and more prominent pale line running back from eye, and pale eye surround. Extremely gregarious during migration and in winter. **ADULT MALE** Spectacular, the rather oversized-looking blue head bearing a red bill and large orange basal knob. Black lines demarcate areas of color on head. Breast is pinkish orange and rest of body is mainly black, with a white patch on side of vent, and a horizontal white line on flanks. Raised, sail-like scapulars can be discerned at close range. In flight, note the white wing coverts, above and below. **ADULT FEMALE** Warm brown, marbled plumage and dark gray bill. In flight, note the pale underwing coverts. **JUVENILE** Similar to adult female. **VOICE** Male utters a purring sound. **STATUS AND HABITAT** Locally common, nesting beside coastal tundra pools in Canadian Arctic. Most winter in coastal waters of North Atlantic seaboard. **OBSERVATION TIPS** Easiest to see on coasts in winter.

PLAIN CHACHALACA
Ortalis vetula L 21–22in

Long-tailed, rather secretive southern Texas specialty. Best located by listening for call. Typically found in social groups. Sexes are similar. **ADULT** Has gray-brown head and neck, grading to warm brown on back and wings, and warm buff on underparts. Tail is relatively long, mostly dark, but with striking white feather tips. Bare throat skin becomes reddish in breeding male. **JUVENILE** Similar to adult but duller, with pale feather margins. **VOICE** A loud and harsh *cha-chalac*. **STATUS AND HABITAT** Local woodland resident in southern Texas; range extends into Central America. **OBSERVATION TIPS** Listen for the distinctive call.

ADULT

MALE

MALE, SUBADULT

COMMON EIDER

FEMALE

MALE

KING EIDER

FEMALE

Phasianidae

GRAY PARTRIDGE *Perdix perdix* L 12–13 in

Subtly attractive and non-native partridge. Usually wary due to hunting. Typically seen in small groups (coveys) that prefer to run from
danger rather than fly. Sexes are separable with care. **ADULT MALE** Has
orange-buff face and finely marked blue-gray nape, neck, and breast. Note the
striking maroon horseshoe marking on otherwise mostly white belly. Body
plumage is otherwise reddish brown, but with intricate markings, fine streaks
on back, and maroon stripes on flanks. **ADULT FEMALE** Similar to male, but
marking on belly is indistinct or absent and plumage is duller overall. **JUVENILE**
Gray-buff, but with a suggestion of adult's dark markings. **VOICE** Male utters a
choked and harsh *kierr-ikk* call. **STATUS AND HABITAT** Native of Eurasia. Introduced for hunting and now
local, but scarce and possibly declining. Favors open grassland and arable farmland. **OBSERVATION TIPS**
Easiest to observe outside breeding season when small groups can be seen feeding in open fields.

RING-NECKED PHEASANT *Phasianus colchicus*

L 26–35 in (male) L 21–30 in (female)

Male is colorful and unmistakable; adult female is also distinctive.
Takes to the air noisily and explosively when flushed. Sexes are strikingly
dissimilar. **ADULT MALE** Has orange-brown body plumage, blue-green sheen
on head, striking red wattle, and long, orange and barred tail; white collar
is absent in some birds. Captive-bred violet-blue forms are sometimes
released and can be confused
with male Japanese Green
Pheasant (*P. versicolor*, some-

MALE

times classified as a separate species). **ADULT FEMALE**
Mottled buffy brown, with a shorter tail than male.
JUVENILE Resembles a small, short-tailed, and dowdy
female. **VOICE** Territorial male utters a loud, shrieking
call, followed by bout of vigorous wing beating. In
alarm, utters a loud *ke-tuk, ke-tuk, ke-tuk* as bird flies
away. **STATUS AND HABITAT** Native to Asia and introduced for hunting. Now locally common and populations
are boosted each fall by release of captive-bred birds for
hunting. Favors mixed agricultural landscapes with
scattered woodland and brushy borders. **OBSERVATION
TIPS** Male's territorial call is distinctive in spring and
displaying birds are entertaining to watch.

WILD TURKEY *Meleagris gallopavo*

L 45–46 in (male) L 36–37 in (female)

Unmistakable and iconic native bird. Male's display is impressive with
puffed-up body feathers and fanned tail. Feeds mainly on seeds, fruits, nuts,
and invertebrates. Sexes are dissimilar. **ADULT MALE** Dark brown overall, but
with a bronzy, greenish sheen on back, neck and underparts. Tail is reddish
brown and proportionately long with chestnut feather tips, upper tail
coverts, and rump feathers; these appear as concentric rings in fanned tail.
Note tuft of feathers on breast. Head and upper neck are bare, bristly, and
mainly blue, but red on throat. **ADULT FEMALE** Smaller and duller than male and
lacks tuft of feathers on breast. **JUVENILE** Similar to adult female. **VOICE** Displaying male utters familiar gobbling call. All birds utter subdued clucking calls. **STATUS AND HABITAT** Hunted to local extinction in many places by start of 20th century. Now locally common due to hunting regulations and
breeding for release programs. **OBSERVATION TIPS** Easiest to find in spring, when males display noisily. **COMMENT** Western subspecies (seen mainly outside range of this book) has white feather tips on
tail. Released, formerly domesticated turkeys sometimes show this character.

FEMALE

MALE

GRAY PARTRIDGE

FEMALE

RING-NECKED PHEASANT

MALE

FEMALE

MALE, EASTERN

MALE, SOUTHWESTERN

WILD TURKEY

Tetraonidae

RUFFED GROUSE *Bonasa umbellus* L 17–18 in

Plump grouse. Intricate plumage patterns afford it superb camouflage on woodland floor. Feeds mainly on buds, shoots, and fruits.
Gray and reddish brown color forms occur throughout, but birds from east
are palest and grayest, while those from west typically are darkest and
brownest. All adult birds show a striking subterminal black band on otherwise brown or gray tail, most noticeable in flight. Sexes are similar. **ADULT
MALE** Has either gray or brown plumage, darker above than below, with pale
streaks on upperparts and dark bars on underparts. Dark tail feather bars
appear as concentric rings on fanned tail. Black feathers on neck form a ruff
when displaying; otherwise hard to see. **ADULT FEMALE** Similar to adult male, but smaller and with
shorter tail. **JUVENILE** Similar to adult female, but duller; dark subterminal tail band is absent. **VOICE**
Utters various squeaks. Male's drumming display is created by rapid wingbeats. **STATUS AND HABITAT**
Locally common in deciduous woodland, especially where Aspen *Populus tremuloides* is common (buds
and shoots feature in diet). **OBSERVATION TIPS** The wonderfully cryptic camouflage makes it hard to
spot. Listen for male's drumming in spring.

SPRUCE GROUSE *Falcipennis canadensis* L 16–16.5 in

Beautifully marked, well-camouflaged grouse. Two forms exist: represented in east by taiga forms (comprising several subspecies); ssp.
franklinii ("Franklin's Grouse") occurs in west, from Cascades and Rockies.
Feeds on conifer shoots and needles, and berries. Sexes are dissimilar. **ADULT
MALE** Has mainly dark brown plumage; white feather edges create scaly
appearance, particularly on belly and flanks. Breast and neck are mainly
black; black throat is defined by white border. Red wattles above both
eyes are striking in display. Taiga subspecies have dark tail with rufous terminal band. "Franklin's" has uniformly dark tail, with white tips to upper tail
coverts. **ADULT FEMALE** Either mainly gray or brown, with dark scaling above and white spots on belly.
JUVENILE Similar to brown morph female. **VOICE** Mostly silent. **STATUS AND HABITAT** Fairly common
in dense, young conifer forests. **OBSERVATION TIPS** Tame, often allowing close approach; camouflaged
plumage makes it hard to spot initially.

NORTHERN BOBWHITE *Colinus virginianus* L 9–10 in

North America's most familiar quail. Male's white throat and stripe
above the eye are distinctive; plumage otherwise shows regional
variation in extent of rufous. Diet includes seeds, fruits, bulbs, and inverte-

MALE, FLORIDA

brates. Gregarious outside breeding season when it forms coveys.
Sexes are dissimilar. **ADULT MALE**
Has white throat and stripe above
eye; dark elements of head pattern
vary from black to rufous, according
to region; lower margin of white throat is defined by black
"necklace." Body plumage is brown overall, but with pale barring on underparts and streaking on flanks. "Masked Bob-
white" (ssp. *ridgwayi*) has mainly rufous orange body plumage
and largely black face and throat; its southwestern U.S. range
is outside the scope of this book. **ADULT FEMALE** Rufous
brown overall, palest below, with streaked flanks and marbled
upperparts. Shows hint of male's head pattern, but pale elements of this are buff-yellow. **JUVENILE** Similar to adult
female, but duller. **VOICE** Male utters a strident *bob-white* call.
STATUS AND HABITAT In decline, but still locally common.
OBSERVATION TIPS Wary where hunted.

ADULT, RUFOUS

ADULT, GRAY

RUFFED GROUSE

SPRUCE GROUSE

FEMALE

MALE, TAIGA FORM

NORTHERN BOBWHITE

MALE

FEMALE

Tetraonidae

ROCK PTARMIGAN *Lagopus mutus* L 13–15 in

Hardy northern grouse. Feeds unobtrusively among rocks and seasonal plumage variation provides good camouflage at all times of the year. In flight, always shows striking white wings and prominent black tail feathers. Forms small flocks outside breeding season. Sexes are separable. **ADULT MALE** Pure

MALE, WINTER

white in winter, except for dark eye, lores, and bill; upper tail coverts often conceal black tail feathers. In spring, acquires marbled grayish buff upperparts; extent of white on back decreases gradually. Belly and legs remain white and note striking red wattle. **ADULT FEMALE** In winter is mainly white; only eye, bill, and tail are black. In spring and summer, has barred yellowish buff and gray upperparts; extent of white on back diminishes with time. **JUVENILE** Similar to summer female. **VOICE** Utters a rattling *kur-kurrrr* call. **STATUS AND HABITAT** Common on rocky tundra but range in east is limited to high Arctic. Mostly sedentary, but some limited altitudinal and southerly movement in winter. **OBSERVATION TIPS** Easiest to see when unseasonal winter thaw or summer snowfall makes camouflage inappropriate.

WILLOW PTARMIGAN *Lagopus lagopus* L 14–16 in

Similar to Rock Ptarmigan, but larger. Both have white wings, but black tail feathers are often concealed by white upper tail coverts. Willow's larger bill is not easy to discern, but difference in calls is more obvious. In summer, Willow has reddish plumage tone overall (gray-buff in Rock). Separation in winter is problematic: pure white plumage including lores, plus dark eye and bill is common to both sexes of Willow, and to female Rock. If alarmed takes flight explosively: bouts of rapid wingbeats are interspersed with long glides on bowed wings. **ADULT MALE** In winter is pure white, except for black tail, bill, and eye; hint of red eye wattle is sometimes seen. Acquires summer plumage through gradual spring molt; finally appears mainly reddish brown, but with white wings and belly. Note red wattle above each eye. **ADULT FEMALE** Has paler, more buffy red and marbled plumage than male; well camouflaged when nesting. **JUVENILE** Resembles summer female. **VOICE** Call is a distinctive, nasal *go-back, go-back*.... **STATUS AND HABITAT** Usually common, but numbers fluctuate. Favors willow scrub (diet includes shoots and buds). Mainly sedentary, but some move south in winter. **OBSERVATION TIPS** Easiest to see in spring.

SHARP-TAILED GROUSE

Tympanunchus phasianellus L 15–18 in

Plump grouse. Mostly unobtrusive but in spring males display at leks with neck wattle sacs inflated; erect tail is shaken, accompanied by foot-stamping. **ADULT MALE** Yellow-buff with white spots on back and wings, and barring on neck and underparts. Tail is yellow-buff above, fringed with barred feathers. When not displaying, note dark eyestripe. **ADULT FEMALE** Similar to

GREATER PRAIRIE-CHICKEN

male, but smaller, with less striking markings; neck sacs and wattles are absent. **JUVENILE** Similar to adult female. **VOICE** Displaying male utters hoots and clucks. **STATUS AND HABITAT** In decline due to habitat destruction but still locally common in sagebrush and grassland. **OBSERVATION TIPS** Easily overlooked except in breeding season. **SIMILAR SPECIES Greater Prairie-Chicken** *T. cupido* (L 16–18 in) is mainly western U.S. with a few prairie outposts in East. Plumage is dark-barred and buff. Male has bolder markings than female; when displaying (at lek) shows inflated orange neck sacs, yellow wattles above eyes, and raised head feathers.

ADULT MALE DISPLAYING

FEMALE, SUMMER

MALE, SUMMER

ROCK PTARMIGAN

FEMALE, SUMMER

MALE, SUMMER

WILLOW PTARMIGAN

MALE, SPRING

ADULT, WINTER

SHARP-TAILED GROUSE

ADULT MALE DISPLAYING

ADULT

Gaviidae and Podicipedidae

COMMON LOON *Gavia immer* L 32–33 in

Elegant waterbird. Long, pointed bill held horizontally or only slightly elevated. In flight, head and neck held outstretched and feet and legs trailing behind (true of all loons). Dives for fish. Sexes are similar. **ADULT** In summer has iridescent greenish black head and neck; note two rows of white stripes on neck. Blackish upperparts have checkerboard-like pattern of white spots on mantle and smaller white spots elsewhere. Underparts are white and bill is dark. In winter, has dark gray upperparts and whitish underparts; note dark half collar. Pale gray bill has noticeably darker culmen. **JUVENILE** Similar to winter adult, but upperparts are brownish gray, scaly-looking on back. **VOICE** Utters evocative, wailing cry and eerie yodeling sound on breeding grounds. **STATUS AND HABITAT** Fairly common on large lakes in breeding season. In winter, favors rocky coasts and large lakes inland. **OBSERVATION TIPS** Most fish-rich lakes within breeding range support a pair in summer. **SIMILAR SPECIES Yellow-billed Loon** *G. adamsii* (L 34–35 in) has similar summer and winter plumage. Pale yellow bill is straight, with paler culmen (concave and dark in Common); bill and head are held tilted upward. Juvenile is similar to winter adult with scaly-looking back. Locally common high Arctic breeder. Scarce on east coast in winter. **Pacific Loon** *G. pacifica* (L 24–26 in) is smaller, with a daintier bill. In summer, has black back with white checkerboard-like pattern of white spots, white underparts, black throat, and otherwise gray head and neck, with black and white stripes on side; in winter, has mainly dark upperparts and white underparts, throat, and front of neck. Breeds in Arctic, west from Hudson Bay. Winters mainly on Pacific; rare in East.

ADULT, WINTER — ADULT, SUMMER — **YELLOW-BILLED LOON**

ADULT, WINTER — ADULT, SUMMER — **PACIFIC LOON**

RED-THROATED LOON *Gavia stellata* L 24–25 in

Elegant loon that holds head and daggerlike bill tilted upward. Sexes are similar. **ADULT** Has blue-gray on face and sides of neck, red throat, and black and white lines on back of neck and, lower down, on sides of neck too. Upperparts are otherwise gray-brown while underparts are whitish. In winter, has gray upperparts, spangled with small white spots. Underparts are white. **JUVENILE** Similar to winter adult, but upperparts are browner and underparts appear grubby. **VOICE** Utters a gooselike *kaa-kaa-kaa* in flight. **STATUS AND HABITAT** Nests beside small pools and fairly common within Arctic range. Outside breeding season, found in shallow coastal seas. **OBSERVATION TIPS** Easiest to find in winter.

ADULT, SUMMER

RED-NECKED GREBE *Podiceps grisegena* L 18–20 in

Swims buoyantly and dives frequently for fish. Has striking white panels on wings, obvious in flight. Sexes are similar. **ADULT** In summer has dark gray-brown upperparts, including nape. Neck and upperparts are brick red, cheeks are pale gray bordered with white, and cap is dark with hint of crest. Underparts are otherwise whitish, with gray streaking on flanks. Bill is stocky and yellow with a dark culmen. In winter, neck color is lost, but often retains hint of reddish collar. Cheek pattern is less well defined and ear coverts are grubby-looking. **JUVENILE** Recalls winter adult, but shows more extensive red on neck; note striking dark stripes on cheeks. **VOICE** Utters subdued wails during breeding season. **STATUS AND HABITAT** Fairly common, breeding on shallow, northern freshwater lakes; more widespread in west than east. Winters mainly on sheltered coasts.

1ST-WINTER

COMMON LOON

ADULT, SUMMER

ADULT, WINTER

RED-THROATED LOON

ADULT, SUMMER

ADULT, WINTER

ADULT, SUMMER

RED-NECKED GREBE

HORNED GREBE *Podiceps auritus* L 12–14 in

Elegant waterbird that swims buoyantly and dives frequently in search of small fish and aquatic invertebrates. All birds have a beady red eye. Flattish crown and bill shape (both mandibles are curved) allow separation from similar Eared Grebe at all times; note also whitish tip to bill. In flight, wings show white patches on both leading and trailing edges. Sexes are similar. **ADULT** In summer, has reddish orange neck and flanks. Back is black and black head is adorned with golden yellow plumes. In winter, has mainly black upperparts and white underparts. Note clear demarcation between black cap and white cheeks. **JUVENILE** Similar to winter adult. **VOICE** Utters territorial calls including various rattling trills and squeals. **STATUS AND HABITAT** Locally common. In breeding season, favors ponds and shallow lakes with abundant emergent vegetation. In winter, mainly coastal, but also on ice-free freshwater lakes in south. **OBSERVATION TIPS** In winter, search sheltered stretches of coast on calm days. Unobtrusive in breeding season, except when displaying in spring.

EARED GREBE *Podiceps nigricollis* L 11–13 in

Distinguished from Horned Grebe by slightly upturned bill and steeper forehead. All birds have beady red eyes. In flight, note white patch on trailing edge of wing. Dives for aquatic invertebrates. Sexes are similar. **ADULT** In summer has blackish head, neck, and back; face is adorned with golden yellow tufts. Flanks are chestnut. In winter, has mainly blackish upperparts and white underparts; separable from similar Horned Grebe by greater extent of dark coloration on cheeks, as well as head shape. **JUVENILE** Similar to winter adult, but white elements of plumage are buffy. **VOICE** Calls include various whistles and squeaks. **STATUS AND HABITAT** Common. Favors shallow, well-vegetated inland lakes and ponds in breeding season. In winter, moves south to freshwater and brackish lakes and sheltered coasts. **OBSERVATION TIPS** Breeding birds have stunning plumage and are an impressive sight: easiest to find in spring when displaying. Winter concentrations are mainly in west, but can be found on Gulf coast.

PIED-BILLED GREBE

Podilymbus podiceps L 11–13 in

Stocky, plump-bodied grebe. Note the pale "powderpuff" of fluffy feathers at rear end. Bill is proportionately large and thick; black band is absent during winter months. Dives frequently for small fish and aquatic invertebrates. Sexes are similar. **ADULT** In summer, has gray-brown plumage, palest on flanks and neck. Bill is pale gray with a striking black band. In winter, plumage is more orange-buff, particularly on neck. Throat is pale and bill is uniformly yellowish gray. **JUVENILE** Has head stripes at first, but after molt acquires plumage like winter adult. **VOICE** Utters various clucking and chattering calls. **STATUS AND HABITAT** Widespread and common. Breeds on well-vegetated ponds and lakes and in winter moves south to ice-free similar freshwater habitats. **OBSERVATION TIPS** Usually indifferent to observers but seldom remains at water surface for long. **SIMILAR SPECIES Least Grebe** *Tachybaptus dominicus* (L 9–10 in) recalls a tiny version of Pied-billed Grebe but note the darker plumage overall in summer, beady yellow eyes (dark in Pied-billed), and daintier bill. Locally common only in southern Texas, on well-vegetated ponds and lakes.

LEAST GREBE

ADULT, SUMMER

ADULT, WINTER

HORNED GREBE

ADULT, SUMMER

ADULT, WINTER

EARED GREBE

ADULT, SUMMER

ADULT, WINTER

PIED-BILLED GREBE

ADULT, SUMMER

Procellariidae

NORTHERN FULMAR

PALE MORPH

DARK MORPH

Fulmarus glacialis W 40–42 in
Medium-sized, superficially gull-like
seabird relative of shearwaters and petrels. Easily distinguished from gulls at close range by
its long tubular nostrils and, in flight, by its
more stiffly held wings and effortless gliding.
Exceptionally buoyant, rides very high on
water, and often gathers in groups where feeding is good, for example around fishing boats.
Generally sociable and nests in loose colonies on sea cliffs. At nest, may
regurgitate oily and smelly crop contents in a projectile fashion if alarmed
by an intruder. Sexes are not separable, but different color morphs occur.
ADULT Pale morph has blue-gray upper wings, back, and tail. Head
and underparts are white. Note dark smudge around eye. Dark morph is
variably dark blue-gray, uniform in color, except for paler primaries.
JUVENILE Similar to the adult, once chick's fluffy white down has been
lost. **VOICE** Utters various gurgling cackles and grunts at colonies, but
otherwise silent. **STATUS AND HABITAT** Common and found year-round
in Arctic and sub-Arctic waters. Nests on ledges on sea cliffs and locally forms sizeable colonies on sea cliffs. In winter, range extends south
down Atlantic seaboard. **OBSERVATION TIPS** Seen on pelagic trips, but
also occasionally from headlands, especially during onshore gales. Many
sub-Arctic birds linger in vicinity of nesting colonies throughout year.

SOOTY SHEARWATER *Puffinus griseus* W 40–41 in

Medium-sized shearwater with a slender, hook-tipped bill and tubular nostrils. Relatively long, stiffly held wings allow it to bank
and glide effortlessly; particularly impressive in strong winds. Angle and
intensity of light affects appearance of plumage colors, particularly on body
and underwing. Sexes are similar. **ALL BIRDS** (not possible to age birds in the
field in our region) Can appear all-dark at a distance, but at close range,
and in good light, note sooty brown plumage and silvery white underwing
coverts that form a striking bar, palest and broadest toward wingtip. Bill
is rather long and more narrow in middle. **VOICE** Silent at sea. **STATUS AND
HABITAT** Breeds in southern hemisphere (during our winter). Undertakes clockwise circum-Atlantic
nonbreeding travels and present in North Atlantic May–Aug. **OBSERVATION TIPS** Easy to see on pelagic trips during summer months and very occasionally gathers close to shores in Jul–Aug if feeding is good.

CORY'S SHEARWATER

Calonectris diomedea W 44–45 in
Large and impressive seabird. Flight is effortless: banks and
glides on wings held stiffly or bowed. Only seen at sea and views are typically distant and brief, except where birds gather at a good feeding source
(e.g. fishing boat). Sexes are similar. **ALL BIRDS** (not possible to age birds
at sea in our region) Have mainly buffish brown upperparts with darker
wingtips and a dark tip to tail (sometimes shows a limited amount of white
at base of tail). Underparts are white, the wings having dark margins. Bill is
dark-tipped and yellow. **VOICE** Mostly silent, but cackles when squabbling over
food. **STATUS AND HABITAT** Common summer visitor (mainly Jun–Aug) from its east Atlantic island
breeding grounds. Numbers vary from year to year. **OBSERVATION TIPS** Usually easy to see in small
numbers on pelagic trips in summer.

NORTHERN FULMAR

ADULT

SOOTY SHEARWATER

ADULT

ADULT

CORY'S SHEARWATER

Procellariidae

GREATER SHEARWATER *Puffinus gravis* W 42–43 in

Similar to Cory's (*see* p.63) but separable by plumage differences, and because generally it flies on stiffer wings. Effortless flight is masterful in strong winds. Sometimes gathers in large flocks in areas of good feeding (e.g. where fish are shoaling, or around fishing boats). Sexes are similar. **ALL BIRDS** (ages are not separable in the field) Have dark grayish brown upper wing coverts and mantle, contrasting with darker wingtips. Note the darker tail and contrasting white upper tail coverts. Dark cap is separated from mantle by incomplete white collar. Underparts are mainly white with dark markings. **VOICE** Silent in the region. **STATUS AND HABITAT** Breeds on South Atlantic islands (in our winter) and undertakes circum-Atlantic nonbreeding travels; present in North Atlantic in summer months and commonest Jul–Sep. Numbers vary from year to year but usually common in offshore waters. **OBSERVATION TIPS** Only very occasionally comes close enough to shore to be seen from land but easy to see on pelagic and whale-watching trips, typically well out of sight of land.

AUDUBON'S SHEARWATER
Puffinus lherminieri W 26–27 in

Fast-flying, narrow-winged shearwater that flashes alternately black and white as it banks and glides, skimming low over water. Sometimes gathers in sizeable groups if feeding is good, and dives after fish. Seldom comes close to land except when nesting, and then only after dark. Sexes are similar. **ALL BIRDS** (ages are not separable at sea) Have blackish brown upperparts and mostly white underparts except for dark flight feathers and leading margin to wing. Note the dark undertail coverts and longer tail end (cf. Manx Shearwater). Bill is slender and hooked with small tube nostrils. **VOICE** Silent at sea but utters weird cackling calls after dark at breeding colonies. **STATUS AND HABITAT** Summer visitor (present mainly Jun–Sep) to Gulf of Mexico and Atlantic, breeding on islands in Caribbean. Favors warm waters for feeding hence range is determined by influence of Gulf Stream and extends further north as summer progresses. **OBSERVATION TIPS** Seldom seen from shore but easy to see on pelagic trips within range.

MANX SHEARWATER *Puffinus puffinus* W 33–35 in

Appreciably larger than Audubon's and separable by noting the white undertail coverts, relatively shorter tail, and greater extent of white on underwings. Contrast between dark upperparts and mainly white underparts are revealed as it banks and glides. Invariably seen at sea flying low over the water on stiffly held wings. Typically seen in sizeable groups. Sexes are similar. **ALL BIRDS** Have more blackish upperparts (not so dark brown, as in Audubon's) and mainly white underparts, although wing margins are dark. **VOICE** Silent at sea but at breeding colonies weird, strangled coughing calls are uttered after dark by nesting birds. **STATUS AND HABITAT** Summer visitor to North Atlantic, present mainly Jun–Sep; winters in South Atlantic. Breeds on remote islands, mainly in northeast Atlantic but recently in Canada too, in small numbers. Fairly widespread in offshore Atlantic waters during spring and summer and favors cooler waters than Audubon's. **OBSERVATION TIPS** Sometimes seen from whale-watching trips operating out of New England ports.

ADULT

ADULT

ADULT

ADULT

GREATER SHEARWATER

AUDUBON'S SHEARWATER

MANX SHEARWATER

ADULTS

ADULT

Hydrobatidae

WILSON'S STORM-PETREL
Oceanites oceanicus W 16–18 in

Tiny seabird that looks all-dark at a distance, but with a striking and contrasting white rump and undertail coverts. At close range, note the square-tipped tail (may appear a bit notched when not spread), the relatively long legs (when outstretched, the toes project beyond the tail), and the pale panel on the upper wing coverts. It glides on outstretched, flat wings and also flutters low over the water, pattering the surface with its dangling feet. Sexes are similar. **ALL BIRDS** Have dark gray-brown plumage, palest on underside of flight feathers and with pale bar on upper wing coverts. Rump is white. Legs are dark and feet have yellow webs. **VOICE** Silent at sea. **STATUS AND HABITAT** Breeds on islands in southern oceans (in our winter) and moves to North Atlantic outside its breeding season. Common offshore visitor (present mainly May–Sep) and seldom seen within sight of land. **OBSERVATION TIPS** Easy to see on pelagic and whale-watching trips during summer months. Sometimes gathers in large concentrations where feeding is good, e.g. around fishing boats.

BAND-RUMPED STORM-PETREL
Oceanodroma castro W 17–19 in

Small seabird with mostly all-dark plumage and a relatively narrow, bandlike white rump. Flight is reminiscent of a shearwater, with glides interspersed with burst of rapid wingbeats. Told from similar-sized Wilson's by shorter legs (feet do not project beyond tail in flight), much less distinct pale bar on upper wing coverts, and different flight pattern. Told from Leach's by tail shape (only slightly notched in Band-rumped but deeply forked in Leach's), narrow white rump (elongated and divided centrally by dusky bar in Leach's), and different flight patterns. Sexes are similar. **ALL ADULTS** Have mostly very dark blackish brown plumage except for white rump; upper wings have faint pale carpal bar. **VOICE** Silent at sea; purring calls uttered at nest by breeding birds. **STATUS AND HABITAT** Breeds on Azores and other islands in east Atlantic and common in offshore waters in west Atlantic and Gulf of Mexico, May–Sep. **OBSERVATION TIPS** Usually easy to see on deep sea pelagic trips in summer. Most records occur far beyond the sight of land.

LEACH'S STORM-PETREL
Oceanodroma leucorhoa W 18–20 in

Tiny by seabird standards, but with relatively long wings and a deeply forked tail. Flight direction and pattern are ever-changing, often bounding with deep, powerful wingbeats, but occasionally gliding in an almost shearwater-like fashion. Combination of forked tail and white, wedge-shaped rump (divided down middle by gray line) is diagnostic. Sexes are similar. **ALL BIRDS** Sooty gray, but can look all-dark at a distance,

ADULT

except for pale panel on upper wing coverts. Note that tail's fork is not always easy to discern and pale gray line that divides rump is visible only at very close range. Underwings are all-dark. **VOICE** Silent at sea, but at breeding colonies birds utter a bizarre-sounding gurgling rattle. **STATUS AND HABITAT** Oceanic, seldom approaching land except during breeding season at night. Nests in burrows on remote islands off Canadian coast with some sizeable colonies. **OBSERVATION TIPS** Tricky to observe since it shuns land and typically does not follow boats. Chance encounters from pelagic trips offer the best opportunities.

ADULT

WILSON'S STORM-PETREL

ADULT

BAND-RUMPED STORM-PETREL

LEACH'S STORM-PETREL

ADULT

Pelecanidae

AMERICAN WHITE PELICAN
Pelecanus erythrorhynchos L 61–63 in

Huge and unmistakable waterbird with the typical pelican form: plump body, proportionately long neck, and extremely long, hooked-tip bill with expandable gular pouch. Essentially white plumage, seen in standing and swimming bird, is transformed when bird takes to the air, revealing contrasting black flight feathers. Wingspan is immense (W 108 in), allowing bird to soar and glide with ease; note the distinctive wing pattern, proportionately short tail, and forward-projecting bill. Swims with ease, by means of large, webbed feet. Feeds on fish by engulfing shoals in huge, yellow gular pouch; often feeds collectively. Sexes are similar. **ADULT** Appears mainly white, but in breeding season breast is flushed faintly with yellow-buff and crown sometimes appears grubby looking. Black flight feathers are mostly hidden in swimming and standing birds. Legs are reddish orange; bill and bare skin surrounding eye are reddish orange in breeding season but more yellowish in winter. **JUVENILE** Similar to adult, but with faint gray feathering on neck and upper wing coverts, and duller bill colors. **VOICE** Mostly silent, although soft grunts are uttered by nesting birds. **STATUS AND HABITAT** Locally common breeding species, nesting colonially on large lakes with abundant fish, mainly in midwestern prairie states. Outside breeding season, moves south to southern U.S. states and Mexico, favoring large freshwater lakes and coastal lagoons and estuaries. **OBSERVATION TIPS** Large enough to not be easily missed, and usually tolerant enough of people, allowing good views, especially during winter months. Soaring flocks are an amazing sight, as are groups engaged in collective feeding.

BROWN PELICAN *Pelecanus occidentalis* L 48–51 in

Huge and impressive waterbird. Unmistakably a pelican, given the body shape, huge bill, and expandable gular pouch; mainly dark plumage allows easy separation from American White Pelican. Swims effortlessly and with grace, using large, webbed feet. Also extremely impressive in flight and capable of sustained gliding and soaring. Feeds in a spectacular manner: dives from a considerable height, pulling back the wings at the last second and engulfing fish in expanded gular pouch when submerged. Sexes are similar. **ADULT** Has streaked, silvery gray upperparts and pale-streaked, brown underparts. Head and neck are whitish in winter, variably flushed with orange-yellow on crown and forehead, with yellowish pink bill and gray-brown gular pouch; breeding bird is similar but has dark brown on rear of neck. **JUVENILE** Mainly brown plumage, but with a whitish belly; seen from below in flight, note the pale margin to underwing coverts that forms a subtle stripe. **VOICE** Mostly silent. **STATUS AND HABITAT** Locally fairly common resident on Gulf coast, especially in south Texas and Florida. Feeds in both sheltered bays and relatively exposed seas. Often seen perched on boat moorings and posts. Seldom seen on inland freshwater lakes. **OBSERVATION TIPS** Usually easy to see in suitable coastal locations and typically not bothered by the presence of people, allowing superb views to be obtained. Fishing birds provide a wonderful spectacle and the activities of one diving bird usually quickly attracts a small gathering of feeding pelicans.

ADULT, NONBREEDING

AMERICAN WHITE PELICAN

JUVENILE

ADULT

ADULT

BROWN PELICAN

JUVENILE

ADULT, BREEDING

Fregatidae and Sulidae

MAGNIFICENT FRIGATEBIRD
Fregata magnificens W 87–90 in

Huge and unmistakable seabird with something of a prehistoric look about it. Has extremely long, pointed, and angular-looking wings, long and deeply forked tail, and long, hook-tipped bill. Aerial mastery is aided by excellent weight:wing area ratio (its feathers weigh more than its bones). Soars and glides effortlessly but capable of amazing speed and agility when in pursuit of food (it picks fish from the surface of the sea) or when parasitizing other feeding birds (forces them to regurgitate or drop their last meal). Breeds colonially in trees, notably coastal mangroves; nest is a stick platform. Sexes are dissimilar. **ADULT MALE** Mostly all-dark, but purple sheen is seen in good light. Bright red throat sac is inflated in display. **ADULT FEMALE** Lacks male's throat sac and has white on belly. **JUVENILE** Mainly dark, but note the white head, neck, and belly patch, and brown upper wing coverts. **VOICE** Mainly silent. **STATUS AND HABITAT** Breeds on the Dry Tortuga islands, Florida; outside the protracted breeding season, wanders and mainly pelagic, or coastal around Caribbean islands, but also visits the Gulf coast. **OBSERVATION TIPS** Usually easy to see on the Florida Keys throughout the year.

JUVENILE

NORTHERN GANNET *Morus bassanus* L 35–38 in

A distinctive species, and one of the largest seabirds in the region. Recognized in flight by its cigar-shaped body and long, narrow wings. Flies with deep, powerful wingbeats, but in strong winds it glides effortlessly on stiffly held wings. Bill is large and daggerlike. When a shoal of fish is discovered, groups of birds plunge-dive from a considerable height (100ft or so), providing an extraordinary spectacle. Sexes are similar, but adult plumage is acquired through successive molts over a five-year period. **ADULT** Has essentially white body plumage with black wingtips (primaries). Note the buffy yellow wash to the head. **JUVENILE** Has dark brown plumage, speckled with white dots. **2ND-WINTER** Similar to juvenile, but underparts are mainly white; typically the head and neck are white except for a dark cap. **3RD-WINTER** Recalls adult, but shows extensive dark feathering on the back and inner wings. **4TH-WINTER** Similar to adult, but some of the secondaries on the inner wing are dark. **VOICE** Silent at sea, but nesting birds utter harsh grating calls. **STATUS AND HABITAT** Very locally common in North Atlantic, nesting in dense concentrations on precipitous sea cliffs, inaccessible to ground predators. Six colonies exist in North America, three on Atlantic coast of Newfoundland and three in Gulf of St. Lawrence. Outside breeding season, moves south down Atlantic seaboard. **OBSERVATION TIPS** Superb views can be had (May–Jul) at Cape St. Mary's Ecological Reserve on Newfoundland's Avalon Peninsula. Otherwise, seen on pelagic trips and from headlands. **SIMILAR SPECIES Masked Booby** *Sula dactylatra* (L 32–33 in) adult is similar to adult Northern Gannet, but note that all flight feathers (not just primaries) are black and has black tail; face has black "mask" at base of bill. Juvenile is similar to juvenile Northern Gannet, but note the white neck and entirely white underwing coverts (only inner underwing coverts are white in Northern Gannet). Breeds on the Dry Tortuga islands and seen at sea in Gulf of Mexico in spring and summer; outside breeding season, range is oceanic and sometimes wanders north along Atlantic seaboard.

JUVENILE

ADULT

MASKED BOOBY

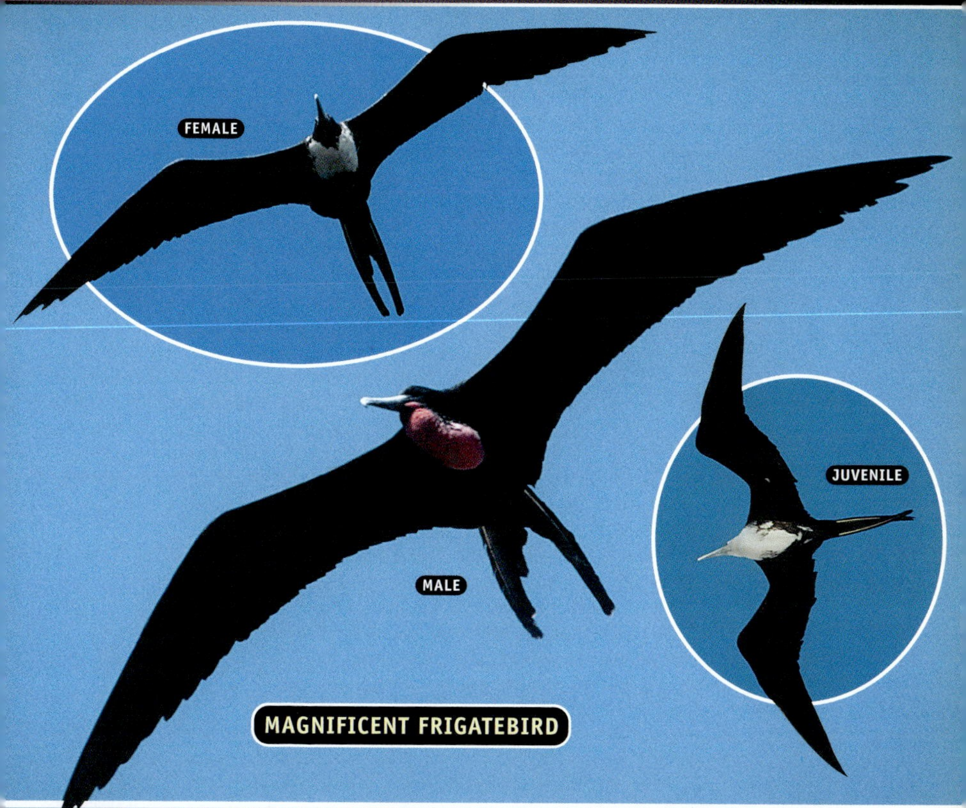

FEMALE

JUVENILE

MALE

MAGNIFICENT FRIGATEBIRD

NORTHERN GANNET

ADULT

NESTING

ANHINGA *Anhinga anhinga* L 34–35 in

Bizarre and unmistakable slim waterbird. Swims well, often so low in water that only its long, slender head and neck are visible. Note also the very long tail, broad wings, and yellow daggerlike bill. Dives well and catches fish. Often perches on branches with wings outstretched to dry. Sexes are separable. **ADULT MALE** Has blackish plumage, except for silvery feathers on upper wing coverts and silvery, elongate feathers on back and scapulars.

FEMALE

ADULT FEMALE Similar to male, but has a buffy brown head, neck, and breast. **JUVENILE** Similar to adult female, but silvery elements of upper wing and back plumage are duller and show less contrast. **VOICE** Mostly silent, but agitated nesting birds utter rattling croaks. **STATUS AND HABITAT** Associated with swamps rich with fish; also lakes and sluggish rivers. Found year-round near coasts but, in summer, breeding range extends inland. **OBSERVATION TIPS** Easy to see on Gulf coast, but for spectacularly close views visit the Everglades.

GREAT CORMORANT *Phalacrocorax carbo* L 35–37 in

Large, dark waterbird with a heavy, hook-tipped bill. Found mainly in coastal waters. Swims low in water and dives (typically with a noticeable leap) for fish, propelling itself with large webbed feet. Flies with head and neck held forward and often perches on rocks or posts with wings outstretched to dry. Sexes are similar. **SUMMER ADULT** Often looks mainly dark, but plumage's oily sheen and black-bordered brownish wing feathers are seen in good light. Eye is green and skin at base of bill is yellow, grading to white. In full breeding plumage, has white thigh patch and white on head and neck. **WINTER ADULT** Loses white feathering. **JUVENILE** Has brown upperparts and whitish underparts; acquires adult plumage over next 2 years. **VOICE** Utters nasal and guttural calls at breeding colonies but otherwise silent. **STATUS AND HABITAT** Nests colonially on undisturbed rocky coasts from Newfoundland to Maine. Present in nearby coastal seas year-round, but many birds move south down Atlantic seaboard in winter. **OBSERVATION TIPS** Most widespread in winter.

DOUBLE-CRESTED CORMORANT
Phalacrocorax auritus L 32–33 in

Robust waterbird with relatively long neck and hook-tipped bill. Compared to larger Great Cormorant, neck and bill are more slender and breeding birds (in our region) lack white in plumage (western birds have white crests). Swims low in water, diving frequently for fish. Flies with head and neck outstretched; often perches with wings outstretched. North America's most widespread cormorant and the one most likely encountered near fresh water. Sexes

ADULT, WINTER

are similar. **ADULT** has mainly dark plumage, but pale feather centers on back and upper wings create a scaly appearance. Acquires black head plumes in breeding season. Note orange gular pouch, base to lower mandible and skin in front of eye; color is most intense in breeding birds. **JUVENILE** Has gray-buff plumage, darkest on back and usually palest on breast and throat. Bill, bare skin around eye, and gular pouch are yellowish orange; note truncated rear margin. Acquires darker adult plumage over 3-year period. **VOICE** Mostly silent. **STATUS AND HABITAT** Locally common on coasts, freshwater marshes and lakes. Present year-round on coast, but a summer visitor to many interior freshwater habitats. **OBSERVATION TIPS** Easy to find in a range of wetland habitats.

ANHINGA

FEMALE

MALE

ADULT, SUMMER

ADULT, SUMMER

ADULT, BREEDING

ADULT

GREAT CORMORANT

DOUBLE-CRESTED CORMORANT

ADULT, WINTER

ADULT

JUVENILE

Ardeidae

LEAST BITTERN *Ixobrychus exilis* L 13–14 in

A tiny, well-marked heron whose unobtrusive habits and largely inaccessible favored habitats make it fairly hard to observe. Sometimes seen climbing up a tall cattail stem or more typically observed briefly in flight, flying low over marsh vegetation with rapid wingbeats. If alarmed, "freezes" with body, neck, and head elongated and pointing vertically. Feeds on fish and small freshwater invertebrates. Sexes are dissimilar. **ADULT MALE** Mainly yellow-buff, palest on underparts, with buff stripes on throat and breast. Cap and back are blackish, latter contrasting with pale buff panel on wings (striking in flight when dark flight feathers are obvious). Has yellow legs and facial skin (this turns pink at height of breeding season), and dull yellow bill with dark culmen. **ADULT FEMALE** Similar to male, but black elements of plumage are dark brown. **JUVENILE** Similar to female, but cap and back are gray-buff. **VOICE** Utters a quacking alarm call. Singing male utters a short succession of cooing notes. **STATUS AND HABITAT** Locally common summer visitor (present mainly May–Aug) to cattail swamps, but easily overlooked. Most migrate south of region for winter, but a few linger in south. **OBSERVATION TIPS** Presence is easiest to detect by recognizing male's song. Patient observation may then yield a brief view, perhaps of a flying bird.

AMERICAN BITTERN
Botaurus lentiginosus L 28–29 in

Bulky and distinctive wetland bird. Despite its large size, the cryptic plumage (that blends in particularly well with dead cattail stems) makes it very hard to spot. Its behavior enhances the effect: moves at a slow, stealthy pace and alarmed birds "skypoint," swaying with same motion as surrounding wetland vegetation. Flies with deep, powerful wingbeats, head and neck held hunched; dark flight feathers contrast with otherwise brown plumage. Feeds on amphibians, fish, and aquatic invertebrates, and often hunts at dawn and dusk. Sexes are similar. **ADULT** Has beautifully patterned brown plumage. Neck and breast have chestnut stripes on paler background and feathers on back and upper wing are marbled and finely marked. Note the white throat and supercilium, and black malar stripe. Daggerlike bill is yellow and legs are greenish. **JUVENILE** Similar to adult, but facial markings are less striking. **VOICE** Territorial birds utter a far-carrying, booming *BOonk-aLOonk*. **STATUS AND HABITAT** Widespread across Canada and northern U.S. in spring and summer, but seldom common. Associated with well-vegetated freshwater marshes and present in breeding range mainly Apr–Sep. Moves south and west in winter and then found mostly in coastal wetlands with large stands of cattail. **OBSERVATION TIPS** Presence often detected by "song" in spring. Persistent observation may be rewarded by a view of a flying bird.

ADULT

MALE

LEAST BITTERN

FEMALE

AMERICAN BITTERN

ADULT

ADULT

ADULT

Ardeidae

SNOWY EGRET *Egretta thula* L 24 in

Pure white heron-like bird. Superficially similar to Cattle and Great egrets but adult Snowy Egret's bright yellow feet, contrasting with otherwise black legs, and its black bill, are diagnostic. Long periods of time are spent roosting and preening. Sometimes adopts a patient, wait-and-see approach to feeding but also employs more energetic tactics in pursuit of fish, amphibians, and crustaceans. Sexes are similar but immatures and adults can be separated with care. Beware confusion with immature Little Blue Heron (*see* p.80), which is all white but has yellowish legs as well as feet, and a two-toned bill. **ADULT** Has pure white plumage with elegant plumes evident during breeding season. Legs are black and feet are yellow (orange tinged at height of breeding season). Daggerlike bill is dark and lores are yellow for much of the time, but are flushed red in breeding season. **JUVENILE** Similar to adult, but backs of legs are yellow. **VOICE** Mostly silent. **HABITAT AND STATUS** Associated with wetland habitats, ranging from sheltered coasts and brackish lagoons to freshwater lakes and rivers. Present year-round near coasts; summer breeding range extends inland. **OBSERVATION TIPS** Easy to see in suitable habitats.

CATTLE EGRET *Bubulcus ibis* L 20 in

Stocky, mainly white heron-like bird with a proportionately large head and bulbous throat. Gregarious and often associates with grazing livestock, chasing after insects and other prey disturbed by feeding animals. Sexes are similar but breeding adults are more colorful than nonbreeding and immatures. **ADULT** Has pure white plumage for much of year but at height of breeding season it becomes flushed yellowish buff on crown, breast, and back. Bill is yellow for most of year, turning orange-red in breeding season; legs are dark for most of year but turn orange-yellow during breeding season. **JUVENILE** Similar to nonbreeding adult. **VOICE** Mainly silent. **HABITAT AND STATUS** Originates from Old World and is a relatively recent arrival to our region; first noted in South America (presumably from Africa) and reached Florida in mid 20th century. Now a widespread resident in coastal districts in southeast, favoring grassland and wetlands; from spring to fall, also occurs inland during summer breeding season. **OBSERVATION TIPS** Usually found in drier habitats than other egret species.

ADULT

GREAT EGRET *Ardea alba* L 39 in

A stately, pure white, heron-like bird, appreciably larger than Snowy Egret; size and color alone are often enough to allow certain identification. Visitors to south Florida could confuse it with white morph of Great Blue Heron (*see* p.82). Great Egret uses its daggerlike bill to good effect when capturing prey, which includes fish and the occasional aquatic mammal or bird. Sexes are similar and outside breeding season adults and immatures are not easily separable. **ADULT** Has pure white plumage; during breeding season, long back plumes trail beyond tail. At all times, legs are dark and bill is yellow. Lores are yellow for much of year but turns bluish green in breeding season. **JUVENILE** Similar to nonbreeding adult. **VOICE** Mainly silent. **HABITAT AND STATUS** Much reduced (by persecution and habitat loss) compared to, say, a century ago. Nevertheless, still relatively common in wetland habitats (mainly freshwater and brackish). Resident year-round in coastal districts within its range (except in parts of West Coast), numbers boosted in winter by birds abandoning inland sites occupied from spring to fall. **OBSERVATION TIPS** So large and conspicuous that you should have no difficulty finding it; size and bill and leg color help separate it from superficially similar smaller species, and from white morph Great Blue Heron.

SNOWY EGRET

ADULT

ADULT, BREEDING

CATTLE EGRET

ADULT, BREEDING

ADULT, SPRING

ADULT

GREAT EGRET

ADULT

ADULT

BLACK-CROWNED NIGHT-HERON
Nycticorax nycticorax L 24–25 in

Stocky heron with proportionately large head and hunchbacked appearance at rest. Typically roosts during day and feeds actively only at night; prey includes amphibians, fish, and invertebrates. Nests and roosts communally. Flies on broad, rounded wings, with neck hunched up. Sexes are similar. **ADULT** Has dark, daggerlike bill, black crown and back, gray wings, and pale face and underparts; eyes are large and red, legs are yellowish, and head is adorned with white plumes. **JUVENILE** Has mainly brown plumage, heavily marked with white spots; bill is dull yellowish. Acquires adult plumage gradually over subsequent 2 years. **VOICE** Utters a barking *quaak* call in flight. **STATUS AND HABITAT** Locally fairly common in wetland habitats; usually roosts in waterside trees or bushes. Present year-round in coastal districts, but summer range extends well inland and north. **OBSERVATION TIPS** Most active at dawn and dusk.

YELLOW-CROWNED NIGHT-HERON
Nyctanassa violacea L 23–24 in

Has similar proportions to Black-crowned but plumage is mainly blue-gray with striking black and white markings on head. In flight, note the entirely dark underwings (white in Black-crowned). Most active after dark and typically roosts in trees during daytime, adopting hunchback appearance. Sexes are similar. **ADULT BREEDING** Blue-gray overall with pale streaks on back and wings and striking face markings: whitish yellow crown and black face with white cheeks. Note the long white head plumes, bright reddish orange legs, and large, red eyes. **ADULT NONBREEDING** Similar, but crown is blue, leg color is dull yellow, and head plumes are smaller. **JUVENILE** Similar to juvenile Black-crowned, but darker brown overall; back and breast in particular are adorned with white spots (smaller than on juvenile Black-crowned); note the blackish (not yellow) bill. **VOICE** Utters a harsh *waak* or *wok*. **STATUS AND HABITAT** Favors dense swamps, coastal marshes, mangroves, and beaches; present year-round in coastal districts, but range extends inland and north in summer. **OBSERVATION TIPS** Easy to see in Everglades.

GREEN HERON *Butorides virescens* L 17–18 in

Small, compact heron. Colorful adult blends in surprisingly well with dappled waterside vegetation. Often perches on branches overhanging water, remaining motionless for minutes on end while waiting for prey such as fish and amphibians to pass within stabbing range. Bill is proportionately long and daggerlike. Sexes are similar. **ADULT** Has dark green crown, rufous-maroon face and neck, and white running from throat down center of neck and breast to whitish belly. Upperparts are otherwise greenish gray; wing feathers have pale margins. **JUVENILE** Mainly brown, tinged rufous on face and with rufous streaks on otherwise paler throat, neck, and breast. **VOICE** Utters a sharp *skeeow* call in flight. **STATUS AND HABITAT** Locally common wetland bird. Summer migrant to north and interior parts of range, present mainly May–Sep; moves south and to coastal districts outside breeding season and winter range extends to Central America. **OBSERVATION TIPS** Unobtrusive, but not unduly wary; easy to see in Everglades in winter.

ADULT

ADULT

JUVENILE

BLACK-CROWNED NIGHT-HERON

ADULTS, COURTSHIP DISPLAY

ADULT

YELLOW-CROWNED NIGHT-HERON

GREEN HERON

SUBADULT

JUVENILE

80

Ardeidae

TRICOLORED HERON *Egretta tricolor* L 24–26 in

Striking and unmistakably slender, coastal heron. Feeds mainly on fish and often wades in a stately manner in deep water, or more actively pursues prey in shallows. Nests colonially, often alongside other heron species. Sexes are similar. **ADULT BREEDING** Has mostly blue-gray head, neck, back, and upper wings, with white underparts and rufous-tinged pale line down center of throat and neck. Note the purplish plumes on scapulars and lower neck. Lores and base of dark-tipped bill are bluish. **ADULT NONBREEDING** Similar, but lores and base of bill are yellowish and line down center of throat and neck is white. **JUVENILE** recalls nonbreeding adult but blue-gray elements of plumage on head, neck, scapulars, and wing covers are reddish chestnut. **VOICE** Utters a harsh *waaah*. **STATUS AND HABITAT** Fairly common in coastal swamps on Gulf and Atlantic coasts; resident in warmer, southern regions with range extending further north in spring and summer. **OBSERVATION TIPS** Easy to see in Florida's Everglades and Mississippi bayous.

ADULT

LITTLE BLUE HERON *Egretta caerulea* L 23–25 in

Distinctive, dark-looking heron that feeds in a slow, deliberate manner and often remains motionless for minutes on end; feeds on amphibians and fish in both freshwater and brackish habitats. Sexes are similar. **ADULT BREEDING** Has mostly dark blue-gray plumage but a rich purplish maroon head and neck. Has long plumes on head, lower neck, and back. Legs are dark, eyes are yellowish, and bill is blue-gray with a dark tip. **ADULT NONBREEDING** Similar, but loses plumes, and colors on head and neck are less intense. **JUVENILE** Has mostly pure white plumage although tips of primaries are subtly darker. Bill is dull yellow (turning grayish with age) with a long dark tip; legs are yellowish. Confusion possible with Snowy Egret but note that species' all-dark bill, yellow lores, and striking contrast between black legs and yellow feet. **VOICE** Utters a harsh *aarrk*. **STATUS AND HABITAT** Common wetland bird in coastal districts of Atlantic and Gulf coasts. Present year-round in many districts but breeding range extends inland. Nests colonially, sometimes alongside other herons. **OBSERVATION TIPS** Easy to see in most coastal wetlands and superb views can be obtained in Florida, where birds are often oblivious to observers.

ADULT

REDDISH EGRET *Egretta rufescens* L 30 in

Distinctive coastal heron with a relatively long bill, strikingly bicolored (pink base and dark tip) in breeding season but otherwise rather dull. Occurs as two very different color morphs. Legs are dark in all birds. Given morph differences, sexes are not separable. **ADULT WHITE MORPH** Has pure white plumage; shaggy plumes are seen on head and lower neck in breeding season. **ADULT DARK MORPH** Has dark bluish gray body plumage and reddish orange head and neck; has shaggy plumes on head and lower neck in breeding season. **JUVENILE WHITE MORPH** Similar to adult white morph but with uniformly dark bill. **JUVENILE DARK MORPH** Similar to adult dark morph but plumage is much paler overall with rufous feather edges on back and uniformly dark bill. **VOICE** Utters a subdued croaking *eeuuah*. **STATUS AND HABITAT** Locally and generally scarce resident of saltwater wetlands on Florida coast and Gulf coast. **OBSERVATION TIPS** Easiest to see well in Florida's Everglades.

ADULT, WHITE MORPH

TRICOLORED HERON

ADULT, NONBREEDING

JUVENILE

ADULT

LITTLE BLUE HERON

IMMATURE

ADULT

REDDISH EGRET

ADULT, DARK MORPH

ADULT, DARK MORPH

GREAT BLUE HERON *Ardea herodias* L 45–47 in

Huge heron with long legs and neck and huge, daggerlike bill. Typical blue-gray form is unmistakable but white morph ("Great White Heron") could be mistaken for smaller Great Egret, which has dark (not yellowish legs) and a proportionately smaller bill. Diet of all birds is highly variable and includes fish, amphibians, and crustaceans, and even mammals and birds on occasion. Flies with deep, powerful wingbeats, neck hunched up and legs trailing. Sexes are similar. **ADULT** Typical morph appears blue-gray overall, but neck is tinged pinkish and adorned with black and white streaks down center. Note the mainly white face and crown, separated by broad black stripe that ends in short plumes. Lower breast feathers form shaggy plumes; note also the reddish "trousers." Lores are blue at height of breeding season. In flight, seen from above, note the dark flight feathers; from below, wings look uniformly dark gray, except for reddish leading edge to inner wing. White morph has pure white plumage; intermediate forms also occur with variably pale pinkish

ADULT

blue body plumage and white head. **JUVENILE** Similar overall to adult, but blue morph birds are less strikingly marked, particularly on head: crown is dark and head plumes are absent. **VOICE** Utters a hoarse *fraarnk* call in flight; otherwise mostly silent. **STATUS AND HABITAT** Locally common, nesting colonially in vicinity of wetlands. Present year-round in much of southern U.S., but range extends north in spring and summer and contracts south to ice-free habitats outside breeding season; often seen on coasts in winter. White morph ("Great White Heron") and intermediates are restricted to Florida. **OBSERVATION TIPS** Given this species' size and often bold nature, it is hard to miss in most suitable wetlands.

WOOD STORK *Mycteria americana* L 40 in

Large and impressive wetland bird with a long, thick bill that is slightly downcurved at tip, and very long, powerful legs. Bald head and neck of adult is distinctive and black and white plumage is striking both in flight and at rest. Perches on dead branches and builds large stick nests in trees. Feeds on fish and other aquatic animals by wading in water, sweeping bill from side-to-side and catching prey upon contact. Late winter colonial breeding is timed to coincide with seasonal drying of pools and concentration of food. Flies with head, neck, and legs held outstretched and soars and glides with ease. Sexes are similar. **ADULT** Has bald, dark head and

ADULT

neck and otherwise mostly white plumage, except for black flight feathers and tail; plumage contrast is most obvious in flight. Bill is dark and legs are dark with pinkish feet. **JUVENILE** Similar in terms of plumage overall, but has grubby feathers on head and neck, and yellowish bill. Acquires plumage and appearance of adult over 4 years. **VOICE** Utters various cackles, hisses, and grunts at nest, but otherwise silent. **STATUS AND HABITAT** Local resident in coastal swamps in Florida, Georgia, and South Carolina; sometimes wanders inland and away from favored habitats after breeding has finished. Endangered, notably by manipulation of water levels by man. **OBSERVATION TIPS** Still easy to view in Florida's Everglades.

WHITE MORPH

GREAT BLUE HERON

ADULT

ADULT

WOOD STORK

JUVENILE

Threskiornithidae

GLOSSY IBIS
Plegadis falcinellus L 22–24 in

Long-legged waterbird with long neck, bulbous head, and long, downcurved bill. Plumage looks colorful in good light. Feeds by probing for aquatic invertebrates. In flight, neck and head are held outstretched, with legs trailing. Sexes are similar. **ADULT BREEDING** Has maroon plumage overall with metallic green sheen on back and wing coverts. Bill is brownish yellow, face is dark and has narrow white line framing eye, running from base of bill. Legs are dull reddish yellow. **ADULT NON-BREEDING** Less colorful, with pale streaks on head and neck. **JUVENILE** Recalls nonbreeding adult, but is browner overall. **VOICE** Mostly silent, but nesting birds utter grunting calls. **STATUS AND HABITAT** Locally fairly common resident of coastal marshes and wetlands from Texas to South Carolina; breeding range extends north to New England in summer. **OBSERVATION TIPS** Easy to see.

WHITE-FACED IBIS *Plegadis chihi* L 23–24 in

Similar to Glossy Ibis and ranges overlap in Louisiana and Texas. Breeding adult is fairly easy to separate from Glossy: facial skin is red (not dark), surrounding white border is more striking, and legs are brighter red. In other plumages, specific identification is a challenge: White-faced has a reddish (not brown) eye, retains pinkish face (dark in Glossy), but loses white border (retained in nonbreeding Glossy). Sexes are similar. **ADULT BREEDING** Has mainly maroon plumage with green sheen on wing coverts and lower back. Bill is grayish and beady red eyes and red facial skin have a white border. Legs are pinkish red. **ADULT NONBREEDING** Similar, but duller (*see also* description above). **JUVENILE** Similar to adult, but duller; facial markings are absent until first spring. **VOICE** Utters a *huerr-huerr-huerr* call. **STATUS AND HABITAT** Locally common resident of Gulf coast wetlands. **OBSERVATION TIPS** Easy to see, but separation from Glossy Ibis can be tricky.

WHITE IBIS *Eudocimus albus* L 25 in

Unmistakable wetland bird. Sexes are similar. **ADULT** Has mostly white plumage with black wingtips, most obvious in flight. Legs, face, and long, downcurved bill are red; color is most intense in breeding

season. **JUVENILE** Recalls adult, but has brown upperparts, streaked brown head and neck, white underparts, and dull orange-pink legs, bill, and face. Begins to acquire elements of adult's white plumage by first summer. **VOICE** Mostly silent. **STATUS AND HABITAT** Locally common resident of coastal belt of Gulf coast and Atlantic coast north to North Carolina. Favors wetlands and adjacent grassland (sometimes even feeds on lawns). **OBSERVATION TIPS** Easy to see.

ROSEATE SPOONBILL *Platalea ajaja* L 32 in

Unmistakable waterbird with diagnostic horizontally flattened, spoon-shaped bill, swept side-to-side through water when feeding. Sexes are similar. **ADULT** Has bald head and dark nape. Rest of body is feathered, mostly white on neck, but flushed pink elsewhere with scarlet bar on wings and spot on breast center. Legs are reddish. **JUVENILE** Recalls adult, but head is feathered (remains so until second winter), plumage is paler overall, and scarlet elements are absent. **VOICE** Mostly silent. **STATUS AND HABITAT** Locally common in coastal wetlands of Texas and south Florida. **OBSERVATION TIPS** Easy to see in Florida's Everglades.

GLOSSY IBIS

ADULT

WHITE-FACED IBIS

ADULT, NONBREEDING

ADULT, BREEDING

WHITE IBIS

ADULT

ADULT

ADULT

JUVENILE

ROSEATE SPOONBILL

JUVENILE

Cathartidae and Pandionidae

TURKEY VULTURE *Cathartes aura* W 67–69 in

The larger and more widespread of our two vulture species. Soars and glides with consummate ease with wings held in a shallow "V";

JUVENILE

active flight is labored. Confusingly, referred to as a "Buzzard" by many nonbirders. Bald head helps reduce feather contamination when feeding on carrion; this is located by both sight and smell. Often perches with wings spread. Sexes are similar. **ADULT** Appears mainly blackish in harsh light, but brownish plumage tone is revealed at close range. Bald head is reddish and bill is pale. In flight, seen from below, silvery gray flight feathers contrast with otherwise dark plumage; note the proportionately long tail. **JUVENILE** Similar to adult, but with browner plumage and dark head and bill. **VOICE** Mostly silent. **STATUS AND HABITAT** Fairly common summer visitor throughout U.S. and into southern Canada. Range contracts south in fall, many birds migrating to Central America. Found mainly in open and lightly wooded country. **OBSERVATION TIPS** Easiest to see on sunny mornings before too many thermals have been generated.

BLACK VULTURE *Coragyps atratus* W 57–59 in

Compact vulture with all-dark plumage. In flight, note the broad wings and silvery white tips (primary feathers), most striking when seen from below; tail is proportionately short. Soars and glides with wings almost level. Gregarious when feeding on carrion, and when roosting. Often perches with wings outstretched. Sexes are similar. **ADULT** Has blackish plumage, except for silvery white primaries. Bald head and upper neck are gray with a wrinkled texture. Bill is relatively slender and pale-tipped. **JUVENILE** Similar to adult, but with dark head, neck, and bill. **VOICE** Mostly silent. **STATUS AND HABITAT** Very common resident in southeast, favoring range of open habitats; visits garbage dumps. Some birds migrate south of region in fall. **OBSERVATION TIPS** Hard to miss.

OSPREY *Pandion haliaetus* W 60–65 in

The classic fish-eating raptor, invariably seen near water. In soaring flight, with its rather long, narrow wings, it can look rather gull-like. However, fishing technique is unmistakable: typically hovers and then plunges, talons first, into water. **ADULT** Has mainly brown upperparts, except for the pale crown; underparts generally look pale white; body is mostly unmarked, except for streaked chest band (most obvious in females). In flight, seen from below, inner wing coverts are pale except for dark carpal patch, while flight feathers have dark brown barring; note the dark terminal band on the barred tail. **JUVENILE** Similar to adult, but dark elements of plumage are paler,

ADULT, WITH NEST MATERIAL

back and upper wing covert feathers have pale margins, and nape and chest are often flushed orange-buff. **VOICE** Utters various whistling calls. **STATUS AND HABITAT** Fairly common summer visitor to northern half of region. Associated with fish-rich lakes, rivers, and coasts. Most migrate south to Central and South America, but in southern states (notably Florida and Gulf coast) present year-round. **OBSERVATION TIPS** Usually easy to find on suitable wetland habitats within range. Spends long periods perched, often on a dead tree, and so careful scrutiny of waterside trees may be required. In some areas, they are bold enough to build their twiggy nests on manmade structures such as powerline poles and towers.

ADULT

ADULT

TURKEY VULTURE

BLACK VULTURE

ADULT

ADULT

OSPREY

ADULT

MISSISSIPPI KITE
Ictinia mississippiensis W 30–35 in

Small raptor with pointed wings and a relatively long tail. Flight is buoyant and it soars and glides on flat wings in a falcon-like manner, sometimes with the tail fanned. Feeds primarily on insects, often caught in flight. Sexes are dissimilar. **ADULT MALE** Has mainly plain gray plumage, dark tail, darker gray back and upper wing coverts and primaries, paler gray on head (note dark patch surrounding red eye), and white upper surface of secondaries. Close view reveals chestnut-colored shafts on upper surface of primaries. **ADULT FEMALE** Similar, but has darker head and paler undertail coverts. **JUVENILE** Recalls adult, but underparts and underwing coverts are streaked and mottled chestnut color, and tail is barred. **VOICE** Utters whistling calls. **STATUS AND HABITAT** Locally common migrant visitor (mainly Apr–Aug) to open country, including farmland, with scattered woods. Nests colonially. Winters in South America. **OBSERVATION TIPS** Gathers in groups where feeding is good.

WHITE-TAILED KITE *Elanus leucurus* W 39–42 in

Attractive and distinctive raptor that is larger and much paler than Mississippi Kite. In flight, often looks all-white, but close view reveals distinctive pattern of gray and black on upperparts. Frequently hovers, while searching for prey, but also glides with wings held in a "V"; also perches on roadside posts. Sexes are similar. **ADULT** Has mainly pale gray back and upper wings, except for black "shoulders" (inner upper wing coverts). Head is paler whitish, but

ADULT

note the large, red eye with black surrounding patch. Tail is pure white when seen from below, but gray-centered seen from above. Underparts are mainly white, but seen from below in flight, note the dark wingtips and carpal patch. Legs and feet are yellow. **JUVENILE** Similar to adult, but breast, nape, and crown are flushed and streaked orange-buff, and back feathers have pale margins. **VOICE** Utters whistling calls. **STATUS AND HABITAT** Local resident of grassland habitats with scattered trees; seldom numerous. **OBSERVATION TIPS** Often active at dawn and dusk when white plumage shows up particularly well.

SWALLOW-TAILED KITE
Elanoides forficatus W 47–51 in

Stunning and unmistakable raptor with extremely long wings and diagnostic long, deeply forked tail. A superbly maneuverable aeronaut capable of seemingly effortless flight, soaring and gliding with ease; tail is twisted and flexed to aid directional control. Usually captures prey (frogs, reptiles, and insects)

while in flight, often plucking prey from ground or foliage. Sexes are similar. **ADULT** Has white head, neck, and underparts (including underwing coverts), and otherwise blackish plumage. At close range, note the red eye. In flight, from below, blackish flight feathers and tail contrast with otherwise white plumage. **JUVENILE** Similar to adult, but tail is shorter and eye is brown. **VOICE** Utters yickering, shrill whistles. **STATUS AND HABITAT** Scarce breeding visitor (present mainly Mar–Jul) to southeastern wetlands. Winters in South America. **OBSERVATION TIPS** Florida's Big Cypress and Corkscrew swamps are hotspots for the species.

ADULT

JUVENILE

MISSISSIPPI KITE

JUVENILE

MALE

ADULT

JUVENILE

WHITE-TAILED KITE

ADULT

SWALLOW-TAILED KITE

ADULT

Accipitridae

SNAIL KITE *Rostrhamus sociabilis* W 42–45 in

Southern Florida and Everglades specialty whose slender and extreme- ly hooked bill is adapted to "winkle out" body of its favorite prey— apple snails *Pomacea* sp.—from shells. The distribution of this wetland mollusk dictates that of the kite. Soars slowly over marshy habitat on broad, rounded wings and flexes tail to assist directional control. Sexes are dissimilar. **ADULT MALE** Has mainly dark gray plumage (flight feathers are subtly darker), with broad white band at base of relatively short, blackish tail. Legs are orange-red. **ADULT FEMALE** Has mostly dark brown upperparts, with pale patches on forehead, above and behind eye, and on cheeks; underparts are pale overall, but heavily marked with dark teardrop spots on breast and belly. Shares male's broad white band at base of tail. Legs are orange. **JUVENILE** Similar to adult female, but with rufous wash to plumage. Legs are dull yellow. **VOICE** Call is a croaking rattle. **STATUS AND HABITAT** A mainly South American raptor whose range extends to Caribbean wetlands in Central America; southern Florida represents the northern limit

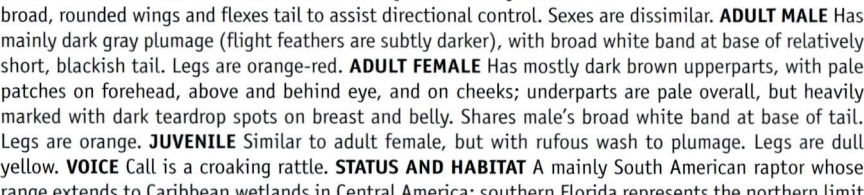

of its world range and here it is an endangered resident, num- bering just a few hundred pairs. Wetland habitat loss and degradation (partly through inappropriate water level man- agement) are the species' major threats. **OBSERVATION TIPS** Usually easy to see in Everglades and wetlands around Lake Okeechobee. **SIMILAR SPECIES Hook-billed Kite** *Chondro- hierax uncinatus* (W 33–36 in) has a massive, hook-tipped bill used for feeding on tree snails. Broad, rounded wings (narrowing toward base) and long tail are obvious in flight. Adult male is dark overall with barred underparts and white bar and white tip to tail. Other plumages are paler and more heavily barred, females flushed rufous below on body and underwing coverts. Rare resident in Rio Grande valley; Santa Ana National Wildlife Refuge is a hotspot.

NORTHERN HARRIER *Circus cyaneus* W 40–46 in

Long-winged, long-tailed raptor that is typically seen gliding at slow speeds low over the ground with almost effortless ease and seldom a wingbeat. Often quarters the ground in a fairly systematic manner, search- ing for prey: feeds mainly on small mammals and birds, located in part by hearing. In direct flight, wingbeats are deep and powerful. Sexes are dissim- ilar in plumage terms and males are smaller than females. **ADULT MALE** Has pale blue-gray head and upperparts and a striking white rump (only obvious in flight); underparts are mainly pale, but note the reddish streaks, most intense on chest. In flight, dark trail- ing edge to wings and black wingtips are most striking when seen from below. Note the faintly barred, black-tipped tail. **ADULT FEMALE** Brown, with darker barring on wings and tail, streaking on body underparts, and narrow white rump; white head markings create an owl-like facial disk. **JUVENILE** Similar to adult female, but plumage is tinged reddish orange, particularly on underparts. **VOICE** Mostly silent. **STATUS AND HABITAT** Widespread and fairly common although seldom seen in large numbers, except when gathering at communal winter roosts. Favors marshes, grassland, and open country with plen- ty of small mammal prey. Summer breeding visitor (present mainly May–Aug) to much of northern North America, present year-round across Midwest belt and a winter visitor further south. **OBSERVATION TIPS** Easiest to find in winter.

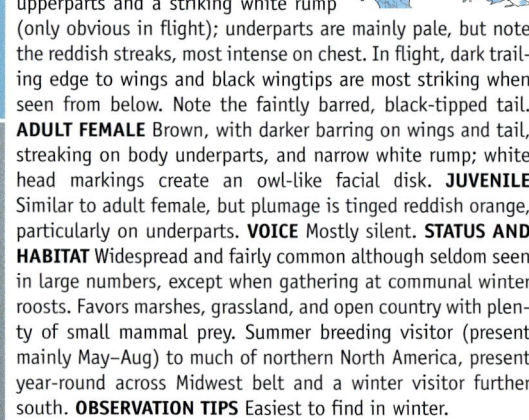

MALE

JUVENILE

SNAIL KITE

FEMALE

MALE

NORTHERN HARRIER

MALE

MALE

MALE

Accipitridae

BALD EAGLE *Haliaeetus leucocephalus* W 75–90 in

A huge, iconic bird of prey and the national symbol of the U.S. Adult is unmistakable. Immature birds, which lack adult's white head and tail, could possibly be confused with a Golden Eagle. However, note Bald Eagle's distinctive flight silhouette with much broader wings and proportionately shorter tail than its cousin; thicker neck and larger head and bill are also useful pointers. Fish are important in the diet and are snatched from water with surprising agility for a bird of this size. Carrion is eaten, mainly in winter when fish are less active at water's surface and sometimes protected from predation by ice. **ADULT** Has a white head, neck, and tail, contrasting with dark brown upperparts and belly. Powerful bill and feet are yellow. **JUVENILE** Mainly uniformly dark brown

JUVENILE

although underparts, including underwings and undertail, are rather irregularly marked with white; bill and cere are dark (latter feature is yellowish in juvenile Golden Eagle) while legs and feet are yellow. **SUBADULT** Gradually acquires adult plumage through successive molts over several years. **VOICE** A variety of hoarse and rather plaintive whistling calls. **HABITAT AND STATUS** Usually seen near water, except occasionally on migration; occurs both on coasts and beside fish-rich rivers and freshwater lakes. Once widespread but suffered badly in the past from pesticide accumulation and habitat destruction in many parts. Numbers are now recovering and before long it may no longer be classed as threatened. Mainly a summer visitor to north of its range although often occurs year-round in coastal districts; northwest is a particular stronghold. Most northern breeders migrate south in fall and are widespread but generally scarce in winter across U.S., some joining resident populations. **OBSERVATION TIPS** Bald Eagles are easiest to observe in the Pacific Northwest but are nevertheless fairly widespread, if not common, in range covered by this book; Florida harbors good numbers.

GOLDEN EAGLE *Aquila chrysaetos* W 80–90 in

A large and majestic raptor. Seen distantly, it could be confused with certain soaring *Buteo* raptors. However, even in silhouette, a closer view reveals Golden Eagle's proportionately long wings (which narrow towards base) and relatively long tail. An active predator, it catches live prey typically the size of hares and ptarmigan; also feeds on carrion, especially in winter. Sexes are similar but adults, juveniles, and immature subadults are separable with care. **ADULT** Has mainly dark brown plumage, with paler margins to feathers on back, and golden-brown feathers on head and neck. Tail is dark-tipped and barred but, in flight and against the sky, it can look uniformly dark. **JUVENILE** Similar to adult but note striking white patches at base of outer flight feathers; tail is white with a broad, dark tip. **SUBADULT** Gradually loses white elements of juvenile plumage by successive molts over several years. **VOICE** Mainly silent. **HABITAT AND STATUS** Favors mountains and hilly terrain, typically soaring over hilltops and hunting over bare slopes and open plains; often at lower altitudes in winter. Widespread summer visitor (mainly May–Sep) to northern Canada; winters across much of central North America. Be advised, however, that most sightings will involve rather distant views of soaring individuals or birds patrolling ridges, riding the updrafts.

2ND-YEAR

ADULT

ADULT

JUVENILE

BALD EAGLE

ADULT

ADULT

GOLDEN EAGLE

JUVENILE

Accipitridae

SHARP-SHINNED HAWK *Accipiter striatus* W 20–25 in

North America's smallest accipiter. Employs rapid, agile, low-level flight to catch small songbirds in surprise attacks. Similar plumage, but different proportions to larger Cooper's: in flight note Sharp-shinned's relatively short, broad, and rounded wings, shorter square-ended, barred tail and short neck. Soars with wings angled forward and active

JUVENILE

flight involves stiff-winged flapping action. Seen perched, note relatively small head, steep forehead and rather dainty bill. Sexes are similar, but female is larger than male. **ADULT** Has mainly dark blue-gray upperparts, barred orange-rufous underparts, and fluffy white vent feathers. Eye is reddish and legs are yellow. **JUVENILE** Has brown upperparts (note white streaks on mantle) and paler underparts with brown, blotchy rufous streaks that can create barred effect. Eye is yellow. **VOICE** Mostly silent, but agitated nesting birds utter *kiew-kiew-kiew* calls. **STATUS AND HABITAT** Common and widespread, favoring wooded country in breeding season. Migrates south in fall, often wintering in more open terrain. **OBSERVATION TIPS** Soaring birds are easy to see in spring. Otherwise unobtrusive and encountered by chance.

COOPER'S HAWK *Accipiter cooperii* W 30–34 in

Medium-sized accipiter. Catches larger prey than does Sharp-shinned. Compared to that species, note relatively longer wings, longer and rounded (not square-ended) tail, and appreciable neck. Plumage differences are little use in flying birds, but note Cooper's more fluid wing action in active flight, and wings held out straighter (not

MALE

angled forward) when soaring. Seen perched, gentle slope of forehead is more continuous with line of thick bill (steeper forehead in Sharp-shinned). Sexes are similar; female is larger than male. **ADULT** Has dark blue-gray upperparts, darkest on crown and palest on nape (creating capped effect). Underparts are paler and barred orange-rufous. **JUVENILE** Has brown upperparts and pale underparts with bold dark brown streaks. **VOICE** Utters *kiek-kiek-kiek* call at nest; otherwise silent. **STATUS AND HABITAT** Widespread and common in wooded country. Northern populations move south in fall. **OBSERVATION TIPS** Seen mainly by chance. **COMMENTS** Tolerate hunting by both Cooper's and Sharp-shinned at bird feeders: they are part of nature, just as much as the songbirds they catch.

NORTHERN GOSHAWK *Accipiter gentilis* W 40–44 in

North America's largest accipiter (*Buteo*-sized). Feeds on medium-sized birds and mammals, caught in agile surprise attacks. In flight, broad, rounded wings and relatively long, broad and barred tail are noticeable. Fanned tail (seen when soaring) looks round-

JUVENILE

ed, with striking white, fluffy undertail coverts. Close view of perched bird reveals differences from appreciably smaller Cooper's: large head and striking pale supercilium, and pale gray (not rufous) underparts. Sexes are similar; female is larger than male. **ADULT** Has mainly gray-brown upperparts; pale underparts are finely barred with gray. Legs are yellow and eye is orange. **JUVENILE** Has brown upperparts; buffy underparts are marked with dark, teardrop-shaped spots. Eye is yellow and supercilium is pale. **VOICE** Utters a harsh *kie-kie-kie* at nest; otherwise silent. **STATUS AND HABITAT** Widespread, but not common, favoring mature forests. **OBSERVATION TIPS** Displaying birds are obvious in spring; otherwise secretive and encountered by chance.

ADULT

ADULT

JUVENILE

COOPER'S HAWK

ADULT

SHARP-SHINNED HAWK

ADULT

ADULT

NORTHERN GOSHAWK

FEMALE

ADULT

Accipitridae

RED-SHOULDERED HAWK
Buteo lineatus W 38–41 in

Familiar and well-marked hawk. Subtle plumage variations exist among the several recognized subspecies that occur across its wide range, but all adults show striking reddish orange "shoulders." Adopts an upright posture when perched and mostly employs a sit-and-wait hunting approach, scanning ground from an unobtrusive woodland perch (typically a branch); feeds on small mammals, amphibians, reptiles, and large insects. In flight, note broad, rounded wings and rounded tail, which is often

ADULT

fanned. Sexes are similar, but geographical variation is discernible with care. **ADULT** ssp. *lineatus* (the typical subspecies in east) Has mostly faintly barred reddish orange underparts, dark streaking on breast; vent feathers are whitish. Head is streaked brown, and feathers on upperparts are boldly marked with black, white, and brown; note the reddish "shoulders." In flight, seen from below, body and wing coverts are barred pale reddish orange, while flight feathers and tail are barred black and white (black bands wider than the white); note pale bases to primaries, which form a narrow band. From above, reddish inner wing coverts ("shoulders") and head contrast with otherwise dark plumage,

ADULT

but note the strongly barred tail. Southern subspecies are similar, but without streaks on breast. Florida ssp. *extimus* is very pale overall. Represented in California, outside region covered by this book, by ssp. *elegans*, which is more rufous overall and has wider tail bands. **JUVENILE** Recalls adult counterparts but is dark brown above and paler below, heavily streaked on breast, with dark-tipped primaries and more evenly barred tail. **VOICE** Breeding birds utter a shrill, repeated *Kee-yur* call. **STATUS AND HABITAT** Common in riverside and swamp woodland, usually near water. Mostly resident but northern birds move south in fall. **OBSERVATION TIPS** Easiest to see displaying in spring.

BROAD-WINGED HAWK *Buteo platypterus* W 33–35 in

Our smallest *Buteo* hawk. Unobtrusive and easily overlooked: perches for long periods in woodland cover. In flight, note broad and rather pointed wings and medium-length tail. Sexes are similar; rare dark morph exists. **ADULT** Light morph has brown upperparts including head; throat is pale, with dark malar stripe, breast is reddish brown and otherwise pale underparts are marked with broad, reddish brown bars. In flight, seen from below, note mainly pale wings with dark tips and trailing edge, barred brown body and inner wing coverts, pale vent, and striking, broad white band on otherwise dark tail (indis-

ADULT, DARK MORPH

tinct, narrow second band sometimes discernible near base of tail feathers). Adult dark morph is uniformly dark brown when perched, except for pale band on tail; in flight, flight feathers are pale, but with dark trailing edge and primary tips. **JUVENILE** Light morph is similar to adult, but underparts are usually paler, with less extensive brown barring; in flight, from below, looks pale except for gray trailing edge and wingtips, and gray-barred tail. **VOICE** Utters a shrill, almost electronic-sounding, *tuee-ee-ee-ee-ee-ee* call. **STATUS AND HABITAT** Common summer visitor (mainly May–Aug) to forests. Winters in South America. Migrants avoid crossing water and in fall funnel through southern Texas before passing south through Central America; spring migrants follow reverse route. **OBSERVATION TIPS** Migrates in huge numbers and sizeable groups ("kettles") utilize thermal updrafts to gain lift. Well-known migration watchpoints are easy to find on the web.

ADULT

JUVENILE

ADULT

RED-SHOULDERED HAWK

ADULT, LIGHT MORPH

ADULT, LIGHT MORPH

BROAD-WINGED HAWK

JUVENILE, LIGHT MORPH

Accipitridae

RED-TAILED HAWK *Buteo jamaicensis* W 48–51 in

Our most widespread *Buteo*. Detailed discussion of extensive plumage variation is beyond this book's scope but adults of all sub-species and morphs seen in summer in east have diagnostic reddish tail. Pacific Northwest breeder Harlan's (ssp. *harlani*, with gray tail) winters in range of this book. All juvenile Red-taileds share characteristics with other juvenile *Buteo* species. Sexes are similar. **ADULT** Has brown head, back, and upper wings, and reddish tail. Most eastern birds have pale underparts faint-ly flushed buff and variably streaked dark brown, mainly on belly; in flight, from below, pale flight feathers have dark trailing edge and tips, and plumage is otherwise pale buff with diagnostic dark leading edge to inner wing. Western birds (seen mostly outside range of this book) occur as dark morphs (uniformly dark brown except for red tail) and light

HARLAN'S RED-TAILED HAWK

morphs (similar to eastern birds but washed rufous below). **JUVENILES** Similar to adult counterparts, but reddish elements of plumage are replaced by whitish; tail has fine, even barring. Compared to Rough-legged, note dark (not pale) leading edge to inner wing and indistinct dark carpal patch; Rough-legged has dark subterminal band or barring on otherwise white tail, and juvenile and adult female have striking dark belly. **VOICE** Utters whis-tles and screams. **STATUS AND HABITAT** Common in a range of habitats; range contracts south in winter. **OBSERVATION TIPS** Easy to observe.

ROUGH-LEGGED HAWK *Buteo lagopus* W 52–55 in

Large long-winged raptor with feathered legs and dainty (by *Buteo* standards) bill. Hunts at low level for rodents and small birds; often hovers. Perches for long periods and looks plump, with wings roughly same length as tail. Plumage is variable, but in all light morphs white upper tail contrasts with otherwise dark upperparts. Sexes are dissimilar. **ADULT MALE** Light morph has gray-brown upperparts and pale head. Underparts are pale but streaked heavily dark brown on breast, with dark feathers on flanks. In flight, from below, wings look pale except for dark carpal patch, tips, and trail-ing edge, while tail is white with broad, dark subterminal band; from above, tail

JUVENILE

is white with dark barring toward tip. Dark morph looks uniformly dark when perched; in flight, looks all dark from above, but from below, note whitish flight feathers (except for wingtips and trailing edge) and whitish tail with dark subterminal band. **ADULT FEMALE** Light morph is similar to male, but note dark belly patch and (in flight) more contrasting black and white pattern on tail and on underwings (except for streaked brown underwing coverts); from above, tail is white with broad black terminal band. Dark morph is similar to dark morph male, but plumage is browner; underwing coverts are noticeably paler than dark carpal patches. **JUVENILE** Light morph is similar to adult female, but in flight note cleaner, paler underwing coverts and gray (not black) subterminal band on tail seen from below; from above, wing coverts and inner primaries are paler than rest of upper wing. Dark morph is similar to dark morph female, but with paler subterminal band on tail underside. **VOICE** Mostly silent. **STATUS AND HABITAT** Breeds across Arctic North America; winters from southern Canada southward when widespread, but seldom numerous in open country including farmland; prefers marshes and open tundra. **OBSERVATION TIPS** A hovering *Buteo* in winter, with a pale upper tail, is an obvious contender for this species.

ADULT

ADULT,
DARK
MORPH

ADULT,
RUFOUS

MALE

JUVENILE

RED-TAILED HAWK

FEMALE

MALE

MALE

ROUGH-LEGGED
HAWK

FEMALE

WHITE-TAILED HAWK *Buteo albicaudatus* W 51–52 in

Specialty of southern Texas. Adult's short, mostly white tail with black subterminal band, and red "shoulders," are striking and diagnostic in combination. Immatures have less distinctive plumage and longer tail than adult but in all birds wingtips extend well beyond tail when perched.

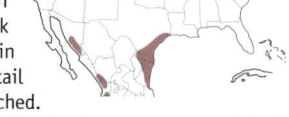

Sexes are similar. **ADULT** Has gray head and back, rufous "shoulders" (inner wing coverts), dark wings, and white underparts; tail is white with a broad, black subterminal band. In flight, white body, underwing coverts, inner flight feathers, and tail contrast with dark primaries (note the white patch near tips of outer flight feathers), dark trailing edge to wing and dark tail band. From above, white tail and rump, and red "shoulders" are striking. **JUVENILE** Mainly dark with white breast and vent, and white marks on head; tail is buffy gray, barred, and with a pale base on upperside. Adult plumage is acquired gradually over successive molts. **VOICE** Utters a shrill *kee-ke-kee-ke'de-ke'de...* **STATUS AND HABITAT** Widespread in Central and South America; resident in southern Texas on prairies and agricultural grassland and coastal scrub. **OBSERVATION TIPS** Visit Attwater National Wildlife Refuge.

JUVENILE

SHORT-TAILED HAWK *Buteo brachyurus* W 36–37 in

Occurs as light and dark morphs. Could be confused with Broad-winged juveniles (*see* p.96), which also occur as two color morphs. Note Short-tailed's dark secondaries and tertials seen from below (Broad-winged's are pale in both morphs) and, at rest, wingtips that reach tip of tail (wingtips are shorter than tail in Broad-winged). Given morph variation, sexes are similar. **ADULT LIGHT MORPH** Has mostly dark brown upperparts with rufous patch on side of neck; white patch in front of eye, and throat and underparts are clean white. In flight, white body, underwing coverts, and pale primary bases contrast with black primary tips and trailing edge to wing, and dark-barred secondaries and tertials. **ADULT DARK MORPH** Looks uniformly dark brown when perched. In flight from below, dark body and wing coverts (and black primary tips and trailing edge) contrast with pale primary bases and barred gray secondaries and tertials. **JUVENILE LIGHT MORPH** Similar to adult but upperparts are paler and underwing shows less distinct dark trailing edge. **JUVENILE DARK MORPH** Similar to adult but body and underwing coverts are barred. **VOICE** Utters shrill screams. **STATUS AND HABITAT** Common in Central and South America, with small resident population in Florida, rare sightings in southern Texas; favors grassland with scattered trees. **OBSERVATION TIPS** Visit the Everglades.

CRESTED CARACARA *Caracara cheriway* W 49–51 in

Large and unmistakable raptor with long legs, neck, wings, and tail, and large, flat-crowned head with a massive eagle-like bill. Sits on fence posts and soars with ease. Sexes are similar. **ADULT** Has dark crown and red cere (changes color quickly) that contrast with otherwise whitish neck and barred white breast. Back, underparts, and wings are dark brown except for barred pale base to primaries and barred, pale tail with a dark terminal band. Wings look nearly square-tipped in flight. Legs are yellow. **JUVENILE** Similar, but has pale spots on back and wings; leg and cere colors are duller. **VOICE** Mostly silent. **STATUS AND HABITAT** Common in Neotropics, resident in southern Texas and southern Florida; favors arid, open country. **OBSERVATION TIPS** Fairly easy to see in southern Texas.

WHITE-TAILED HAWK

ADULT

ADULT

ADULT, LIGHT MORPH

SHORT-TAILED HAWK

ADULT, DARK MORPH

JUVENILE, DARK MORPH

ADULT

JUVENILE

CRESTED CARACARA

Falconidae

AMERICAN KESTREL *Falco sparverius* W 21–23 in

A familiar raptor, eastern North America's smallest falcon and the one most likely to be seen hovering along roadsides. Feeds on small mammals and insects. In flight, note typical falcon outline with relatively narrow, pointed wings and proportionately long tail; latter is fanned when hovering or soaring, but otherwise straight. Sexes are dissimilar and males are well marked and colorful. **ADULT MALE** Has dark-spotted rufous back and blue-gray wing coverts; striking head pattern includes blue-gray cap with central rufous spot, brown nape with twin dark spots, and two vertical black lines running down from eyeline and framing white cheek. Underparts are pale buff with dark spots on belly. Tail is rufous with black subterminal band and white tip. In flight, from above, rufous

back and tail contrast with blue-gray and black pattern on wings; from below, underwings are barred gray and well-patterned tail is most striking feature. **ADULT FEMALE** Has mainly dark-spotted rufous brown upperparts, except for dark primaries; head pattern is similar to male's, but duller. Underparts are pale, with lines of rufous spots on breast and belly. In flight, looks mainly rufous brown above and pale buff below. **JUVENILE** Similar to adult counterparts, but male is more streaked below and less colorful overall. **VOICE** Utters a screaming *killy-killy-killy* or rapid *kee-kee-kee*. **STATUS AND HABITAT** Widespread and common in open country, including farmland. Mainly a summer migrant to Canada (present mainly Apr–Aug), birds moving south in fall and boosting resident numbers in southern U.S. **OBSERVATION TIPS** Easy to find in open country, perched on poles or overhead wires, or hovering while scanning ground for prey.

MERLIN *Falco columbarius* W 22–24 in

Small falcon, often seen flying low over ground in dashing hunting flight while pursuing small bird prey. Perches for extended periods on lookout, using fence posts or rocky outcrops. Soaring Merlin could perhaps be confused in silhouette for a small Peregrine, but its low, dashing flight is vaguely reminiscent of Sharp-shinned Hawk. Sexes are dissimilar and northern birds ("Taiga Merlin," ssp. *columbarius*) are smaller and darker than birds breeding further south ("Prairie Merlin," ssp. *richardsoni*); Pacific Northwest residents ("Black Merlin," ssp. *suckleyi*) are darker overall still but occur outside range covered by this book. The following descriptions apply to ssp. *columbarius*. **ADULT MALE** Has blue-gray upperparts and buffy, streaked, and spotted underparts. In flight, and from above, blue-gray back, inner wings, and tail contrast with dark wingtips and dark terminal band on tail. **ADULT FEMALE** Has brown upperparts and pale underparts with large, brown spots. In flight, from above, upperparts are rather uniform brown with numerous faint bars on wings and tail; from below, body is streaked, while tail is distinctly barred. **JUVENILE** Similar to adult counterparts. **VOICE** Mainly silent although a shrill *kee-kee-kee* is uttered in alarm. **STATUS AND HABITAT** Widespread and fairly common in open country. In region covered by this book mainly a summer visitor to Canada (present mostly May–Aug) and winter visitor to U.S.; widespread in winter in west, but in east mainly associated with coastal and southern states. **OBSERVATION TIPS** Easiest to find in winter.

MALE

AMERICAN KESTREL

FEMALE

MALE

MERLIN

FEMALE

Falconidae

PEREGRINE FALCON *Falco peregrinus* W 39–42 in

Robust and stocky falcon. Soars on broad, bowed wings, but stoops at phenomenal speed with wings swept back after prey, such as pigeons. Often perches for long periods on clifftop outcrops or manmade structures, such as pylons or tall buildings. In flight, long, broad-based and pointed wings, stocky body, and long tail are good features. Striking head pattern and contrast between dark upperparts and paler, well-marked underparts are useful in identifying perched birds. Geographical variation in plumage confuses matters but, given this, sexes are similar, although female is appreciably larger than male. **ADULT** Tundra race (ssp. *tundrius*) has dark blue-gray upperparts and pale, barred underparts. Note the dark facial mask (dark "mustache" extends well behind eye and borders white cheek) and powerful, yellow legs and feet. In flight, from above, looks rather uniform; from below, pale underparts are barred, and contrast between pale cheeks and throat, and dark "mustache" is usually striking. Interior ssp. *anatum* is similar, but underparts are flushed peachy buff. Pacific race (sometimes released in east, outside its normal range) is sim-

JUVENILE

ilar, but pale elements of underparts are flushed buff, and dark on head is more extensive (white on cheek is reduced). **JUVENILE** Similar to adult, but upperparts are brownish while paler underparts are suffused with buff. **VOICE** Utters a loud *kek-kek-kek...* call. **STATUS AND HABITAT** Once widespread in open habitats, pesticides decimated interior populations in 1960s by thinning eggshells. Reintroduction program is aiding recovery here. Tundra populations, less affected by pollution (except in winter), remain stable and these birds winter further south and are those most usually to be seen in coastal east. Many large towns and cities in east also have resident, breeding pairs. **OBSERVATION TIPS** Panic attacks in winter flocks of waders and ducks may mean that a hunting Peregrine is nearby.

GYRFALCON *Falco rusticolus* W 47–53 in

Huge and impressive falcon. *Buteo*-sized, but note its typical falcon shape with long, pointed wings and long tail. White morph (the real prize for birders) is unmistakable. Dark and gray morphs could perhaps be confused with Peregrine, but note Gyrfalcon's much larger size, more bulky body, and broader, less pointed wings. Hunts up to goose-sized prey, and nests, roosts, and often perches on rocky outcrops. Legs and cere are yellow in

ADULT, GRAY MORPH

all birds. Sexes are similar, although female is appreciably larger than male. **ADULT PALE MORPH** Has mainly white head and underparts; upperparts including upper tail are white with variable amounts of dark barring, and black-tipped primaries. **ADULT GRAY MORPH** Has gray head and upperparts; underparts are pale with dark barring. **ADULT DARK MORPH** Has dark brown head and upperparts, with paler but heavily streaked underparts. **JUVENILE** Similar to adult counterparts. **VOICE** Mostly silent. **STATUS AND HABITAT** Widespread, but scarce Arctic breeder. Most birds move south in winter but extent of movement is unpredictable and many remain in snowbound areas. **OBSERVATION TIPS** Seen mainly by chance unless you visit the Arctic tundra in summer.

JUVENILE

ADULT

PEREGRINE FALCON

ADULT, GRAY MORPH

GYRFALCON

ADULT, GRAY MORPH

JUVENILE, PALE MORPH

Rallidae

KING RAIL *Rallus elegans* L 15–16 in

Secretive, long-billed wetland bird that is easier to hear than see. Laterally flattened body allows it to move through dense vegetation with ease.
Confusion is possible with Clapper: King favors freshwater marshes while
Clapper prefers brackish; adult King is warmer rufous than grayer adult Atlantic
coast Clapper and has bolder dark markings than rufous adult Gulf coast Clapper. Juveniles are harder to separate although King's upper wing coverts are
brighter rufous than on Clapper. Sexes are separable. **ADULT MALE** Looks
rufous-orange overall with blackish rear flanks and undertail, marked with striking white stripes. Centers of many upperpart feathers are black. **ADULT FEMALE**
Similar to male, but is paler and duller overall. **JUVENILE** Has back, wing covert, and upper tail pattern reminiscent of adult, but duller, grubby looking underparts. **VOICE** Utters a series of harsh *tchek-
tchek-tchek...* notes. **STATUS AND HABITAT** Locally common but declining in freshwater wetland
habitats. Present year-round in coastal belt of southern U.S.; summer range extends north and inland,
but precise distribution is patchy. **OBSERVATION TIPS** Should you hear a calling bird, patience and quiet
observation may allow a sighting.

CLAPPER RAIL *Rallus longirostris* L 14–15 in

Similar in habits and appearance to King Rail; *see* that species'
description for details of differences. Many subspecies exist; within
range of this book, Gulf coast birds are recognizably different from those on
Atlantic coast. Sexes are similar. **ADULT** From Gulf Coast has grayish face, dark
crown, and dull orange-buff neck and breast. Rear flanks are gray-brown with
white vertical stripes, and back is brown with dark-centered feathers. Tail is
often cocked and has pale, gray-barred undertail coverts. Atlantic coast adults
are duller and have orange-buff elements of plumage replaced by gray-buff.
JUVENILE Gray-brown overall and lacks white vertical lines seen on adult's rear
flanks. **VOICE** Utters a distinctive clattering call; responds to playback. **STATUS AND HABITAT** Generally
rather scarce resident of coastal brackish marshes. **OBSERVATION TIPS** High tides sometimes force birds
to swim from inundated vegetation to drier ground.

VIRGINIA RAIL *Rallus limicola* L 9–11 in

Small, long-billed rail. Shy, furtive, and heard more often than it is
seen. Laterally compressed body allows it to pass with ease through
dense emergent wetland vegetation. Long toes enable it to walk on yield-
ing mud. Sexes are similar. **ADULT** Has orange-buff throat, neck, and breast,
contrasting with black and white stripes on rear flanks, gray cheeks, and dark
brown crown. Upperparts are orange-brown with dark feather centers. Bill
is long, slightly decurved, and reddish, and legs are reddish pink; note the
beady red eye. **JUVENILE** Similar to adult, but orange elements of plumage are
gray or dark brown, and bill is dark. **VOICE** Utters a distinctive *wik-wiDik-wiDik*
in breeding season; piglike squeals heard year-round. **STATUS AND HABITAT** Common summer visitor
to freshwater marshes. Present year-round on parts of Atlantic coast, but most winter in southern U.S.
and Mexico, then favoring both brackish and freshwater marshes. **OBSERVATION TIPS** Scan wetland
margins where emergent vegetation meets open mud for the best chances of observation.

KING RAIL

ADULT

CLAPPER RAIL

ADULT, GULF COAST

VIRGINIA RAIL

ADULT

ADULT

ADULT

SORA *Porzana carolina* L 8–9 in

Dumpy and rather secretive waterbird. Heard more often than it is seen. Typically skulks along marsh margins, its long toes allowing it to walk over soft mud or floating plants. Walks with a bobbing action and occasionally swims short distances. Feeds mainly on aquatic invertebrates. In flight (typically brief and low), note white trailing edge to inner wing (above and below) and white leading edge to underside of inner wing. Sexes are separable with care in summer. **ADULT MALE** In breeding season has blue-gray face, neck, and breast, but note black between base of bill and eye, continuing as line down to center of chest. Belly is pale and flanks are barred brown, black, and white. Upperparts are brown, spangled with white on back; undertail is creamy white. Bill is yellow and legs are yellowish green. Nonbreeding bird is similar, but with duller bill and leg colors, and less extensive black on face. **ADULT FEMALE** Similar to nonbreeding male. **JUVENILE** Recalls adult female, but blue-gray elements of plumage are buff and bill is darker. **VOICE** Utters a whinnying squeal, and a loud *keek* in alarm. **STATUS AND HABITAT** Widespread and common summer visitor to freshwater marshes. Migrates south in fall and winters from southern U.S. to northern South America. Migrant and winter birds favor similar habitats, but also turn up in coastal wetlands. **OBSERVATION TIPS** Learn to recognize a Sora's call and you are likely to soon detect its presence in your local wetland. Seeing one is a different matter, but with patience it well may emerge from cover. Typically, a feeding Sora will follow a circuit around its territory, appearing in the same spot every hour or so.

YELLOW RAIL *Coturnicops noveboracensis* L 6–7 in

Tiny wetland bird. Habits are so secretive, and favored habitat so impenetrable, that few people ever get a good look at this enigmatic species. Most satisfy themselves with hearing the call or catching a glimpse of a flushed bird in brief flight (note white secondaries and underwing coverts). Sexes are similar. **ADULT** In breeding season has buff-yellow plumage overall, palest on throat, with darker feathering on crown, through eye, and on flanks; back feathers have dark centers. Back and flanks are spangled with fine white bars. Bill is yellow and legs are dull pinkish. Nonbreeding adult is similar, but with dull bill. **JUVENILE** Similar to adult, but head, neck, and breast are darker overall, but with more extensive white spangling. **VOICE** Utters a rhythmic clicking *tic-tic-tic-tic*; imitate this by tapping two stones together. **STATUS AND HABITAT** Threatened and declining as a result of wetland habitat destruction. Endemic to North America and entire world population may number just a few tens of thousands of birds. In breeding season, favors freshwater marshes with abundant, emergent grasses and sedges. Winters on Gulf and south Atlantic coasts of U.S., favoring grassy wetlands and rice fields. **OBSERVATION TIPS** Tricky to observe, so consider yourself lucky if you succeed. Perhaps least difficult to see in winter in flooded agricultural fields.

BLACK RAIL *Laterallus jamaicensis* L 4–6in

Diminutive rail and the smallest of its kind in Eastern North America. Has a dumpy, short-tailed appearance, recalling perhaps a small chick of a larger species. Behavior is positively furtive and consequently Black Rails are far easier to hear than to see. Sexes are very subtly dissimilar. **ADULT MALE** Can appear all dark, but in good light note the dark rich-brown crown, nape, and back. Underparts are dark blue-gray with black and whitish barring on flanks, belly, and undertail coverts. Has dark bill and beady red eye. **ADULT FEMALE** Similar, but has less well-marked upperparts and is marginally paler on underparts. **JUVENILE** Recalls adult female but is browner overall. **VOICE** Territorial male utters a sharp, repeated *ki'ki durr, ki'ki durr…*, mainly after dark. **STATUS AND HABITAT** Local and easily overlooked. Threatened by habitat loss. Breeds on inland freshwater marshes and coastal salt marshes; birds migrate to coastal habitats for winter. **OBSERVATION TIPS** One of the hardest North American species to observe. Very occasionally seen dashing from one area of flooded dense vegetation to another—mostly in the winter, when high tides force birds to flee cover as it becomes inundated by rising water levels. If flushed by an observer from wetland vegetation quickly drops back into cover and is seldom seen again. Count yourself extremely lucky if you see one!

SORA

ADULT

MALE

YELLOW RAIL

ADULT

FEMALE

MALE

BLACK RAIL

Rallidae

PURPLE GALLINULE *Porphyrio martinica*
L 12–14 in

Colorful, plump-bodied wetland bird whose very long toes allow it to walk on floating vegetation. Swims well, but also clambers through vegetation. Sexes are similar. **ADULT** Has mostly deep bluish purple head, neck, and underparts, and green back and wing coverts. Note the entirely white undertail coverts. Legs are yellow, eye is red, and bill is red with yellow tip; note the pale blue frontal shield. **JUVENILE** Has mostly warm orange-buff head, neck, and flanks, white underparts including undertail coverts, and grayish green back and wing coverts. Bill and legs are dull brown. **VOICE** Utters various shrill squeaks and cackles. **STATUS AND HABITAT** Locally common in freshwater wetlands with dense vegetation. Present in breeding range mainly May–Sep, but present year-round in southern half of Florida. Much more widespread in Central America. **OBSERVATION TIPS** Easy to see in Florida's Everglades.

COMMON MOORHEN *Gallinula chloropus* L 13–14 in

Dark-looking wetland bird that swims with jerky movements and flicks its tail constantly. Flight looks labored with dangling legs. Very

long toes allow it to walk on soft mud and on floating plant debris. Feeds on aquatic invertebrates and plants. Sexes are similar. **ADULT** Can look all-dark, but has dark blue-gray head, neck, and underparts, and brownish back, wings, and tail. Note the yellow-tipped red bill, red frontal shield on forehead, and yellowish legs and toes. Sides of undertail are white; note white line on flanks. **JUVENILE** Grayish brown, but with white on throat, sides of undertail coverts, and on flanks. **VOICE** Utters a far-carrying *kurrrk*. **STATUS AND HABITAT** Favors well-vegetated freshwater (sometimes brackish) wetlands. Present year-round in many coastal states but summer breeding range extends north and present there mainly May–Sep. **OBSERVATION TIPS** Not unduly shy and easy to see.

JUVENILE

AMERICAN COOT *Fulica americana* L 14–16 in

Dumpy waterbird with long, lobed toes that facilitate swimming. Feeds by upending or by making shallow dives, but also grazes waterside vegetation. In breeding season, constructs large mound nests of water-

plants. Outside breeding season, often forms large flocks. When taking off from water, typically runs along surface, splashing its feet before finally getting airborne. Sexes are similar. **ADULT** Has essentially all dark plumage, darkest on head and neck; note white on outer undertail coverts. Bill and frontal shield are mainly white, except for dark subterminal band on bill and red patch on forehead shield; note the beady red eye. Legs are greenish yellow. In flight, note white trailing edge to otherwise dark, rounded wings. **JUVENILE** Has dark grayish brown upperparts and white on throat and front of neck. Bill is dull pink. Recalls an oversized winter plumage Pied-billed Grebe (*see* p.60). Acquires adult-like plumage by first winter, but bill is pure white and red on forehead is absent. **VOICE** Utters a loud *kwoot* call. **STATUS AND DISTRIBUTION** Widespread and common on freshwater wetlands. Mostly a summer visitor to northern half of its range in the east, and a winter visitor further south, but present year-round near Gulf and Atlantic coasts. **OBSERVATION TIPS** Easy to observe.

ADULT

ADULT

PURPLE GALLINULE

1ST-WINTER

ADULT

COMMON MOORHEN

ADULT

AMERICAN COOT

ADULT

Aramidae and Gruidae

LIMPKIN *Aramus guarauna* L 25–27 in
Large and distinctive wetland bird with the body of a heron (plumage recalls
that of immature night-heron), but a massive bill reminiscent of an ibis or
a large shorebird. Note also the long, powerful legs. Feeds mainly on apple
snails, curvature of bill tip assisting in extraction of snail's body from its shell.
In flight, wings are broad, appear relatively long and square-ended. Sexes are similar. **ADULT** Has rich
brown plumage overall, darkest on belly and flight feathers and palest on face. Head, neck, and back
are adorned with white, streaklike spots; those on back and wing coverts are largest and most arrowhead like. Bill is dull yellow and legs are dark. **JUVENILE** Similar, but with smaller, less distinct white
markings. **VOICE** A loud, far-carrying and vaguely crane-like screeching *kee-ow*. **STATUS AND HABITAT**
Widespread in Central and South America, but restricted here to wetlands in Florida where it is a scarce
resident. **OBSERVATION TIPS** Easiest to see in Everglades; despite size, surprisingly easy to overlook.

SANDHILL CRANE *Grus canadensis* L 40–46 in
Large and almost unmistakable bird with a stately posture and gait.
Confusion with Great Blue Heron (*see* p.82) is possible, but note differences in plumage, structure, and head markings. Outside breeding season, Sandhill is invariably seen in large flocks, whereas Great Blue is usually
solitary. In flight, Sandhill holds head and neck outstretched, while Great
Blue has neck hunched into an "S" shape. Seen from below in flight, note
mainly pale flight feathers. Arctic nesters are appreciably smaller and short-
er-billed than southern breeders. Sexes are similar. **ADULT** Has mainly blue-
gray plumage, palest on face. Note red crown and variable rufous feathering on

wings. Legs and daggerlike bill are dark. **JUVENILE** Has
variably blue-gray and rufous plumage, but typically
rufous predominates on head, neck, and back. Bill is dull
pink and red on crown is absent. **VOICE** Utters evocative,
rattling, bugling calls. **STATUS AND HABITAT** Very locally common. Vast majority of population nests on remote
tundra or expansive northern wetlands, and winters in
wetland areas with adjacent farmland in southern U.S.
and Mexico. Small population (4,000–5,000 birds) is resident in Florida, numbers boosted in winter by migrants.
OBSERVATION TIPS At traditional migration staging
areas and winter roosts, the massive numbers of Sandhill
Cranes provide one of the greatest wildlife spectacles.

WHOOPING CRANE *Grus americana* L 50–55 in
Tall, upright bird; adult is unmistakable. One of North America's most
endangered species and subject to considerable conservation interest. Sexes are similar. **ADULT** Has mainly white plumage with black primaries,
black mask, and red crown. Bill is dull yellowish and legs are dark. **JUVENILE**
(seldom seen away from adult's company) Recalls adult, but unmarked

head and neck are flushed orange-
buff and has extensive reddish buff
feathering on back and wing coverts.
Bill and legs are gray. **VOICE** Utters
loud, trumpeting and bugling calls. **STATUS AND HABITAT**
Rare, breeding on undisturbed wetland marshes. The only self-
sustaining population nests in Wood Buffalo National Park,
Alberta, and winters at Aransas National Wildlife Refuge, Texas.
Small, captive or feral (non-migratory) populations exist elsewhere (e.g. in Florida). **OBSERVATION TIPS** Visit Aransas NWR
in Texas in winter to see wild birds (the population was
estimated to be 249 birds in 2009).

LIMPKIN
ADULT

SANDHILL CRANE
ADULT

WHOOPING CRANE
ADULT

Charadriidae

SNOWY PLOVER *Charadrius alexandrinus* L 6.25–6.5 in

Dumpy little plover that looks mostly very pale. Typically feeds near water's edge, running at speed then pausing momentarily to pick invertebrates from surface of sand. Sexes are separable. **ADULT MALE** In summer, has pale sandy brown upperparts and white underparts. Note black patches at front of sandy crown, behind eye and on the side of breast. Legs and bill are black. In winter, resembles adult female. **ADULT FEMALE** In summer is similar to male, but black elements of plumage are a paler dark brown. In winter, plumage shows even less contrast. **JUVENILE** Resembles winter female. **VOICE** Utters a soft *bruip* call. **STATUS AND HABITAT** Scarce and threatened species, favoring wide-open sandy habitats or mudflats. Occurs year-round on a few coastal beaches but more widespread in winter. Human disturbance badly affects breeding success and seldom thrives unless nests are protected. **OBSERVATION TIPS** Heat haze and harsh sunlight make it hard to spot, so easiest to see on dull days.

MALE

PIPING PLOVER *Charadrius melodus* L 7–7.5 in

Another pale and endangered plover. Easily told from Snowy by orange (not blackish) legs and orange base to bill in summer adults (otherwise dark, and similar to Snowy). Runs in short bursts at great speed; hard to locate when it stops because it blends so well with favored sandy habitats. Sexes are separable with care. **ADULT MALE** In summer, has mainly pale sandy upperparts and white underparts. Note narrow black collar and (usually incomplete) breast band, and black band on forehead. Legs are orange and dainty orange bill is black-tipped. In winter, black elements of plumage are brown and bill is dark. **ADULT FEMALE** In summer is similar to male, but black elements of plumage are brown. In winter, resembles winter male. **JUVENILE** Similar to winter adult. **VOICE** Utters a piping *peep-lo*. **STATUS AND HABITAT** Scarce and endangered. In summer, favors drying margins of Great Plains lakes and beaches of northeastern Atlantic coast; breeding success badly affected by disturbance from humans and their dogs and cats. In winter, moves mostly to Gulf coast sandy beaches. **OBSERVATION TIPS** Easiest to spot when it runs. To minimize disturbance, look for it in winter.

ADULT

WILSON'S PLOVER *Charadrius wilsonia* L 7.5–8 in

Stocky, coastal plover with a large bill and long legs. Feeds in typical plover manner by running a few steps, pausing, and tilting forward to pick up invertebrate prey. **ADULT MALE** Has mostly brown upperparts; note the white collar, throat, forehead, and supercilium, that contrast with the brownish crown (black at front) and ear coverts. Has a black chest band, but underparts are otherwise white. In flight, note the blackish flight feathers and narrow white bar on upper wings. Legs are dull pinkish and bill is dark. **ADULT FEMALE** Similar, but black elements of plumage are pale brown. **JUVENILE** Recalls adult female, but brown feathers have paler margins and breast band is often incomplete. **VOICE** Call is a sharp, agitated *whit-whit*. **STATUS AND HABITAT** Widespread on coasts of Mexico, Caribbean, and northern South America. Summer breeding range extends to U.S. Gulf and Atlantic coasts: nests on sandy beaches and adjacent dunes; scarce and declining, badly affected by disturbance from humans, their dogs and cats, and habitat destruction. Migrates south in fall with some birds wintering in Florida. **OBSERVATION TIPS** Look for it in winter, in Florida.

ADULT, WINTER

MALE, SUMMER

SNOWY PLOVER

PIPING PLOVER

ADULT, SUMMER

ADULT, WINTER

WILSON'S PLOVER

ADULT, SUMMER

ADULT, WINTER

Charadriidae

SEMIPALMATED PLOVER
Charadrius semipalmatus L 7–7.5 in

Small, dumpy wader that is seldom seen far from water. Runs at speed (as if powered by clockwork) and then stands still for a few seconds before picking a food item from ground. Webbing between outer toes is hard to discern, except in very close views. Sometimes forms flocks on migration. Sexes are separable with care. **ADULT MALE** Has mainly sandy brown upperparts and white underparts, with a continuous black breast band and collar. Note the distinctive black patch through the eye and on the forecrown, defining the white patch in front of eye

ADULT

and very narrow and short white supercilium. Legs are orange-yellow and bill is orange with a dark tip. In winter, black elements of plumage on head are mainly brown, especially on forecrown; bill is mainly dark, but with dull orange at base of lower mandible. **ADULT FEMALE** Similar to male, but black elements of plumage on head are brown. **JUVENILE** Similar to winter adult, but breast band is small and often incomplete. **VOICE** Utters a soft *tchu-eep* call. **STATUS AND HABITAT** Common and widespread in breeding season, nesting beside lakes and rivers across Arctic North America and present there mainly May–Aug. Fall migrants can appear in any suitable open, damp habitats, but are obvious on Atlantic coast. Occurrence in winter is extremely wide-ranging: found on coastal shores and estuaries from Atlantic and Gulf coasts to southern South America. **OBSERVATION TIPS** Easy to find on coasts in winter, or in spring if you visit the Arctic.

KILLDEER *Charadrius vociferus* L 10–11 in

Boldly marked, long-legged, and noisy plover. The two black breast bands are striking and diagnostic. Long wings and tail give standing bird a more elongated appearance. Feeds in characteristic plover manner: runs at speed for short distances, then pauses to pick invertebrate prey from ground. In flight, its long wings with a bold white wing stripe, and long, wedge-shaped tail with an orange rump are striking features. Sexes are similar. **ADULT** Has mainly brown upperparts and white underparts, but note the two black breast bands (upper one continues as a narrow collar) and

ADULT

striking black and white markings on face (black forecrown, and white forehead and supercilium). Bill is slender and dark, and legs are pale. Tail darkens toward tip, but note the terminal white margin. **JUVENILE** Similar to adult, but black elements of plumage are brown or dark brown and initially, for brief period, it has just one breast band. **VOICE** Utters a shrill, piping *kiu-dee* or *tee-dee-dee*. **STATUS AND HABITAT** Common and widespread in summer across much of the region south of the Arctic, favoring short grassy areas, including urban sites, such as roadside verges, golf courses, parks, and playing fields. Migrates south in fall and winters in southern half of region. Seen in the vicinity of water far less frequently than most shorebird family members. **OBSERVATION TIPS** Easy to see and identify. **COMMENTS** Breeding birds, with eggs or chicks, are famous for feigning injury, with a broken wing display, to distract the attention of predators away from the nest.

ADULT, WINTER

ADULT, SUMMER

SEMIPALMATED PLOVER

JUVENILE

KILLDEER

ADULT

Charadriidae

BLACK-BELLIED PLOVER
Pluvialis squatarola L 11.25–11.5 in

Plump-bodied, well-marked plover. In flight, all birds reveal striking black "armpits" (axillaries) on otherwise white underwings, white upper tail, and white wing stripe. Mostly solitary outside breeding season. Sexes are separable with care in summer plumage. **ADULT MALE** In summer has striking black underparts, separated from spangled gray upperparts by broad white band. In winter, looks gray overall. Close view reveals spangled black and white upperparts and whitish underparts. Legs and bill are dark. **ADULT**

FEMALE Similar to male, but black on underparts is variably mottled. In winter, similar to male. **JUVENILE** Resembles winter adult, but has pale buffy wash, hence potential for confusion with golden-plovers. **VOICE** Utters a diagnostic *pee-oo-ee* call, like a human wolf-whistle. **STATUS AND HABITAT** Breeds on high Arctic tundra. In winter, almost exclusively coastal, on salt marshes and estuaries. On migration, occasionally stages on lake margins in interior. **OBSERVATION TIPS** Easiest to observe in winter and hence mostly seen in winter plumage. However, summer plumage is often retained briefly by birds in fall newly arrived on wintering grounds and acquired, prior to departure, in spring.

ADULT, WINTER

AMERICAN GOLDEN-PLOVER
Pluvialis dominica L 10–10.5 in

Beautifully marked plover and renowned long-distance migrant. Almost unmistakable in summer plumage when entirely black underparts usually allow separation from Pacific. In other plumages, grayer, less golden-spangled upperparts are a pointer, but greater wing projection beyond tail and relatively shorter tertials are most reliable guides for separation from Pacific. Compared to larger Black-bellied, looks slim-bodied and long-legged with pronounced wing projection (wings roughly same length as tail in Black-bellied), gray underwings (black "armpits" in Black-bellied), dark rump, and only faint wing stripe. Often gregarious outside breeding season. Feeds on invertebrates and berries in summer. Sexes are separable with care in summer. **ADULT MALE** In summer, has striking black underparts,

MALE, SUMMER

PACIFIC GOLDEN-PLOVER

ADULT, WINTER

separated from golden-spangled upperparts by broad white band running from forehead to sides of neck. In winter, looks gray overall, with dark crown, and pale supercilium. **ADULT FEMALE** In summer is similar to male, but black elements of plumage are mottled. In winter, similar to winter male. **JUVENILE** Similar to winter adult, but with a hint of golden spangling on crown and back. **VOICE** Utters a mournful *quee-dle*. **STATUS AND HABITAT** Fairly common breeding species in western Arctic, favoring dry tundra. Winters in southern South America, favoring dry grassland. Typically flies nonstop from Arctic to northeastern South America, then nonstop to southern South America. Fall sightings often involve juveniles. Flocks of returning migrants are sometimes seen in spring, typically in grassland and agricultural fields. **OBSERVATION TIPS** Most reliably found by visiting Arctic breeding grounds in summer. **SIMILAR SPECIES Pacific Golden-Plover** *P. fulva* (L 9.75–10 in) has a shorter wingspan, but longer tertials than American, and longer bill and legs. In summer, black on underparts is usually marbled white on flanks and undertail. In other plumages, especially juvenile, looks golden-spangled on back and crown, with yellow flush to face and chest. Main breeding range is Arctic Asia, but also nests in west Alaska. Most winter in South Pacific, but small numbers occur in fall on East Coast.

ADULT, WINTER

BLACK-BELLIED PLOVER

ADULT, SUMMER

JUVENILE

AMERICAN GOLDEN-PLOVER

ADULT, SUMMER

ADULT, WINTER

Haematopodidae and Recurvirostridae

AMERICAN OYSTERCATCHER
Haematopus palliatus L 17–19 in

Robust and stocky coastal shorebird. Black and white plumage and bright red bill make it almost unmistakable. Feeds on intertidal invertebrates, using chisel-like bill to hammer mollusks from rocks and break shells of mud-flat species. Sometimes roosts in flocks outside the breeding season. Sexes are similar. **ADULT** Has black-ish head and neck and a dark brown back; under-parts are white. Bill is red, legs are dull pink, and eye is yellow with a red eyering. **JUVENILE** Similar to adult but bill is paler and dark-tipped and back feathers have pale margins. **VOICE** Utters a shrill, piping *kweep*. **STATUS AND HABITAT** Specialty of Atlantic and Gulf coasts, found on estuaries, mudflats, and rocky shores, and often nests on sandy and shingle beaches, and dunes. Fairly common but human distur-bance excludes it from many potentially suitable areas in breeding season. Res-ident in much of its range but northernmost populations migrate south in fall. **OBSERVATION TIPS** Easy to find and identify in suitable habitats.

ADULT, SUMMER

AMERICAN AVOCET
Recurvirostra americana L 17–18 in

Elegant wading bird. Despite seasonal differences in plumage, unmis-takable with black and white plumage overall, extremely long pale bluish legs, and slender, upcurved bill. Long, thin bill is swept from side-to-side in shal-low water, collecting tiny invertebrate prey. Looks striking in flight: seen from above, black wingtips, outer wing coverts, and scapular stripes contrast with otherwise white plumage. Sexes are similar, but male's bill is straighter than female's. **ADULT** In summer, has orange-buff flush to head and neck. Underparts are white and upperparts are black with white on scapulars and upper back. In winter, buffy elements of plumage become whitish. **JUVENILE** Similar to dull summer adult with washed out orange-buff coloration and pale edges to back feathers. **VOICE** Utters a sharp *kweet*. **STATUS AND HABITAT** Locally common in breeding season but mostly outside range of this book; favors shallow lakes, muddy ponds, and marshes. In winter, mainly coastal, found on pools and mudflats along Gulf coast and on Atlantic coast to North Carolina. **OBSERVATION TIPS** Easy to observe and identify.

BLACK-NECKED STILT
Himantopus mexicanus L 13–14 in

Unmistakable, elegant wading bird, with ridiculously long, red legs, striking black and white plumage, and a long, straight, and very thin bill. Long legs allow it to feed in deep water, but it also forages in shallows, pick-ing small invertebrates from surface with precision. In flight, uniformly black wings and long, trailing legs make identification straightforward. Sexes are separable with care. **ADULT MALE** Has mainly black upperparts and white underparts; sometimes acquires pinkish flush to underparts in breeding season. Throat and front of neck are white and note white patch above eye on otherwise black face. **ADULT FEMALE** Similar to male, but back is brownish, not jet-black. **JUVENILE** Similar to adult, but with less extensive black on neck, and pale feather edges on back. **VOICE** Utters an insistent *kleet*. **STATUS AND HABITAT** Locally fairly common on shallow ponds, lake mar-gins, and marshes. Summer range contracts south and west in fall and mainly coastal in winter, often favoring brackish lagoons; coastal belt of Texas and southern Florida are good. **OBSERVATION TIPS** Easy to observe and identify if suitable habitats are visited.

MALE

AMERICAN OYSTERCATCHER

ADULT, SUMMER

ADULT

ADULT

AMERICAN AVOCET

FEMALE

BLACK-NECKED STILT

MALE

Scolopacidae

GREATER YELLOWLEGS
Tringa melanoleuca L 13–14 in

Robust, elegant wading bird. Extremely long, orange-yellow legs and long, relatively thick and slightly upturned bill make identification easy. However, confusion is possible with Lesser Yellowlegs, which is smaller and an altogether more dainty bird (*see* that species' description for further distinctions). Feeds primarily in shallow water, catching aquatic invertebrates and small fish, but equally at home on open mudflats. Often chases wildly, like a thing possessed, after prey. Seen from above in flight, all birds have mainly dark upperparts, with contrasting white rump and pale-barred tail. Typically rather wary and nervous. Sexes are similar. **ADULT** In summer plumage, has beautifully patterned brown, black, and white feather markings on back and upper wings. Head, neck, and breast are streaked with brown, and underparts are mainly white, but with brown spots and barring on flanks. Bill is usually all-dark. In winter, looks more pale with gray-brown overall feathers on back, and upper wings marked with marginal white spots and scallops. Bill is pale at base. **JUVENILE** Similar to winter adult, but feathers on back have buffy marginal spots and breast has obvious dark streaking. Bill is paler at

base. **VOICE** Utters a strident *tiu-tiu-tiu* in flight. Song is a yodeling *twee-ooo*. **STATUS AND HABITAT** Widespread and common breeding species in open, boggy, boreal forests. Long-distance migrant that winters from southern U.S. to South America. Usually found on coast (mudflats and lagoons) outside breeding season but, during migration, sometimes stages on lakes. **OBSERVATION TIPS** Distant birds can sometimes be identified with reasonable certainty because of their frenetic feeding habits. Close views allow separation from Lesser Yellowlegs: concentrate on relative body sizes, and bill size and shape.

LESSER YELLOWLEGS *Tringa flavipes* L 10–11 in

Elegant wading bird with long, orange-yellow legs. Bill is thin, long and straight; it only just exceeds head length, whereas Greater's bill is much longer than head length. Note also that Lesser's bill is always all dark, whereas Greater's is pale-based in juveniles and winter adults. Feeds in a more precise manner than Greater (which runs around wildly) and generally much less wary. In flight, dark upperparts contrast with white rump and pale-barred tail. Sexes are similar. **ADULT** In summer, has back feathers beautifully patterned with brown, black, and white. Head and neck are heavily streaked brown and underparts are mainly white (Greater's flanks have dark barring). In winter, looks much paler grayish overall. Head, neck, and upperparts are pale gray-brown,

feathers on back being marked with pale marginal spots and scallops. Underparts are white. **JUVENILE** Similar to winter adult, but with more streaking on neck and breast, and buffy marginal spots and scallops on back feathers. **VOICE** Utters a sharp *tew* or *tew-tew* in flight. Song is a yodeling *tweedle-ee*. **STATUS AND HABITAT** Common breeding species in taiga or lightly wooded tundra habitats. Watchful nesting birds sometimes perch on stunted trees. Long-distance migrant, wintering as far south as southern South America. Widespread on migration throughout North America and winters in smaller numbers than Greater on Gulf coast. **OBSERVATION TIPS** Bill length and more controlled feeding habits are pointers allowing separation from Greater.

GREATER YELLOWLEGS

JUVENILE

ADULT, SUMMER

LESSER YELLOWLEGS

JUVENILE

Scolopacidae

SOLITARY SANDPIPER *Tringa solitaria* L 8–8.5 in

Compact, medium-sized sandpiper. As its common name suggests, it is typically solitary and usually feeds unobtrusively around muddy pool margins or in shallow marshes. Characteristically bobs body up and down as it walks. Flight is rapid and often rises steeply if flushed: note wings are dark above and below and tail has dark center and white margins, barred toward tip. Sexes are similar. **ADULT** In summer plumage, has dark brown upperparts, feathers on back are finely marked with pale marginal spots. Head and neck are streaked brown; crown is darkest and note white eyering. Underparts are white, with faint barring on flanks. Legs are dull yellowish green and relatively long bill is dull pinkish gray, darkening toward tip. Winter adult is similar, but is duller overall with less intense pale spots on back, and only faint streaking. **JUVENILE** Similar to winter adult, but has more striking white spots on back and upper wings, but only very faint streaking on otherwise uniformly buffy brown head and neck. **VOICE** Utters a shrill *peet-wheet* or *peet-wheet-wheet* when flushed. Song includes elements of call-like notes. **STATUS AND HABITAT** Widespread in breeding season in taiga marshes and bogs. Nests in abandoned songbird nests in trees. Winters almost exclusively in South America (only very rarely in southern U.S.), but widespread across region during migration, often stopping off at surprisingly small pools for a few hours or days. **OBSERVATION TIPS** Displaying or watchful breeders will sometimes perch on dead branch. Migrants are easiest to find on southbound journey, mainly late Jul–Sep; juvenile migration follows that of adults.

SPOTTED SANDPIPER *Actitis macularius* L 7–8 in

Widespread and familiar sandpiper with distinctive habits and unique and diagnostic summer plumage. Typically seen feeding on the margins of pools, streams, and lakes; as it walks, constantly bobs its body up and down. Usually flies low over water on bowed wings with shallow, rapid wingbeats; tail looks rather long and in fact, at rest, it extends well beyond wings. Feeds on aquatic invertebrates and is usually solitary. Sexes are similar. **ADULT** In summer plumage, has rich brown upperparts marked with dark spots and streaks on back. Underparts are whitish, but boldly marked with dark spots; these are particularly intense on throat and chest. Note the dark eyestripe and pale white supercilium. Bill is pale pinkish orange and legs are more pinkish yellow. In winter plumage, upperparts are uniform gray-brown. Head is mainly buffy brown, but note pale supercilium and throat. Chest is buffy brown and note clear demarcation from otherwise white underparts. Bill is pale and legs are pale pink. **JUVENILE** Similar to winter adult, but note the black and buff barring on wing coverts. **VOICE** Utters a sharp *weet* or *peet-weet-weet*.... Display song comprises whistling notes. **STATUS AND HABITAT** Widespread and common in breeding season, typically found along stony or gravelly shores and steep banks of streams and lakes. Winters mainly in Central and South America but some linger in southern U.S., particularly on coasts. Migrants turn up on inland pools and lakes, and on coastal lagoons and estuaries. **OBSERVATION TIPS** Almost any unpolluted, relatively undisturbed stream or lake within summer range is likely to accommodate the species.

ADULT

SOLITARY SANDPIPER

ADULT, SUMMER

ADULT, SUMMER

SPOTTED SANDPIPER

1ST-WINTER

Scolopacidae

MARBLED GODWIT *Limosa fedoa* L 18–19 in

Large and subtly patterned shorebird. Bill is extremely long and nearly straight (distal half is slightly upturned), allowing easy separation from similarly-sized Long-billed Curlew (*see* p.128), which has downcurved bill; bill is used to probe mud and soft sand for invertebrates. In flight, wings are mainly uniformly orange-buff above and below but with dark carpal patch on upper wings. Typically tolerant of observers. Outside breeding season, often roosts at high tide with flocks of other, similarly-sized shorebirds. Sexes are similar. **ADULT** Looks pale buffy orange overall, darkest on back and wings. In summer plumage, close inspection reveals intri-

ADULT

cate dark marbling on back and upper wings and subtle barring on underparts. Bill is mostly pink with a dark tip. Legs are dark and relatively long. In winter, plumage looks paler overall and less colorful, with much less intense barring on underparts; pink on bill is more extensive. **JUVENILE** Similar to winter adult. **VOICE** Utters a loud *ker-Wik* in flight. **STATUS AND HABITAT** Fairly common, breeding in wet grassland and marshes, mostly in the northern Great Plains. Winters on coasts, mainly south of our region, but reasonable numbers remain on Gulf coast (mainly Texas) and Atlantic coast (mainly Florida to North Carolina); favors mudflats, estuaries, and sandy beaches. Common during migration along suitable areas of coastline. **OBSERVATION TIPS** Easiest to see in spring and fall on coasts.

HUDSONIAN GODWIT

Limosa haemastica L 15–16 in

Large and distinctive shorebird whose summer plumage is colorful and fabulously intricate. On breeding grounds, watchful territorial birds sometimes perch on stunted trees. The long bill is slightly upturned toward the tip and is distinctly bicolored, pink along much of its length, but with a dark tip. Bill is used to probe soft ground for invertebrates. Legs are dark in all birds. In flight, all birds show a striking tail pattern (white at base, black at tip), white wing stripes and, from below, bold and contrasting black underwing coverts. Sexes are usually separable in breeding season and female is larger than male. **ADULT SUMMER MALE** Has beautifully patterned feathers on back, tertials, and upper wing coverts, with black centers and scalloped white and chestnut margins. Head and neck are streaked gray-brown

ADULT, WINTER

and underparts are barred and flushed rich chestnut. **ADULT SUMMER FEMALE** Paler and less colorful overall, in particular with less chestnut on underparts. **ADULT WINTER** Has rather uniform gray-brown upperparts and paler gray-buff underparts. **JUVENILE** Similar to winter adult, but feathers on back and wing coverts have pale margins and darker subterminal marks creating a scaly appearance. **VOICE** Mostly silent. **STATUS AND HABITAT** Nests on wet tundra and breeding range is extremely restricted, with two populations around Hudson Bay, and others west to Alaska. Long-distance migrant that winters in southern South America. On migration (May–Jun and Aug–Sep), stops off at estuaries and mudflats and other coastal wetland habitats. **OBSERVATION TIPS** Visit Churchill, Manitoba, in spring to see this species on its breeding grounds. Or search suitable coastal habitats during migration times.

ADULT, WINTER

MARBLED GODWIT

ADULT, SUMMER

MALE, SUMMER

HUDSONIAN GODWIT

JUVENILE

Scolopacidae

WHIMBREL *Numenius phaeopus* L 17–18 in

Large shorebird with a long, decurved bill, used to probe mud and soil for invertebrates. Head markings are striking and call is a good means

ADULT

LONG-BILLED CURLEW

ADULT

of identification. Sexes are similar. **ADULT** Has gray-brown plumage overall with fine, dark streaking on neck and breast. Back and wing feathers have small, pale marginal spots. Head pattern comprises two broad, dark lateral stripes on otherwise pale crown, and dark stripe through eye. Legs are bluish gray. **JUVE-NILE** Similar to adult, but feathers on wings and back have larger pale spots. **VOICE** Call typically comprises 5–7 whistling notes delivered at same pitch. **STATUS AND HABITAT** Locally fairly common breeding species on tundra, mainly in Alaska and Hudson Bay areas. Long-distance migrant; many birds winter in South America, but fairly common outside breeding season on Gulf and Atlantic coast beaches and rocky shorelines. **OBSERVATION TIPS** Easiest to find outside breeding season on coasts, mudflats, and coastal wetlands. **SIMILAR SPECIES Long-billed Curlew** *Numenius americanus* (L 21–23 in) is much larger, with rufous wash to plumage and much longer legs and bill. Sometimes seen in similar coastal habitats (estuaries and mudflats) in winter, on coast of Texas and Florida.

WILLET *Tringa semipalmata* L 14.5–15 in

Plump-bodied shorebird with a stout, straight, pale-based bill and longish blue-gray legs. Plumage appears undistinguished when feeding but transforms in flight to striking black and white markings on wings. Typically tolerant of observers. Sexes are similar. **ADULT** In breeding season is gray-brown overall, but heavily streaked on head and neck, and with dark

ADULT, WINTER

scallops on lower neck, chest, and flanks. In winter, looks rather uniformly pale gray-brown, palest on underparts. **JUVENILE** Similar to winter adult, but back and upper wing coverts are washed and spotted yellow-buff with pale spots. **VOICE** Utters a sharp *klip* in alarm; song is a ringing *peel-will-willet*. **STATUS AND HABITAT** Locally common, nesting beside marshes and wintering on coastal beaches. Represented in eastern North America by ssp. *semipalmatus*, which is darker (notably in breeding season) than its western counterpart. **OBSERVATION TIPS** Easy to find on coasts in winter.

RUDDY TURNSTONE *Arenaria interpres* L 9–10 in

Robust and pugnacious shorebird. Short, triangular bill is used to turn stones and tideline debris in search of seashore invertebrates. Unobtrusive when feeding among seaweed and rocks. All birds have reddish orange legs and striking black and white pattern in flight. Sexes are similar. **ADULT** In summer, has bold patches of orange-red on back, white underparts, and

ADULT, SUMMER

bold black and white markings on head. Male has brighter back colors than female and more distinct black head markings. In winter, has mainly gray-brown upperparts, including head and neck. Blackish, rounded breast band shows clear demarcation from white underparts. **JUVENILE** Similar to winter adult, but upperparts are paler and back feathers have pale fringes. **VOICE** Utters a rolling *tuk-ut-ut* in flight. **STATUS AND HABITAT** Locally common high Arctic tundra breeder. Outside breeding season, found on range of coastal habitats; rocky shores with extensive strandline are ideal. **OBSERVATION TIPS** Easy to see on coasts, Aug–Apr; early arrivals and late departures sometimes seen in summer plumage.

ADULT

WHIMBREL · ADULT

ADULT, WINTER

WILLET · ADULT, SUMMER

RUDDY TURNSTONE

MALE, SUMMER

ADULT, WINTER

Scolopacidae

PURPLE SANDPIPER *Calidris maritima* L 9–9.5 in

Plump-bodied shorebird that feeds on rocky shores and on jetties, often among breaking waves. All birds have a slender, slightly down-curved bill with dull orange-yellow base, and yellow-orange to dark greenish legs. In flight, uniformly dark upperparts reveal only a faint pale wing stripe. Sexes are similar. **ADULT SUMMER** Has chestnut-brown crown and

ADULT

feather margins on back; face and neck are streaked and note darker ear coverts. Underparts are mainly white, but heavily streaked, and spotted on flanks. **ADULT WIN-TER** Has dark blue-gray upperparts including head, neck, and chest; underparts are whitish, with faint spots on flanks. **JUVENILE** Has streaked buffy brown upperparts with distinct pectoral transition on chest from white underparts. **VOICE** Utters a sharp *kwiit* in flight. **STATUS AND HABITAT** Locally fairly common. Breeds on coastal tundra in northern Canada and Greenland. Winters on rocky shores on Atlantic coast. **OBSERVATION TIPS** Easiest to find in winter on rocky coasts. Usually tame but unobtrusive, hence easy to overlook.

STILT SANDPIPER *Calidris himantopus* L 8–9 in

Elegant shorebird with long, yellowish legs; long bill is downcurved toward tip. In flight, note long, trailing legs, and white rump and upper tail. Usually feeds in deep water, probing mud in deliberate manner. Sexes are similar. **ADULT SUMMER** Beautifully marked with chestnut on crown and ear coverts, broad pale supercilium, and otherwise dark-streaked face and neck. Underparts have distinct dark

ADULT

bars; feathers on back have dark centers. **ADULT WINTER** Has mainly gray upperparts and white underparts; note the pale supercilium. **JUVENILE** Similar to winter adult, but feathers on back have cleaner-looking pale margins. **VOICE** Mostly silent. **STATUS AND HABITAT** Very common locally high Arctic breeding species, from northern Alaska to Hudson Bay. Common on Atlantic coast during fall migration. Winters mainly in Central and South America, but small numbers remain on Gulf coast. **OBSERVATION TIPS** Look for migrants in fall on coasts; breeding birds are easiest to see in Churchill, Manitoba.

RED KNOT *Calidris canutus* L 10–11 in

Dumpy and robust shorebird with short and stout legs and bill. In winter, forms large flocks, which fly in tight formation. Faint white wing stripe is visible in flight but otherwise lacks distinctive features in winter plumage. Sexes are similar. **ADULT SUMMER** Has orange-red on face, neck, and underparts; many back feathers have black and orange-red centers and gray fringes. Legs and bill are dark. **ADULT WINTER** Has uniform gray-brown upperparts and white underparts. Bill is dark and legs are dull yellowish green. **JUVENILE** Similar to winter adult, but back feathers have pale fringes and dark submarginal bands, creating a scaly look. Usually has buff tinge to plumage, particularly on breast. **VOICE** Utters a sharp *kwet* call. **STATUS AND HABITAT** Locally fairly common. Breeds on high Arctic tundra. Migration is mainly coastal, but typically uses regular

ADULTS, WINTER

staging posts away from which only lone individuals are seen. Winters on sandy beaches and estuaries from southern U.S. states southward to South America. **OBSERVATION TIPS** Staging hotspots include Delaware Bay and Tampa Bay, Florida; the latter also hosts wintering birds. The National Audubon Society considers both to be Important Bird Areas.

ADULT, WINTER

PURPLE SANDPIPER

ADULT, SUMMER

ADULT, WINTER

ADULT, WINTER

STILT SANDPIPER

JUVENILE

ADULT, SUMMER

JUVENILE

RED KNOT

ADULT, WINTER MOLTING

ADULT, SUMMER

Scolopacidae

DUNLIN *Calidris alpina* L 8–9 in

The archétypal small, coastal wader in winter. Represented globally by several races, each with subtly different bill lengths; ssp. *hudsonia* breeds in Arctic Canada and is by far the commonest subspecies on the East Coast outside the breeding season. Forms flocks outside breeding season. Sexes are subtly different in summer, but separation is tricky. **ADULT SUMMER** Has a reddish brown back and cap, whitish underparts with bold black belly, and streaking on neck. Males are more boldly marked than females, but considerable variation exists within sexes and hence overlap occurs. Bill and legs are dark in all birds. **ADULT WINTER** Has uniform dull brownish gray upper-

ADULTS, WINTER

parts, mostly dingy white underparts, and dark legs and bill. **JUVENILE** Has pale-fringed reddish brown and black feathers on back; some align so pale fringes form "V" patterns. Underparts are whitish, but with black streaklike spots on breast and (diagnostically for juvenile shorebird) on flanks too; head and neck are brown and streaked. **VOICE** Utters a *preeit* call; display flight "song" comprises a series of whistles. **STATUS AND HABITAT** Locally very common. Nests on Arctic tundra marshes. In winter favors estuaries and mudflats. Occasional at inland wetlands on migration. **OBSERVATION TIPS** Easy to find on coasts in winter. Get to know it in summer and winter plumages—it is the yardstick by which other small waders can be judged.

SANDERLING *Calidris alba* L 7.5–8 in

Characteristic shorebird of sandy beaches during the winter months, seen in small flocks running at speed, and feeding, along edges of breaking waves; looks very white overall underneath and pale gray above at this time of year. Shows a striking white wing stripe, seen in flight, and dark legs and bill are seen at all times. Sexes are similar. **ADULT WINTER** Has mostly uniform dull gray upperparts and white underparts. Black outer margins to flight feathers, and on outer wing coverts and leading edge of inner wing, are visible on rest-

ADULT, WINTER

ing birds as dark wingtips and "shoulder" bar. **ADULT SUMMER** (sometimes seen in late spring or early fall) Flushed rufous on head and neck and has scattering of dark-centered feathers on back; underparts are white. **JUVENILE** Similar to winter adult, but many back feathers are dark in the center. **VOICE** Utters a sharp *plit* call. **STATUS AND HABITAT** Common winter visitor (mainly Sep–Apr) to coastal sandy beaches. Breeds on tundra in Canadian high Arctic and Greenland. Occasional on inland wetlands during migration. Winter range extends to coastal South America but good numbers remain on Atlantic and Gulf coasts. **OBSERVATION TIPS** Easy to see in winter.

ADULT, SUMMER

DUNLIN

ADULT, WINTER

JUVENILE

ADULT, SUMMER

SANDERLING

ADULT, WINTER

JUVENILE

Scolopacidae

SEMIPALMATED SANDPIPER
Calidris pusilla L 6–6.5 in

Tiny shorebird with dark legs; webbing between toes is only notice-able at very close range. Short, dark bill appears "blob-tipped" (longer and tapering in Western). Forms flocks outside breeding season. Sexes are similar. **ADULT SUMMER** Has streaked brown upperparts, neck, and chest, and otherwise white underparts. Many back feathers are dark at center, with rufous margins; has hint of rufous on crown, but never as striking as Western. **ADULT WINTER** Has gray-brown upperparts and white underparts. **JUVENILE** Has brown overall upperparts and white underparts; note the long, bold supercilium (meets at front of head), rather dark crown and ear coverts, and more scaly-looking back (due to pale feather margins). **VOICE** A clipped *tchrrp* call. **STATUS AND HABITAT** Common high Arctic tundra breeder. Most migrate across plains to Gulf and Atlantic coasts in fall; after feeding, most fly direct to wintering grounds in South America; reverse route is followed in spring. **OBSERVATION TIPS** Seen mainly on coast on migration, Apr–May and Aug–Sep.

ADULT

WESTERN SANDPIPER
Calidris mauri L 6.25–6.5 in

Compared to similar Semipalmated, has relatively long, dark legs and rather long, tapering dark bill. Sexes are similar. **ADULT SUMMER** Has striking rufous crown and ear coverts, and dark-centered rufous back feathers. Underparts are white, with streaking on neck and chest, and arrowhead streaks on breast and flanks. **ADULT WINTER** Has gray-brown upperparts and white underparts. **JUVENILE** Recalls summer adult, but lacks streaking on breast and flanks, and has only hint of rufous on crown and ear coverts. **VOICE** A shrill *jeet* call. **STATUS AND HABITAT** Common, more so in west than east. Nests on tundra from Alaska to Siberia, migrates across region and winters from Gulf coast to South America. **OBSERVATION TIPS** On east coast, migrants are commonest in fall.

JUVENILE

LEAST SANDPIPER *Calidris minutilla* L 5.75–6 in

The world's smallest shorebird. Distinguished from Semipalmated and Western sandpipers at all times by its yellow (not dark) legs; collectively, these three birds are known as "peeps." Needlelike bill is dark at all times. All birds show faint white wing stripe and white sides to tail in flight. Sexes are similar. **ADULT SUMMER** Has streaked brown head and neck, with reasonably clear demarcation from mostly white underparts; note the pale, but not very prominent supercilium. Upperparts are brownish overall, with many feathers dark at center and with buff or white margins. **ADULT WINTER** Has gray-brown head and upperparts and streaked gray-brown chest and breast showing clear demarcation from white throat and underparts; note the pale supercilium. **JUVENILE** Recalls summer adult, but upperparts are warmer brown, feather margins are cleanly defined, and pale margins to mantle feathers align to create a striking "V." **VOICE** Utters a thin *kreet* call. **STATUS AND HABITAT** Common. Nests on tundra wetlands and open marshes in boreal forest. Winters on coasts and beside freshwater across southern U.S. southward to South America. **OBSERVATION TIPS** Easy to find outside breeding season; commonest during fall migration.

JUVENILE

ADULT, SUMMER

SEMIPALMATED SANDPIPER

ADULT, WINTER

1ST-FALL

WESTERN SANDPIPER

ADULT, SUMMER

ADULT, WINTER

JUVENILE

ADULT, WINTER

LEAST SANDPIPER

ADULT, SUMMER

Scolopacidae

WHITE-RUMPED SANDPIPER
Calidris fuscicollis L 7–7.5 in

ADULT, SUMMER

Plump-bodied shorebird with a rather elongated-looking "tail-end," the effect created by its long wings (primaries project well beyond tail at rest); this characteristic is shared by the superficially similar Baird's Sandpiper. Its diagnostic white rump (upper tail coverts) is obvious only in flight. The slightly downcurved bill is mainly dark, but has an orange base to the lower mandible, another good feature for identification although close views are needed to appreciate it. **ADULT SUMMER** Has rufous on back and bold streaking on crown, neck, and chest; markings are arrowheaded on breast and flanks. Underparts are otherwise white. **ADULT WINTER** Grayish above and white below. **JUVENILE** Has rufous, dark-centered back feathers with pale margins, some of which align to create a white "V." Dark reddish brown crown and ear coverts contrast with otherwise pale face and long, pale supercilium. **VOICE** A thin *tseet* call. **STATUS AND HABITAT** Common Arctic breeder that favors wet tundra. A long-distance migrant that migrates across plains in spring, and mainly down Atlantic seaboard in fall before flying directly to South America. Staging birds can be found on estuaries and around drying margins of freshwater pools near coasts. Adults migrate before juveniles in fall. Winters in southern South America. **OBSERVATION TIPS** Unless you visit its Arctic breeding grounds in spring, easiest to observe in fall on East Coast, mainly Aug–Oct.

BAIRD'S SANDPIPER *Calidris bairdii* L 7.5–7.75 in

Another long-distance migrant shorebird whose wings extend beyond its tail at rest. This feature gives it a "long-bodied" appearance and allows for confusion with White-rumped Sandpiper. Distinguished from this species by the absence of a white rump, but note also the uniformly dark, tapering, and straight bill (no orange base to lower mandible). Sexes are similar. **ADULT SUMMER** Has gray-brown, almost silvery looking, upperparts with dark centers to some back feathers. Neck and chest are streaked, but underparts are otherwise white. **ADULT WINTER** Has grayish upperparts and white underparts. **JUVENILE** Has scaly-look-

JUVENILE

ing back (feathers have dark centers and pale margins) and buffy wash to face, neck, and chest; note the fairly well-defined pectoral cut-off between streaked brown chest and otherwise white underparts. Indistinct pale supercilium is most obvious in front of eye. **VOICE** A trilling *prrrp*. **STATUS AND HABITAT** Common breeding species on dry tundra in high Arctic. Most birds have an inland migration route across the plains, and pause only briefly before flying to South America where they winter. Consequently, for such a relatively common breeding species, it is tricky to find on migration. **OBSERVATION TIPS** Migrants often favor dry, short grassland and the best chances for observation come by searching suitable habitats on Gulf coast, Apr–May and Aug–Sep. Juveniles occasionally turn up on East Coast in fall, usually favoring short grass habitats but sometimes the margins of drying pools and mudflats.

ADULT, WINTER

WHITE-RUMPED SANDPIPER

ADULT, SUMMER

ADULT

BAIRD'S SANDPIPER

JUVENILE

JUVENILE

Scolopacidae

PECTORAL SANDPIPER *Calidris melanotos* L 8–9 in

Well-marked shorebird. At all times has yellowish legs, gently down-curved, mainly dark bill with a dull orange base, and strongly streaked throat and breast, showing clear pectoral demarcation from otherwise white underparts. Male is larger than female with darker throat and breast markings. **ADULT SUMMER** Has brown upperparts overall, back feathers with dark centers and buff margins. Crown is rufous and contrasts with white supercilium. **ADULT WINTER** Similar, but markings are less intense and less colorful. **JUVENILE** Similar to summer adult, but with brighter upperparts, feathers of back having buff, rufous or white margins (latter align on mantle and scapular feathers). **VOICE** A trilling *krrrk* call and hooting song. **STATUS AND HABITAT** Common Arctic breeder. Fairly common on migration through Midwest, usually beside freshwater or on grassy mudflats; also seen on East Coast. **OBSERVATION TIPS** Easy to find on high Arctic breeding grounds. Otherwise, look for fall migrants beside inland pools or on coasts.

ADULT

TERRITORIAL ADULT

UPLAND SANDPIPER
Bartramia longicauda
L 11.5–12 in

Distinctive, small-headed curlew-colored, dry grassland shorebird with long neck, short, straight bill, and long-bodied appearance (due to long wings and very long tail). Legs are yellow in all birds and note large, dark eye on otherwise rather pale face. Perches on fence posts on breeding grounds. In flight, wingtips are noticeably darker than rest of wings, but with white outer primary shaft. Sexes are similar. **ADULT** Has gray-brown upperparts, feathers on back with dark centers creating barred effect. Underparts are mainly whitish, but with streaking on neck and chevron-shaped markings on breast and flanks. **JUVENILE** Similar to adult, but plumage is subtly flushed buffy brown. **VOICE** Utters a "wolf-whistle" call on breeding grounds, bubbling *quilip-ip-ip* at other times. **STATUS AND HABITAT** Formerly much more abundant. Still widespread, but much declined (hunting and habitat loss). Nests in tall grassland (prairies and seminatural habitats). On migration, favors shorter grassland. Winters mainly on Argentinian pampas. **OBSERVATION TIPS** Easy to find within range and in suitable habitat in breeding season. Scarce on migration.

BUFF-BREASTED SANDPIPER
Tryngites subruficollis L 8–8.5 in

Charming and usually tame shorebird, associated with grassland not water. Plumage is pale buff overall. Dark eye is emphasized by dark cap and otherwise pale buffy face. At all times, note rather short, dark bill and relatively long yellow legs. In flight and display, reveals mainly whitish underwings (dark primary coverts appear as contrasting dark crescent). Sexes are similar. **ADULT** Has streaked crown, nape, and back, and dark centers to otherwise buff feathers on wings. Underparts are buffy and mainly unmarked. **JUVENILE** Similar to adult, but rather uniformly dark-centered, buff-margined feathers on back and wings create a rather scaly appearance to upperparts. **VOICE** Mostly silent. **STATUS AND HABITAT** Once abundant, but decimated (literally) by hunting, mainly during 19th century; still a fairly common breeding species on high Arctic tundra. Long-distance migrant that winters in pampas grassland of southern South America. Migrants pass over Great Plains and occasionally stop off to feed, favoring short, drier grassland; scarce away from this migration route. **OBSERVATION TIPS** Search short grassland e.g. airfields along Gulf coast in September for migrant juveniles.

JUVENILE

ADULT

ADULT

UPLAND SANDPIPER

PECTORAL SANDPIPER

JUVENILE

ADULT

BUFF-BREASTED SANDPIPER

JUVENILE

Scolopacidae

WILSON'S PHALAROPE
Phalaropus tricolor L 9–9.5 in
Elegant shorebird with needlelike bill. Like all phalaropes, has lobed
feet used for swimming (often spins) and exhibits sex role reversal: more
colorful female courts male who incubates eggs. **ADULT BREEDING** Female
is stunning, with black and maroon stripe on side of neck and peachy orange
throat and chest. Back is gray and maroon, underparts are mostly white.
Summer male is similar, but darker overall and less colorful. **ADULT WINTER**
Has pale gray upperparts and whitish underparts. **JUVENILE** Recalls winter
adult, but upperparts are brownish, back feathers with pale margins. **VOICE**
Utters soft croaking calls. **STATUS AND HABITAT** Nests beside muddy ponds, shallow lakes, and reservoirs; common and widespread in west but breeding range in wast is restricted. Winters in South America and migrants gather in large numbers on saline lakes in southwest (outside range of this book) to
molt prior to migration. **OBSERVATION TIPS** Enchanting to watch during nesting season on suitable
pools within breeding range. Scarce during migration in east.

RED-NECKED PHALAROPE
Phalaropus lobatus L 7–8 in
Delightful and often tame little shorebird. Uses all-dark, needlelike
bill to pick small invertebrates from water's surface, typically while swimming. Shows role reversal at nest and breeding females are brighter than
males. **ADULT BREEDING** Female has brown upperparts (many back feathers
have yellow-buff margins), white throat, dark cap, and reddish orange neck;
gray breast and mottled flanks grade into white underparts. Summer male is
similar, but colors are duller.
ADULT WINTER Has mainly
gray upperparts and white underparts, with grayish
hindcrown and nape and black patch through eye.
JUVENILE Recalls winter adult, but has brown upperparts with pale buff fringes to back feathers; gradually acquires gray back feathers in fall. **VOICE** Utters a
sharp *kip* call. **STATUS AND HABITAT** Widespread and
common nesting species beside tundra pools. Winters
at sea off South America. Migration is mainly at sea,
but a few turn up on inland freshwater pools. **OBSERVATION TIPS** Easy to see, mid-May–Jul, in Arctic; otherwise seen on pelagic boat trips during migration or
from coasts during on-shore gales in fall.

JUVENILE

RED PHALAROPE *Phalaropus fulicarius* L 8–8.5 in
Charming little shorebird, typically seen swimming, often spinning
rapidly. Most individuals are oblivious to human observers. Bill is
shorter and stouter than that of Red-necked, and is yellow with dark tip.
Breeding female is more colorful than male. **ADULT BREEDING** Female has
orange-red plumage on neck and underparts, dark crown, and white facial
patch, and buff-fringed dark feathers on back. Summer male is similar but
duller. **ADULT WINTER** Has gray upperparts, white underparts, dark nape,
and black "panda" patch through eye. **JUVENILE** Loosely recalls winter adult,
but breast, neck, and back are tinged buff and back feathers are dark with buff
fringes. **VOICE** Utters a sharp *pit* call. **STATUS AND HABITAT** Common breeding species (Jun–Jul)
beside high Arctic tundra pools. Winters at sea off South America and migration is mainly pelagic.
OBSERVATION TIPS Visit high Arctic for guaranteed sightings. Otherwise pelagic boat trips offer best
chances during migration. Lone migrants sometimes found on coastal pools after gales in fall. Rarely
observed inland.

JUVENILE

FEMALE, BREEDING

WILSON'S PHALAROPE

MALE, BREEDING

MALE, BREEDING

FEMALE, BREEDING

RED-NECKED PHALAROPE

RED PHALAROPE

ADULT, WINTER

FEMALE, BREEDING

ADULT, WINTER

Scolopacidae

SHORT-BILLED DOWITCHER
Limnodromus griseus L 11–11.5 in

Stout-bodied shorebird with long, straight, grayish bill. Very similar to Long-billed and specific identification is often not possible with poor views, and even close views of some individuals. All birds have yellowish green legs, pale supercilium; white rump and lower back is revealed in flight. Feeds by probing mud in deliberate, sewing machinelike manner. Forms flocks outside breeding season. Sexes are similar. **ADULT SUMMER** Has most feathers on

ADULT, WINTER

back beautifully patterned with dark centers and orange margins, although some appear uniform gray. Underparts are flushed orange on neck and breast, grading to white on belly and toward vent; intensity and extent of color, and of dark barring, varies between subspecies, but typical eastern breeding ssp. *griseus* are paler and more buff on upperparts, and with white underparts, than ssp. *hendersoni* that breeds in northern central Canada. **ADULT WINTER** Has gray upperparts, neck, and breast, and otherwise white underparts. **JUVENILE** Has back feathers with dark centers and orange margins; diagnostically, tertials have dark internal bars and stripes on otherwise paler background. Neck and breast are flushed orange-buff; underparts are otherwise whitish. **VOICE** Utters a rattling *tu-dlu* call. **STATUS AND HABITAT** Common, but declining; nests on northern marshes and in boreal forest clearings. Migration is coastal and ssp. *griseus* and *hendersoni* winter on Atlantic coast, mostly on estuaries, mudflats, and brackish lagoons; winter range extends to South America. **OBSERVATION TIPS** Outside breeding season, dowitchers are common on suitable coasts. Specific identification may not be possible with some individuals.

JUVENILE

LONG-BILLED DOWITCHER
Limnodromus scolopaceus L 11–11.5 in

Very similar to Short-billed. Bill length is not useful in identification due to variation within, and overlap between, the two species. However, a bird with a strikingly long bill is likely to be a female Long-billed. Subtle plumage differences (tertial markings in juveniles; extent of orange in breeding birds; gradation from gray to white on underparts in winter birds) and distinctly different calls are most useful diagnostic features. Habits and behavior are similar to Short-billed. Sexes are similar. **ADULT SUMMER** Has beautifully marked upperparts, back feathers with dark centers and orange or white margins. Cap is dark and underparts are flushed orange, more extensively than in Short-billed, and with more extensive dark barring on neck and breast. **ADULT WINTER** Has gray upperparts, neck, and breast, grading less abruptly into otherwise white underparts than in Short-billed. **JUVENILE** Similar to juvenile Short-billed, but note uniformly dark-centered tertials, lacking internal barring seen in juvenile Short-billed. **VOICE** Utters a shrill *kyeep* call. **STATUS AND HABITAT** Common; nests on tundra. Migration is coastal and winters on Gulf coast, south to Central America, favoring mudflats and estuaries but also freshwater marshes further inland. **OBSERVATION TIPS** Easy to see on coasts outside breeding season. Much more likely to be found on inland freshwater habitats, within winter range, than Short-billed.

ADULT

ADULT, SUMMER

SHORT-BILLED DOWITCHER

ADULT, WINTER

ADULT, SUMMER

ADULT, SUMMER

LONG-BILLED DOWITCHER

ADULT, WINTER

JUVENILE

Scolopacidae

WILSON'S SNIPE *Gallinago delicata* L 10.5–11 in

Plump-bodied shorebird with relatively short, yellowish green legs and a long, pale-based bill. This is used to probe soft ground in sewing machinelike manner; the mandible tips are extremely sensitive and able to detect invertebrate prey. Plumage provides extremely good camouflage in favored marshy habitats, blending in well with tangled dead stems of wetland plants. Flight is rapid and zigzagging when flushed. Sometimes seen in flocks outside breeding season in places where feeding is good. Formerly treated as conspecific with Eurasian Common Snipe *G. gallinago*, but now considered to be a separate species. Sexes are similar. **ALL BIRDS** Have brown upperparts overall and pale underparts, dark bars on flanks and unmarked on center of belly.

ADULT

Note beautiful pattern on back and wing feathers, pale margins forming white stripes, and bold dark and white stripes on head. In flight, note the strongly barred underwing. **VOICE** Utters a sneezing *ske-erch* call in alarm. Bleating, whistlelike sound is heard as outer tail feathers vibrate in display flight on breeding grounds. **STATUS AND HABITAT** Common wetland species, with breeding range extending across most of northern North America. Most breeding birds move south in winter when it becomes common across southern half of continent; range extends through Central America. **OBSERVATION TIPS** Most conspicuous when displaying in spring. In winter, easy to overlook until flushed, because it is well camouflaged among dead wetland plants. Subject to considerable hunting pressure during winter months.

AMERICAN WOODCOCK
Scolopax minor L 11–11.5 in

Specialty of eastern North America, this plump-bodied bird has extraordinarily intricate plumage markings that afford it superb camouflage among fallen leaves on the woodland floor. Note the short legs and long, pinkish bill (relatively shorter than that of Wilson's Snipe). Bill is used to probe soft ground for earthworms and other invertebrates. Mostly nocturnal in its feeding habits and typically solitary at all times. Eyes are relatively large and set high on head, giving near all-round vision. At breeding grounds, male performs a distinctive zigzag diving display, accompanied by twittering sounds. Sexes are similar. **ADULT** Has brown upperparts overall, but feathers on back and wings are adorned with narrow black lines; note the pale gray-buff lines on edge of mantle and scapulars. Nape and rear of crown are marked with dark bars, and face and neck are otherwise rather pale gray. Underparts are orange-buff and unmarked and this color extends to underwing coverts, visible in flight. **JUVENILE** Similar to adult. **VOICE** Call is a buzzing, squeaky *beent*. **STATUS AND HABITAT** Widespread and locally common breeding species in damp woodland and brushy forest across much of eastern North America. Northern birds are mostly migratory, heading south in fall, and winter in southern U.S. states, from Texas to Florida. **OBSERVATION TIPS** Easiest to find by visiting suitable habitats at dusk (when birds become active), then looking and listening for displaying males. Otherwise, usually seen by chance, when flushed. Widely hunted in winter.

ADULT, DISPLAYING

ADULT

WILSON'S SNIPE

1ST-WINTER

ADULT

AMERICAN WOODCOCK

Laridae

SOUTH POLAR SKUA
Stercorarius maccormicki L 21–22 in
Powerfully built pelagic seabird. Recalls large, immature gull, but
has thickset, cigar-shaped body, thick neck, and relatively broad, short
tail and wings that are dark brown, except for bold, white "flash" at base
of primaries. Note dark legs and adult's dark, hook-tipped bill. Scavenges,
kills smaller birds, and harasses large ones into regurgitating previous meal.
Sexes are similar, but adults occur in two extreme morphs and intermediate
forms. **ADULT** Dark morph has subtly streaked dark brown plumage, apart
from white wing "blazes," and paler nape. Pale morph has dark wings and tail,
but contrastingly pale buff head, neck, and body. Some morphs are intermediate between these two
extremes. **JUVENILE** Similar to dark morph adult, but with dark-tipped pale bill, paler legs, and no
streaking on body. **VOICE** Silent in North America. **STATUS AND HABITAT** Nests in Antarctic and a nonbreeding visitor to North Atlantic, present mainly May–Jul. Mainly pelagic and offshore. **OBSERVATION
TIPS** Seldom seen from land. Take a pelagic trip to stand a chance of seeing it.

GREAT SKUA *Stercorarius skua* L 22–24 in
Similar in appearance and habits to South Polar. Differences are subtle: slightly larger bodied and broader winged compared to South

ADULT

Polar, also has larger bill, uniform head and neck
color (South Polar's pale neck contrasts with its
darker cap and back), and "warmer," overall more
rufous plumage. Sexes are similar, but pale and
dark adult morphs occur. **ADULT** Dark morph has
dark brown plumage overall, with rufous-buff tips
to many feathers. Note the white wing "blazes"
(pale bases to primaries). Pale adult has pale back and upper wing coverts
(as well as head, neck, and underparts), whereas pale South Polar has contrastingly dark back and upper wings. **JUVENILE** Similar to dark adult, but
more reddish brown overall, although sometimes appearing almost black.
Wing "blaze" is obvious and pale bill is dark-tipped. **VOICE** Mostly silent.
STATUS AND HABITAT Breeds in northeast Atlantic (closest colony is on
Iceland). Pelagic away from breeding grounds. Occasional in Canadian seas
in summer; commoner and more widespread Oct–Mar. **OBSERVATION TIPS**
Seldom seen from land. Take a pelagic trip to stand a chance of seeing it.

POMARINE JAEGER *Stercorarius pomarinus* L 18–23 in
Powerful, stocky seabird with broad, long wings and direct flight.
Adult has diagnostic twisted, spoon-shaped extensions to central tail
feathers. Latter feature, and larger size, allow separation from daintier Parasitic
Jaeger. Harasses other seabirds into regurgitating previous meal, and some-
times kills smaller birds. Sexes are similar, but adults occur in two color morphs.
ADULT Pale morph has dark wings (except for white "flash" at base of primar-

ies) and tail. Head has dark hood, neck is
variably flushed with yellow, especially on
nape, and otherwise whitish underparts have
variable dark breast brand, most striking in females. Dark morph
is uniformly dark brown, except for white wing "blazes." **JUVENILE**
Has brown upper wings, barred brown underparts, and barred gray
underwings except for white "blaze" at base of primaries. Note
stubby central tail extensions and subtly paler rump. **VOICE** Silent
away from breeding grounds. **STATUS AND HABITAT** Nests on high
Arctic tundra. Pelagic at other times. Migrates down Atlantic
seaboard where it is common Jul–Oct; winters in small numbers.
OBSERVATION TIPS Seen from pelagic trips, but seldom from land.

ADULT, PALE MORPH

ADULT

SOUTH POLAR SKUA

ADULT, PALE MORPH

JUVENILE

GREAT SKUA

ADULT

JUVENILE

POMARINE JAEGER

ADULT, PALE MORPH

PARASITIC JAEGER *Stercorarius parasiticus* L 16–20 in

Elegant seabird with buoyant and graceful flight. Deep, powerful wingbeats and narrow, pointed wings can give it an almost falcon-like appearance, especially when aerobatically chasing seabirds such as Arctic Terns and kittiwakes, which it harasses into relinquishing last meal. All birds have a white patch near tip of wing (most noticeable on underwing), but only adults have pointed tail streamers that extend beyond wedge-shaped tail. Female is larger than male, but both occur in two color morphs and take 2 years to acquire full adult plumage. **ADULT** Pale phase has a whitish neck, breast, and belly, with variable yellow

ADULT, DARK MORPH

flush on cheeks and neck; has a dark cap and plumage is otherwise uniform dark gray-brown. Dark phase is uniformly dark gray-brown, darkest on cap. **JUVENILE** Variably rufous brown, palest and distinctly barred on belly, throat, and underwings. Compared to juvenile Pomarine, note rather dainty, dark-tipped pale bill and wedge-shaped tail that bears tiny, pointed central projections. Juvenile Long-tailed has longer, blunter tail projections. **VOICE** Utters nasal calls near nest. **STATUS AND HABITAT** Widespread and common breeding species in marshy tundra and coastal wetlands across North American Arctic. Common passage migrant in spring and fall down Atlantic seaboard and sometimes seen in coastal waters; very occasionally inland too. Winters at sea, mainly south of equator, but some remain as far north as Gulf of Mexico. **OBSERVATION TIPS** Easy to see on Arctic breeding grounds and on pelagic trips during migration. The most likely skua or jaeger species to be seen from land during migration, often harassing terns and other small seabirds.

LONG-TAILED JAEGER
Stercorarius longicaudus L 15–23 in (+ 5–6 in tail)

Elegant and distinctive seabird. Shares some characters with Parasitic, but relatively easy to identify, even distantly. In flight, has rather long, pointed wings that lack white patch seen on Parasitic's outer wing. Adult has extremely long central tail streamers. At close range, note dainty bill. Sexes are similar. **ADULT** Uniform gray-brown on back and upperside of inner wing, contrasting with dark outer half of wing and trailing margin of inner wing. Cap is dark and neck and underparts are whitish, with faint yellow flush on cheeks seen at close range. **JUVENILE** Variably gray-brown, with some indi-

ADULT

viduals being rather dark. Note relatively long and rather wedge-shaped tail; pale morph juvenile has pale belly and nape with a hint of a darker breast band. Compared to juvenile Parasitic, bill is stubbier, outer half being darker than inner half (dark-tipped in juvenile Parasitic); pale morph juvenile is grayer overall than juvenile Parasitic, and pale "wedge" is often obvious on nape. **VOICE** Utters harsh anxiety calls on breeding grounds, but otherwise silent. **STATUS AND HABITAT** Common and widespread Arctic tundra breeding species. Otherwise, exclusively pelagic and mostly offshore, even during migration. Winters at sea, mainly south of equator. **OBSERVATION TIPS** Easy to see on Arctic breeding grounds. Pelagic boat trips, typically venturing beyond sight of land, are required to see migrants (commonest May and Aug–Sep). Only very rarely seen from land or inland on migration, usually after severe gales.

JUVENILE

PARASITIC JAEGER

ADULT, PALE MORPH

JUVENILE

LONG-TAILED JAEGER

ADULT

Laridae

ADULT,
SUMMER

ADULT,
SUMMER

FRANKLIN'S
GULL

1ST-WINTER

LAUGHING GULL

Larus atricilla L 16–17in

Medium-sized gull, with relatively long wings (extend well beyond tail at rest). Alert birds look long-necked, and note dark red legs and rather long and slightly down-curved, reddish bill. Bold and opportunistic feeder in many areas. Sexes are similar. **ADULT SUMMER** Has dark gray back and upper wings, except for white trailing edge and dark tips to wings. Underwings show contrast between mainly dark flight feathers and white wing coverts. Underparts and neck are white, and note dark hood and white "eyelids." Bill is reddish. **ADULT WINTER** Similar, but dark hood is lost except for dark streaking on nape; bill is dark. **JUVENILE** Mainly brown, but molts to first-winter plumage in fall: gray back, gray and brown inner upper wing coverts, and dark outer wing and flight feathers. Plumage is otherwise mainly grubby white, with dark tail band and streaked and gray breast and neck (striking on nape). Bill is dark. **VOICE** Utters laughing, gull-like calls. **STATUS AND HABITAT** Breeds on rocky coasts and mainly coastal in winter. **OBSERVATION TIPS** Easy to see on most coasts. **SIMILAR SPECIES Franklin's Gull** *Larus pipixcan* (L 14–15 in) is daintier than Laughing; bill straight (slightly downcurved in Laughing). Adult has pattern of white-black-white on wingtips (uniformly black in Laughing). In summer, note black hood and pink-flushed white underparts. Compared to Laughing, winter adult retains more extensive dark markings on head; first-winter has narrower dark tail band. Breeds on prairie ponds; migrates in flocks to coasts of South America for winter.

LITTLE GULL

JUVENILE

ADULT,
WINTER

LITTLE GULL

ADULT,
SUMMER

BONAPARTE'S GULL

Larus philadelphia L 13–14 in

Our commonest small gull. Flight is buoyant and, at times, tern like. In flight, all adults show white leading edge and dark trailing margin to primaries. Forms loose flocks outside breeding season. Sexes are similar. **ADULT SUMMER** Has pale gray back and upper wings, white underparts and neck, and blackish hood. Bill is dark and legs are red. **ADULT WINTER** Similar, but dark hood is lost and dark ear coverts contrast with otherwise white head. **JUVENILE** Mainly mottled brown, but acquires first-winter plumage in early fall: similar to winter adult, but with dark trailing edge to entire wing, less striking pale leading edge (some dark feathering), and dark bar on inner upper wing; legs are pale pink. **VOICE** Call is tern like, nasal, and higher pitched than other gulls. **STATUS AND HABITAT** Common breeding species, in colonies in marshes and around lakes in boreal forests; nests in trees. Outside breeding season, found on Atlantic and Gulf coasts, on wetlands across southern U.S. states and on Great Lakes. **OBSERVATION TIPS** Easy to see during breeding season in Arctic. Outside breeding season, locally common. **SIMILAR SPECIES Little Gull** *L. minutus* (L 11–12 in) is a rare breeder and scarce in winter on Atlantic coast and Great Lakes. Adult has dark hood in summer, dark smudges and cap in winter; note pale gray upper wing with white tip and trailing edge, and blackish underwing with white tip and trailing edge. Juvenile has dark back, dark cap and ear spot; first-winter has dark bars on gray upper wing and dark-tipped tail; underwing pale in both.

ADULT, SUMMER

LAUGHING GULL

ADULT, SUMMER

ADULT, WINTER

ADULT, WINTER

1ST-WINTER

BONAPARTE'S GULL

ADULT, SUMMER

ADULT, WINTER

1ST-WINTER

ADULT, WINTER

Laridae

RING-BILLED GULL *Larus delawarensis* L 17–20 in

Our most familiar gull. Often bold and approachable, and an opportunistic feeder, quick to capitalize on manmade sources of food and seasonal natural bounties. Takes 2 years to reach adult plumage. Sexes are similar. **ADULT SUMMER** Has pale gray back and upper wing, except for white-spotted black wingtips and pale trailing edge. Plumage, including tail, is otherwise white. Bill is yellow with dark subterminal band, and iris and legs are yellow. **ADULT WINTER** Similar, but head and neck are streaked brown and leg and bill colors are duller. **JUVENILE** Has mottled gray and brown plumage, palest on head; note also, pinkish legs and dark bill and eye. First-winter plumage (acquired in fall) is similar, but back is gray, bill is pink but dark-tipped, iris is pale, and tail has dark terminal band. By second winter, plumage approaches that of winter adult, but retains faint, narrow dark band on tail. **VOICE** Utters a mewing *kyow* call, higher-pitched than that of larger, similar gulls. **STATUS**

SUMMER

AND HABITAT Widespread and generally common across much of central and southern North America, although range changes seasonally: breeds colonially beside lakes in Canada and northern U.S.; outside breeding season, northern populations move south and in winter found along coasts, and near freshwater and food sources inland. **OBSERVATION TIPS** Easy to see on most coasts, including populated beaches and seafronts, outside breeding season. Some individuals actively seek out people for food and are a common sight in littered parking lots and at garbage heaps.

HERRING GULL *Larus argentatus* L 22–26 in

Large, robust gull with relatively deep body, large head, and thick bill. Wings are long and proportionately broad and all birds have pink legs. Adult is easily distinguished from similar sized Lesser Black-backeds (*see* p.156) by its paler back and pink (not yellow) legs. Immatures are best separated by studying proportions overall and subtle differences in plumage (pale upper tail, head, and neck in Lesser Black-backed). Takes 3 years to reach adult plumage. Represented mainly by ssp. *smithsonianus* (aka American Herring Gull, considered a separate species by some). Sexes are similar. **ADULT SUMMER** Has pale blue-gray back and upper wings, except for white trailing edge and dark wingtips with white "windows". Plumage is otherwise white. Bill is yellow with orange spot on gonys, and eye has yellow iris and orange eyering. **ADULT WINTER** Similar, but head and neck are streaked brown; leg, bill, and eyering colors are duller. **JUVENILE AND 1ST-WINTER** Have mottled brown plumage, dark tail, and dull pink legs. Initially bill is dark, but becomes dark-tipped pink by first winter. Note pale inner primaries create pale panel on upper wing and otherwise uniformly brown upper wings. Adult plumage acquired through successive molts: becomes more uniform gray on back and upper

ADULT

wings and whiter elsewhere. Retains dark band on tail and some brown feathering on upper wings into third winter. **VOICE** Utters distinctive *kyaoo* and anxious *ga-ka-ka*. **STATUS AND HABITAT** Widespread and common, nesting on islands in northern lakes, and on coasts. Winter range is mainly coastal. **OBSERVATION TIPS** Easy to find on coasts outside breeding season. Become familiar with proportions of known adult Herring Gulls then apply what you have learned, especially about bill size or other species shape, and colour, and wing length, to any immatures you happen to come across.

ADULT, SUMMER

RING-BILLED GULL

ADULT, WINTER

1ST-WINTER

ADULT, WINTER

1ST-WINTER

HERRING GULL

ADULT, SUMMER

GLAUCOUS GULL *Larus hyperboreus* L 23–29 in

Large, bulky, and pale gull. All birds have pale wings, pink legs, large head, and massive bill. At rest, wings project only slightly beyond tail (wings are noticeably longer than tail in Iceland). Juvenile acquires adult plumage over 3-year period. Sexes are similar. **ADULT SUMMER** Has very pale gray back and upper wings with white trailing edge and wingtips. Plumage is otherwise white. Bill is yellowish with orange spot on gonys, and iris is pale yellow with orange eyering. **ADULT WINTER** Similar, but head and neck are streaked grubby brown; bill and eye colors are duller. **JUVENILE** Pale mottled brown, but first-winter plumage is whitish overall with pale buff marbling on back and upper wing coverts, and pale buff barring on tail; plumage becomes paler as winter progresses. Bill is dark-tipped pink and eye is dark. Second-winter is paler still, variably pale gray on back and upper wing, with buff barring on tail; iris is usually pale. Third-winter resembles winter adult, but retains faint buff barring on tail. **VOICE** Utters deep *kyaoo* and *ga-ka-ka* calls. **STATUS AND HABITAT** Common breeder on Arctic coastal tundra. Outside breeding season, mainly coastal and range extends along northern half of Atlantic seaboard although precise distribution is unpredictable and in part influenced by severity of winter weather further north. **OBSERVATION TIPS** Easy to see within northerly winter range, typically in good numbers within harbors or at garbage dumps.

ICELAND GULL *Larus glaucoides* L 21–24 in

Attractive, pale gull. Recalls Glaucous Gull in all plumages but note Iceland's smaller size, less bulky body, and longer-winged appearance.

ADULT, SUMMER

THAYER'S GULL

ADULT

2ND-WINTER

THAYER'S GULL

1ST-WINTER

Rather rounded head and relatively small bill lend an almost pigeon-like quality to the head. Relatively short legs are pink. Represented in North America mainly by ssp. *kumleini* (known as "Kumlein's Gull") and to which main description refers. Sexes are similar. **ADULT SUMMER** Has a pale gray back and upper wings with a white trailing edge and pale gray subterminal marks on outer four or five otherwise white primaries. Plumage is otherwise white. Bill is yellowish green with an orange spot; pale yellowish to brown eye has a purplish red eyering. Adult ssp. *glaucoides* (breeds on Greenland) is similar but primaries are pure white. **ADULT WINTER** Similar, but has brown streaking on head and neck. **JUVENILE AND 1ST-WINTER** Pale gray-buff with white primaries. Bill is dark with hint of pink at base. Adult plumage is acquired over next 3 years through successive molts. Second-winter bird looks very pale overall, with faint gray-buff marbling; bill is pale grayish pink with a narrow dark tip or submarginal band. Third-winter is similar to winter adult, but with buff feathers on tail and upper wings. **VOICE** Utters a distinctive *kyaoo* and anxious *ga-ka-ka*, similar to Herring Gull but higher pitched. **STATUS AND HABITAT** Nests on cliffs in Canadian high Arctic and winters mainly on coasts of northern Canadian seaboard; occasionally pushed further south by harsh weather. **OBSERVATION TIPS** In winter, often associates with other gull species. **SIMILAR SPECIES Thayer's Gull** *L. thayeri* (L 22–24 in) is western counterpart of Iceland; sometimes turns up on Great Lakes and Atlantic seaboard in winter. Adult is similar to adult Iceland but has black wingtips with white "windows." Immatures are similar to their Iceland counterparts, but darker and browner.

ADULT, WINTER

ADULT, SUMMER

1ST-WINTER

GLAUCOUS GULL

1ST-WINTER

ADULT, WINTER

ICELAND GULL

ADULT KUMLEIN'S, WINTER

ADULT, WINTER

1ST-WINTER

Laridae

GREAT BLACK-BACKED GULL *Larus marinus* L 29–31 in

Largest gull in the world. Bears a passing resemblance to Lesser Black-backed but always looks bulkier and adult shows little discernible difference between dark overall upper wing color and that of primaries (these always look appreciably darker than upper wing in Lesser Black-backed). Note also the massive bill and pale pink (not yellow) legs in adult birds. Feeds on carrion and also an active predator of seabirds in spring and summer. Territorial pairs typically nest close to colonially nesting birds for food. Sexes are similar. **ADULT SUMMER** Has mostly uniformly dark back and upper wings (wingtips sometimes appear very marginally darker than rest of wings in good light). Has white patch at very tip of wings and broad white trailing edge running along almost entire length of wing. Plumage is otherwise white. Bill is yellow with an orange spot. **ADULT WINTER** Similar, but head and neck have faint gray-brown streaks and bill and leg colors are duller. **JUVENILE** Has mottled and streaked gray-brown plumage. In flight, the brown upper wings reveal pale panels on upper wing coverts and inner primaries. Bill is dark, legs are dull pink and whitish tail has a dark terminal band. By first-winter, head and neck are whiter and cleaner looking. Full adult plumage is acquired over next 3 years. Not until third-winter does back becomes dark; by this time bill is pale pink with a dark tip. **VOICE** Utters a deep *kaa-ga-ga* call. **STATUS AND HABITAT** Locally common, present year-round on northern Atlantic coast and around Great Lakes. Summer range extends north along Canadian coast and winter range extends south down Atlantic seaboard. **OBSERVATION TIPS** Usually easy to see in winter at coastal gull roosts, in harbors, and at garbage dumps.

LESSER BLACK-BACKED GULL

Larus fuscus L 22–25 in

Eurasian gull with similar size and proportions to Herring (*see* p.152), but adult's dark gray back and upper wings are obvious and bright yellow legs clinch identification. Associates with other large gull species outside breeding season. Sexes are similar. **ADULT SUMMER** Has dark gray back and upper wings. Black wingtips are appreciably darker than rest of upper wing (in typical ssp. *graellsii* seen in North America) and note white trailing edge to inner two-thirds of upper wing. Plumage is otherwise white. Bill is bright yellow with an orange spot. Iris is yellow and eyering is red. **ADULT WINTER** Similar, but has streaks on head and neck and duller leg and bill colors. **JUVENILE AND 1ST-WINTER** Have streaked and mottled gray-brown plumage, palest on head. Upper wings appear uniformly dark brown and tail is whitish with dark terminal band. Eye and bill are dark. Full adult plumage is acquired over 3 years though successive molts. Second-winter is similar to first-winter but has gray back with pinkish legs and dark-tipped pink bill; underparts and tail are paler with less streaking. Third-winter bird resembles winter adult but has more streaking on head and neck, and hint of dark terminal tail band. **VOICE** Utters a distinctive *kyaoo* and anxious *ga-ka-ka*. **STATUS AND HABITAT** Scarce but increasing nonbreeding visitor to Atlantic coast, mainly Oct–Mar. Breeding status here is not known. **OBSERVATION TIPS** Search among winter gull roosts to find it. **SIMILAR SPECIES Yellow-legged Gull** *L. michahellis* (L 23–26 in) from Europe is probably overlooked but increasingly detected. Adult recalls Herring but has yellow legs. Juvenile and first-winter have paler head and neck than Herring counterparts.

**YELLOW-LEGGED GULL
ADULT**

ADULT

2ND-SUMMER

GREAT BLACK-BACKED GULL

ADULT, SUMMER

2ND-WINTER

ADULT

ADULT, WINTER

LESSER BLACK-BACKED GULL

1ST-WINTER

ADULT, SUMMER

Laridae

SABINE'S GULL *Xema sabini* L 13–14 in

Graceful gull with a readily diagnostic wing pattern, forked tail, and buoyant flight, reminiscent of a tern. Entire nonbreeding life is spent at sea, typically well beyond the sight of land. Sexes are similar. **ADULT SUMMER** Has gray back and upper inner wing coverts, and mainly white body plumage, except for dark gray hood. Unmistakable in flight: gray on upper wings contrasts with triangle of white on inner wing and triangle of black on leading edge of primaries. Legs are black, bill is dark with yellow tip; eyering is red. **ADULT WINTER** Similar, but head is mainly white except for hint of dark hood; seldom seen here, but molting birds (part way to winter plumage) are encountered regularly. **JUVENILE** Has pale-edged tawny gray feathers on back and inner upper wing coverts, creating scaly appearance. Plumage is otherwise mainly white, except for gray-buff markings on

crown and nape, black wingtips, and black tip to tail. In flight, has similar upper wing pattern to adult (three contrasting triangles of color), but gray is replaced by tawny gray. Legs are pink and bill is dark. **VOICE** Silent in our region. **STATUS AND HABITAT** Nests on coastal tundra in the high Arctic. Migrates down Atlantic seaboard and winters at sea, mainly in southern oceans. **OBSERVATION TIPS** Seldom seen from land, or inland, except during or just after severe weather, but found on pelagic trips, mainly Aug–Sep. Trips to Stellwagen Banks, off New England coast, are usually productive for this species and many adult birds seen in late Jul/early Aug still retain full summer plumage.

ADULT, SUMMER

BLACK-LEGGED KITTIWAKE
Rissa tridactyla L 17–18 in

Elegant, marine gull with buoyant, rather stiff-winged flight and short black legs. Adult is fairly easy to recognize and in flight typically appears very pale with wingtips that look like they have been dipped into black paint. Juvenile recalls juvenile Sabine's Gull but can be separated by differences in upper wing pattern. Sexes are similar. **ADULT SUMMER** Has pale gray back and upper wings, except for white trailing edge and well-defined

black wingtips. Plumage is otherwise white and bill is yellow.

ADULT WINTER Similar, but has gray nape and blackish patch on rear of crown. **JUVENILE** Has gray back and inner upper wing with black line running across coverts and along leading edge of primaries; these two colors contrast with white triangle on trailing half of wing but pattern does not form the clear three triangles of color seen in juvenile Sabine's. Note the black half collar, black tip to tail, and black bill. **VOICE** Utters diagnostic *kittiwake* call at colonies. **STATUS AND HABITAT** Locally common, nesting colonially on sea cliffs on Canadian Atlantic coast. Winters at sea, range extending south down much of Atlantic seaboard. **OBSERVATION TIPS** Easy to see at seabird colonies within breeding range, mainly May–Aug, and a visit to one of these (e.g. Cape St. Mary, Newfoundland) is a "must" for any birdwatcher. At other times, seen from land only during severe gales, but found regularly on pelagic trips to offshore Atlantic waters from fall to spring.

JUVENILE

ADULT, SUMMER

SABINE'S GULL

JUVENILE

JUVENILE

ADULT, SUMMER

BLACK-LEGGED KITTIWAKE

ADULT, SUMMER

ADULT, WINTER

Laridae

BLACK TERN *Chlidonias niger* L 9–10 in

Elegant wetland bird whose plumage varies markedly according to time of year and age. Breeding adults are stunning but seldom remain in pristine plumage for long. Buoyant and aerobatic flight is used to good effect when hawking insects or picking food items from water's surface. Sexes are similar. **ADULT SUMMER** Has mainly gray upperparts, but head and neck, along with breast and belly, are black; note white vent and undertail coverts, slightly forked tail, and gray upperparts. Bill is black and legs are dark red. **ADULT WINTER** (this plumage is acquired gradually Jul–Sep) Has gray upperparts, entirely white underparts; black on head is restricted to cap, nape, and ear coverts. Birds in intermediate stages of molt can look a bit "moth-eaten." Bill is black and legs are dull red. **JUVENILE** Similar to winter adult, but back is brownish gray and scaly-looking due to pale feather margins. First-summer birds resemble winter adults, but with irregular dark spots on underparts. **VOICE** Utters a harsh *scherr*. **STATUS AND HABITAT** Locally common in summer months, but declining due to habitat destruction and degradation. Favors marshes and other freshwater habitats and breeds colonially, building nests on floating vegetation. Migrates mainly overland, sometimes in flocks, and winters on coasts and at sea from Central to South America. **OBSERVATION TIPS** Easy to see at breeding colonies in summer months although sometimes abandons previously used sites if water levels are not suitable. Turns up during migration (Apr–May and Aug–Sep) at inland freshwater sites south of breeding range, but often only pauses to feed for a day or so, sometimes just a matter of hours.

ADULT, WINTER

LEAST TERN *Sternula antillarum* L 8–9 in

Our smallest tern. Flight is rapid and buoyant and it frequently hovers before plunge-diving into shallow water for small fish and shrimp. Sexes are similar. **ADULT SUMMER** Has gray back and upper wings and mainly black cap, although forehead is white; plumage is otherwise pure white. Note the black-tipped yellow bill and yellow-orange legs. In flight, outer two primaries are noticeably dark (show as black wingtips at rest). **ADULT WINTER** (acquires this plumage from late summer onward) Similar, but white on forehead is more extensive and leg and bill colors are duller; upper wing is more uniformly pale. **JUVENILE** Similar to winter adult, but back appears scaly, and outer four or five primaries and leading edge of inner wing are dark. Most first-summer birds resemble winter adult, but with dark leading edge to inner wing and dark outer primaries. **VOICE** Utters a raucous *kree-ick* call. **STATUS AND HABITAT** Declining, but still very common locally. Nests colonially on sandy and pebbly beaches, both on coasts and at inland freshwater sites. Badly and directly affected by man's actions, specifically disturbance, to, or exclusion from, beach nest sites, as well as habitat destruction and degradation. Ground predators compound the problem. Migrates along coasts and river courses and winters on coasts and at sea off Central and South America. **OBSERVATION TIPS** Easy to see at locations where nesting colonies are protected (search the web for sites and access details). If you come across nesting birds elsewhere, keep your distance and avoid disturbing this vulnerable species.

ADULT, SUMMER

ADULT,
SUMMER

BLACK TERN

ADULT, SUMMER

ADULT, SUMMER

LEAST TERN

JUVENILE

Laridae

COMMON TERN *Sterna hirundo* L 11–12 in

Elegant tern that plunge-dives for fish and hawks insects. Sexes are similar. **ADULT SUMMER** Has gray upperparts, black cap, and

whitish gray underparts. Compared to Arctic, note black-tipped orange-red bill, longer red legs, and paler underparts. In flight from below, only inner primaries look translucent and wings have diffuse dark tips; from above, outer primaries have dark tips and shafts, inner ones are dark and appear as a "wedge." **ADULT WINTER** Similar, but has white forehead and dark carpal bar; bill and legs are dark. **JUVENILE** Has white underparts, incomplete dark cap, and scaly gray upperparts; leading and trailing edges of inner upper wing are dark. **VOICE** Utters a harsh *kreeear* call. **STATUS AND HABITAT** Locally common. Breeds beside forest lakes in Canada and on Atlantic coast; present mainly May–Sep. Winters on coasts of Central and South America. **OBSERVATION TIPS** Easy to see in summer. **SIMILAR SPECIES Roseate Tern** *S. dougallii* (L 12–13 in) is paler overall with black on wings limited to narrow wedge on upperside of outer primaries. Adult's bill is mostly black but goes red at base in breeding season. In breeding season has pink flush to underparts and long tail streamers. Rare breeder on Canadian coast and Florida Keys.

ARCTIC TERN *Sterna paradisaea* L 12–13 in

Compared to Common, adult has smaller blood-red (not black-tipped orange-red) bill, different upper wing pattern (inner primaries pale gray in Arctic, seen as dark "wedge" in Common), longer outside tail feathers, shorter legs, and darker belly. **ADULT SUMMER** Has gray upperparts, with black cap; underparts are palest on throat and cheeks and darkest on belly. In flight from below, flight feathers look translucent, with narrow, dark trailing edge to primaries; from above, wings look uniformly gray. **ADULT WINTER** Not seen here. **JUVENILE** Has

white underparts, incomplete dark cap, and scaly gray upperparts. In flight, note dark leading edge and white trailing edge to inner upper wing (leading *and* trailing edges dark in juvenile Common). Legs are dull red, bill is completely or mostly dark. **VOICE** A harsh *krt-krt-krt*. **STATUS AND HABITAT** Locally common nester on tundra and coasts. Migrates at sea and winters in Antarctic. **OBSERVATION TIPS** Easy to see in Arctic, May–Aug. Migrants seen on pelagic trips.

FORSTER'S TERN *Sterna forsteri* L 13–14 in

Paler than Common with longer, more deeply forked tail, longer legs, and different upper wing pattern. Much less pelagic than Arctic and, of the three, the only one likely to be seen here in winter. Sexes are similar. **ADULT SUMMER** Has mainly pale gray back and upper wings, black cap, and otherwise white plumage. Legs are orange-red and bill is orange-red with black tip. In flight, note dark trailing edge to otherwise white primaries (lack dark "wedge" on Common's inner upper primaries). **ADULT WINTER** Looks pale overall, except for dark "mask" through eye, black bill, and darker primaries (especially margins). **JUVENILE** Similar to winter adult, but with buff feathers on back, upper wing, and crown, pale-based bill, and shorter outer tail feathers; first-winter is similar to winter adult but with shorter outer tail feathers. **VOICE** A harsh *kree-err* call. **STATUS AND HABITAT** Nests beside freshwater marshes; other times commonest near coasts. **OBSERVATION TIPS** Easy to see at freshwater sites in summer and coasts in winter.

TERNS

ADULT, SUMMER

ADULT, SUMMER

ADULT, SUMMER

COMMON TERN

ADULT, SUMMER

ARCTIC TERN

ADULT, SUMMER

ADULT, SUMMER

ADULT, WINTER

ADULT, SUMMER

FORSTER'S TERN

ADULT, SUMMER

Laridae

GULL-BILLED TERN *Gelochelidon nilotica* L 13–14 in

Robust, pale tern with controlled flight and relatively deep bill. Does not plunge-dive like other terns and habits are more terrestrial, often hawking insects and picking prey from surface of ground. Sexes are

similar. **ADULT SUMMER** Has pale gray upperparts, black crown and nape, and white underparts. In flight, wings appear almost uniformly white except for dark edges to underside of primaries. Bill and legs are black. **ADULT WINTER** Similar, but head is white except for gray streak from behind eye to nape. **JUVENILE** Similar to winter adult, but back, upper wings, and crown have faint brown feathering. Legs and bill are dark reddish. **VOICE** Utters a *kerr-wick* call. **STATUS AND HABITAT** Local breeding species, nesting on beaches on Atlantic and Gulf coasts and present mainly Apr–Aug. Seen regularly during migration on Gulf coast, wintering from there south to coasts of South America. **OBSERVATION TIPS** Fairly easy to see near Atlantic coasts in spring and summer, where it often feeds over salt marshes and coastal fields rather than open water.

SANDWICH TERN *Sterna sandvicensis* L 14–15 in

Elegant seabird with powerful, buoyant flight on long, narrow wings. Announces its presence with a loud and distinctive call and dives frequently after fish. Sexes are similar. **ADULT SUMMER** Has very pale gray back and upper wings, a dark, crested cap, and otherwise white plumage.

Legs are black and the long, narrow bill is black with a yellow tip. In flight, wings can look almost pure white but at closer range outer primaries appear as subtly darker wedge. **ADULT WINTER** (seen in this plumage from late summer onward) Similar, but forehead is white. **JUVENILE** Similar to winter adult, but back is barred and scaly. **VOICE** Utters a harsh *chee-urrick* call. **STATUS AND HABITAT** Nests along Atlantic and Gulf coasts on beaches and islands; present in summer breeding range mainly Apr–Sep. Winters from Florida and Gulf coasts south throughout Caribbean.

ROYAL TERN *Thalasseus maximus* L 18–21 in

Large, robust tern with buoyant, direct flight. Plunge-dives after fish. Bill is stout and orange and legs are black and long. Tail is deeply forked. Sexes are similar. **ADULT SUMMER** Pale gray above and whitish below, palest on head and neck. Has a black cap and, in flight, note dark upper surface to outer primaries and dark-edged wingtips seen from below. **ADULT WINTER** Similar, but shows only remnant of dark cap on nape. **JUVENILE AND 1ST-WINTER** Similar to winter adult, but with dark spots on back, upper wings, and upper tail, and yellowish legs and bill. **VOICE** Utters a coarse, low-pitched *kree-eh*. **STATUS AND HABITAT** Very locally common on Atlantic and Gulf coasts and present year-round as far north as North Carolina; summer breeding range extends north to New England. Nests on islands and feeds in shallow seas. Disperses outside breeding season and many birds winter south of our region. **OBSERVATION TIPS** Easy to see on coasts. Congregates and mixes with other terns where feeding is good.

GULL-BILLED TERN

ADULT, SUMMER

ADULT, WINTER

SANDWICH TERN

ADULT, SUMMER

ADULT, SUMMER

ROYAL TERN

ADULT, WINTER

ADULT, WINTER

Laridae

CASPIAN TERN *Hydroprogne caspia* L 20–22 in

A giant among terns, and the largest of its kind in the world. Most distinctive and diagnostic feature is huge, daggerlike bill that is dark red with dark subterminal band and small pale tip. Body is plump and robust, with gull-like proportions. Tail is forked, but outer feathers are not particularly long. Flight is powerful, direct, and gull-like. Plunge-dives after fish. Sexes are similar. **ADULT SUMMER** Has pale gray back and upper wing and mainly white underparts. In flight, however, note that upper surface of primaries is marginally darker than rest of upper wing, and trailing margin of primaries is darker still; from below, primaries are blackish. Legs and cap are uniformly black. **ADULT WINTER** Similar, but cap is streaked black and white, darkest below eye, rather than uniformly dark. **JUVENILE** Similar to winter adult, but with paler bill and subtle scaling effect on back and upper tail. **VOICE** Utters a harsh, slightly menacing *kraa-aar* call. **STATUS AND HABITAT**

ADULT

Very locally common breeding species (mainly May–Jul), nesting in colonies on gravel or sand islands and bars in or near freshwater lakes and rivers rich with fish, and coastal estuaries and lagoons. Coastal birds seldom feed far from shore. Disperses and moves south outside breeding season, wintering on Gulf coast, and coasts of Central and northern South America. **OBSERVATION TIPS** Typically rather thinly scattered, but usually easy to see at any freshwater or coastal sites where medium-sized fish are plentiful. Size of bill and stature overall make this species unmistakable.

BLACK SKIMMER *Rynchops niger* L 17–18 in

Extremely distinctive, ternlike waterbird with wonderfully bizarre and laterally flattened diagnostic bill. Lower mandible is appreciably longer than upper one and used in characteristic fashion when fishing: feeds in flight (mostly after dark), skimming low over water, bill open, then snapping at prey that comes into contact with lower mandible as it scythes through the water surface. Tail is slightly forked. Often seen in flocks. Sexes are similar. **ADULT SUMMER** Has mainly black upper wings and back, continuous with black cap and back of neck; forecrown and underparts are white. In flight, note dark center to otherwise white upper tail, dark gray primaries, and white trailing edge to dark upper wing. Legs are short and red and bill is red-based and dark-tipped.

ADULT, SUMMER, FEEDING

ADULT WINTER Similar, but black cap and nape are separated from black back by streaked white hind neck. **JUVENILE** Similar to winter adult, but with paler gray-buff margins to feathers of otherwise dark elements of upperparts. These are molted gradually through first winter. **VOICE** Utters a nasal *kwuup* call. **STATUS AND HABITAT** Local and generally scarce in southwestern U.S., but common and much more widespread on Gulf coast. Nests on sandy beaches. Extremely vulnerable to changing water levels, but more so to human disturbance, both directly and by the presence of aggressive dogs. Present year-round on Gulf coast and Atlantic coast north to North Carolina; summer breeding range extends north to New England. **OBSERVATION TIPS** Usually easy to see on suitable coasts in Florida.

ADULT, WINTER

CASPIAN TERN

ADULT, SUMMER

ADULT, WINTER

BLACK SKIMMER

ADULT, SUMMER

Alcidae

RAZORBILL *Alca torda* L 16–18 in

Bulky seabird with essentially black and white plumage and distinctive bill. Swims well, dives frequently, and flies low over water on whirring wingbeats. Sexes are similar. **ADULT SUMMER** Has a black head, neck, and upperparts, and white underparts; note the neat white wing bar. Bill is large and laterally flattened; at close range, note

ADULT, SUMMER

the vertical ridges and white lines. **ADULT WINTER** Similar, but has partly white face (throat and cheeks); bill is smaller. **JUVENILE** Recalls winter adult, but bill is smaller and lacks markings. **VOICE** Mostly silent, but it sometimes utters croaking calls near nest. **STATUS AND HABITAT** During breeding season, favors rocky coasts and is a constituent member of many seabird colonies on Newfoundland and Labrador coasts. Outside breeding season it is highly pelagic and healthy birds are seldom seen close to land; Grand Banks is a hotspot. **OBSERVATION TIPS** At seabird colonies, those birds that are not incubating often sit around on prominent rocks near nest. Machias Seal Island, New Brunswick, provides good views.

COMMON MURRE *Uria aalge* L 17–18 in

Stoutly built seabird. Nests in dense colonies on sea-cliff ledges. When not nesting, spends entire life at sea; swims well and dives frequently. Flies on whirring wingbeats; like other alcids, wings are also used when swimming—it "flies" underwater. Sexes are similar. **ADULT SUMMER** Has dark chocolate-brown head and upperparts, including upper wings (darker in northern birds than southern ones), and white underparts. Some birds ("Bridled Murres") have a white "spectacle" around eye. Bill is dark, daggerlike and straight in all birds. **ADULT WINTER** Similar, but with more white on head: white cheeks and throat separated by black line running back from eye. **JUVENILE** Similar to winter adult, but with more extensive streaking on head and neck. **VOICE** Utters nasal, growling *har-rrrhr* calls at breeding colonies. **STATUS AND HABITAT** Locally numerous member of selected seabird colonies, nesting on precipitous cliff ledges. Entirely pelagic outside breeding season. **OBSERVATION TIPS** Easy to see, May–Jul, at selected breeding colonies on northeastern Canadian coast. Cape St. Mary's and Baccalieu Island are hotspots.

THICK-BILLED MURRE *Uria lomvia* L 17–18 in

Marginally smaller than similar Common Murre. Has shorter, thicker bill (almost gull-like) with striking white stripe along gape. Neck is thicker than Common, and plumage darker overall, although latter feature is often hard to discern in poor light. Adopts upright posture when resting on cliff. Swims well, dives frequently, and flies on whirring wingbeats. Sexes are similar. **ADULT SUMMER** Has blackish head, neck, and upperparts, with clean demarcation on chest from white underparts. **ADULT WINTER** Simi-

ADULT, WINTER

lar, but throat becomes white (lacks white cheeks seen in winter Common). White gape stripe is less striking. **JUVENILE** Similar to winter adult. **VOICE** Utters rumbling *har-rrrhr* calls at breeding colonies. Otherwise silent. **STATUS AND HABITAT** Restricted mainly to cold northern and Arctic seas; smaller numbers breed in Newfoundland and Nova Scotia. Nests colonially on sea-cliff ledges, often found alongside Common Murre. Pelagic outside breeding season, most remaining in Arctic waters. **OBSERVATION TIPS** Abundant in Arctic, but smaller and more accessible colonies may be observed in Newfoundland and Nova Scotia.

RAZORBILL
ADULT, SUMMER

ADULT, BRIDLED

COMMON MURRE

ADULT, WINTER

COMMON MURRE

THICK-BILLED MURRE
ADULT, SUMMER

ADULT, SUMMER

Alcidae

DOVEKIE *Alle alle* L 8–9 in

Tiny seabird and the smallest Atlantic alcid. Dumpy, compact appearance is accentuated by short neck and tiny, stubby bill. Flies on rapid, whirring wingbeats. Swims well and dives frequently. Sexes are similar. **ADULT SUMMER** Has a black head, neck, and upperparts, and white underparts. At close range, white lines on scapulars, white wing bar (white edge to secondaries), and tiny white eye crescent above eye can be seen. **ADULT WINTER** Similar, but has a black cap, nape, and back with otherwise white plumage. **JUVENILE** Similar to winter adult. **VOICE** Silent in the region. **STATUS AND HABITAT** Abundant breeding species, nesting in huge colonies on

ADULTS, WINTER

boulder slopes in high Arctic Greenland. Outside breeding season, entirely pelagic. Many remain in Arctic seas, but good numbers extend south down Atlantic seaboard and common in winter off coasts of Newfoundland, mainly Oct–Mar. **OBSERVATION TIPS** Sometimes forced close to shore during or just after onshore winter gales.

BLACK GUILLEMOT *Cepphus grylle* L 13–14 in

Rather plump-bodied seabird. Strikingly pied plumage is contrastingly different in summer and winter. Swims well, dives frequently, and flies low over water on rounded wings with whirring wingbeats. All birds have white underwings, red legs, and red inside of mouth (obvious when bird is calling). Sexes are similar. **ADULT SUMMER** Has mainly sooty black plumage with striking white patch on wing. **ADULT WINTER** Has white underparts and mainly white neck with dark streaks down nape. Crown is dark-streaked and has dark-centered gray back feathers and black flight feathers; retains white wing patch. **JUVENILE**

ADULT, WINTER

Similar to winter adult, but with more dark streaking on face, neck, and underparts. **VOICE** Utters high-pitched whistles when in breeding colonies. **STATUS AND HABITAT** Locally common year-round on rocky coasts in Canada and Greenland; nests under boulders and in rock crevices. Usually feeds in inshore waters at all times. **OBSERVATION TIPS** Common on suitable coasts, but mainly Arctic breeding range renders many areas inaccessible. Usually fairly easy to see on coasts of Newfoundland and Nova Scotia; sometimes visits harbors.

ATLANTIC PUFFIN *Fratercula arctica* L 12–13 in

Endearing and unmistakable seabird due to its bill size, shape, and color. Looks rather black and white at a distance and flies on narrow wings with whirring wingbeats. Swims well and dives frequently in search of fish. Sexes are similar. **ADULT SUMMER** Has mostly black upperparts with dusky white face; underparts are mostly white with a clear demarcation from black neck. Legs are orange-red and bill is huge, laterally flattened and marked with red, blue, and yellow. **WINTER ADULT** Similar, but it has a dark gray face and slightly smaller, much duller bill. **JUVENILE**

ADULT, WINTER

Similar to winter adult, but with even smaller, duller bill. **VOICE** Utters strange groaning calls at nest. **STATUS AND HABITAT** Very locally abundant at Canadian seabird colonies. Nests in burrows on grassy, sloping cliffs and islands. Numbers greatly reduced in the past by hunting; species is now threatened by overfishing and marine pollution. Outside breeding season, Puffins are found far out to sea and seldom seen from land. **OBSERVATION TIPS** A visit to a colony is a memorable experience. Some in Newfoundland and Labrador are accessible and Witless Bay and Baccalieu Island are hotspots.

ADULT, WINTER

ADULT, SUMMER

DOVEKIE

ADULT, SUMMER

BLACK GUILLEMOT

ADULT, SUMMER

ADULT, SUMMER

ATLANTIC PUFFIN

ADULT, SUMMER

ADULT, SUMMER

Columbidae

ROCK PIGEON *Columba livia* L 12–13 in

North America's most familiar pigeon, especially in towns and cities. Typically utterly fearless and many depend to large extent on "hand-outs" from people or carelessly dumped refuse. Forms flocks and

ADULT

usually feeds on ground. Nowadays, most birds are free-living, but centuries of domestication have produced a spectrum of color varieties; hence hard to discern sex differences within species' overall variation. **ADULT** Ancestral form has blue-gray plumage overall, palest on upper wings and back, and flushed pinkish maroon on breast. Has two dark wing bars and dark-tipped tail. In flight, note small white rump patch; upper wings have dark trailing edge and narrow wing bar, while underwings are white. Pure white, reddish brown and marbled and mottled color forms are all common too. **JUVENILE** Similar, but duller. **VOICE** Utters various cooing calls. **STATUS AND HABITAT** Old World species, introduced by original European settlers and now common and widespread. Favors urban settings where food is available, but also seen on farmland. **OBSERVATION TIPS** Hard to miss. A positive benefit to urban Peregrine Falcons.

MOURNING DOVE *Zenaida macroura* L 11–12 in

Slim-bodied, long-tailed dove. Feeds on ground (mainly on seeds) and walks with jerky, but rapid manner on short legs. Forms flocks outside breeding season. Sexes are separable with care. **ADULT** Male has pinkish buff plumage overall. Upper wings, back, and rump are buffy brown with black spots on tertials and wing coverts. Head, neck, and breast are paler buff, flushed pink on breast and with iridescent bluish feathers on nape. Note dark crescent on lower margin of ear coverts, dark bill and pinkish red legs. Adult female is similar, but less colorful on neck and breast. **JUVENILE** Similar to adult female, but has spotted and barred appearance to back, neck, and breast, and pale face with dark line through eye. **VOICE** Utters a series of mournful, hooting calls. **STATUS AND HABITAT** Common in open terrain, including arable farmland, parks, suburbs, and roadsides. Northern populations are mostly migratory, present Mar–Sep, wintering south to Mexico. Birds from south of range are often rather sedentary and at best locally nomadic in winter in search of food. **OBSERVATION TIPS** Easy to see.

WHITE-WINGED DOVE *Zenaida asiatica* L 11–12 in

Compact and proportionately plump, arid-country dove. Forms flocks, especially outside breeding season, easily recognized in flight by white, crescent-shaped mark on upper wings; white tip to tail is most obvious when fanned, on takeoff and landing. Sexes are similar. **ADULT** Gray-brown overall, with a pinkish flush most evident on neck and breast. Bill is dark, legs are reddish, and note black crescent below eye, which has red iris

ADULT

and blue orbital skin. In flight, white outer margins to upper wing coverts contrast with blackish outer wing. **JUVENILE** Similar, but with less striking wing markings and subdued colors and markings on head. **VOICE** Series of owl-like cooing calls is sometimes rendered as "who cooks for you." **STATUS AND HABITAT** Mainly Central American species with toehold in parts of southern U.S., favoring arid scrub and adjacent farmland. Locally common summer visitor, but present year-round in southern Florida, Texas, New Mexico, and Arizona. **OBSERVATION TIPS** Easy to see in suitable arid habitats.

ADULT

ADULT

ROCK PIGEON

MOURNING DOVE

ADULT

ADULT

ADULT

WHITE-WINGED DOVE

JUVENILE

JUVENILE

Columbidae

EURASIAN COLLARED-DOVE
Streptopelia decaocto L 12–13 in

Similar to Mourning Dove but with shorter tail, unmarked upperparts and diagnostic dark half collar on nape. Distinctive call is well known in urban areas, as is gliding display flight performed on bowed, outstretched wings. Sexes are similar. **ADULT** Has mainly sandy brown plumage with pinkish flush to head and underparts. Black wingtips and white outer tail feathers are most noticeable in flight. Bill is dark and legs are reddish. **JUVENILE** Similar, but has duller color and black half collar is absent. **VOICE** Utters repetitive (mildly irritating) song that comprises much-repeated *oo-oo-oo* phrase. **STATUS AND HABITAT** Introduced to Bahamas in 1970s and has since spread across much of U.S.; range expansion mirrors that in Europe since 1950s. Often found in urban areas but also near farm buildings and grain spills. **OBSERVATION TIPS** Easy to see within range, which is expected to expand further.

COMMON GROUND-DOVE
Columbina passerina L 6–7 in

Small, plump dove with relatively short tail and large head. Feeds unobtrusively, mainly on ground. In flight, chestnut and black pattern on outer wing is striking, above and below. Sexes are dissimilar. **ADULT MALE** Has

ADULT

WHITE-TIPPED DOVE

ADULT

buffy brown back and gray-buff wing coverts adorned with black spots. Crown and nape are iridescent bluish and face, neck, and underparts are pinkish with dark scaly-looking barring. Pale face shows off beady red eye. Bill is dainty, pale reddish pink, and dark-tipped. **ADULT FEMALE** Similar, but nape and crown are brownish (and lack iridescence) and face and underparts are less colorful. **JUVENILE** Similar to adult female, but browner and with fewer, or no, black spots. **VOICE** Utters monotonously repeated, upslurred *whoo-errp* calls. **STATUS AND HABITAT** Mainly Central American species that is a locally common resident in southern U.S. Favors dry, open, bushy terrain with sandy ground. Often found in disturbed and urban sites such as farms and city parks. **OBSERVATION TIPS** Easy to overlook when feeding on ground in dappled shade. **SIMILAR SPECIES White-tipped Dove** *Leptotila verreauxi* (L 11–12 in) is resident in arid country in southern Texas. Plump bodied with mostly brown upperparts, buffish pink face and underparts, pale eye, and white-tipped tail.

INCA DOVE *Columbina inca* L 8–9 in

Small, plump-bodied and long-tailed ground-feeding dove. Most distinctive and diagnostic feature is "scaly" appearance to feathers on back, wing coverts, and underparts. In flight, note white sides on long tail and striking chestnut pattern on outer flight feathers, above and below; chestnut color is also visible on closed wing. Sexes are similar, although seen side-by-side, male is brighter than female. **ADULT** Has mainly gray-brown upperparts and pinkish gray underparts, palest on belly. Note that all parts of body, but especially back and belly, have black feather margins creating "scaly" look. Bill is dark, legs are pinkish, and eye has red iris and hint of blue orbital skin. **JUVENILE** Similar, but duller and less well patterned. **VOICE** Utters subdued, chuckling and cooing calls including *coo-coo* and *kup-kup-kup kerrWhoo*. **STATUS AND HABITAT** Mainly Central American species with toehold in parts of southern U.S., mainly Texas, where it is a locally common resident. Favors arid and disturbed land, often around human dwellings, on lawns and in gardens. **OBSERVATION TIPS** Easy to see in Texas and usually indifferent to people.

EURASIAN COLLARED-DOVE

ADULT

ADULT

COMMON GROUND-DOVE

FEMALE

MALE

INCA DOVE

ADULT

ADULT

ADULTS

SMOOTH-BILLED
ANI *Crotophaga ani*
L 14–15 in

A Florida specialty and, within its range, unmistakable on account of its mostly black plumage, huge bill, and extremely long tail. Often seen in small groups that usually comprise up to 15 or so individuals, of which several will be breeding pairs; nesting is a cooperative affair. Members of group interact with one another constantly. Flight is rather weak and frequently includes low glides; usually adopts an upright posture when perched. Feeds mainly on insects and other invertebrates, but sometimes also fruits and seeds. Sexes are similar. **ADULT** Has shaggy black plumage; in good light, note the purplish, oily sheen to many of the feathers. Tail is long and broadens toward the tip; wings are relatively short and rounded. Bill is laterally flattened and smooth with a pronounced dorsal ridge; latter feature is useful for separation from vagrant adult Groove-billed Ani. **JUVENILE** Similar to adult. **VOICE** Utters a distinctive, upslurred *kwerr'ipp*, distinctly different from that of Groove-billed Ani. **STATUS AND HABITAT** Widespread in Central and South America, with a resident population in southern Florida. Here it favors open areas of scrub and grassland. **OBSERVATION TIPS** Usually fairly easy to see in southern Florida and typically tame and indifferent to the presence of people. Groove-billed Ani is a rare vagrant to Florida, so be aware of the outside possibility of its occurrence there.

GROOVE-BILLED ANI
Crotophaga sulcirostris L 13–14 in

Engaging and distinctive, long-tailed, all-dark bird with a proportionately large bill. Gregarious and typically seen in groups of 5–10 birds. Usually nests communally and social groups engage in cooperative breeding behavior. Flight is weak and characteristic, involving interspersed glides on rounded wings and brief bouts of flapping; in flight, tail appears to have a mind of its own. Usually adopts an upright posture when perched, with dangling tail. Feeds mainly on insects, caught on ground or while foraging among leaves. Sexes are similar. **ADULT** Appears uniformly black, although oily blue-green iridescence can be seen in good light. Nape and throat appear shaggy. Bill is large, dark, and laterally flattened; curved upper margin continues profile of crown and does not show such pronounced dorsal ridge as in Smooth-Billed Ani. Close inspection of bill reveals obvious horizontal grooves on upper mandible. **JUVENILE** Similar to adult, but bill lacks grooves. **VOICE** Utters a distinctive, repeated, piping *tee-wuup, tee-wuup*. **STATUS AND HABITAT** A mainly Central and South American species with a foothold in southern Texas, where it is present mainly May–Sep. Usually associated with dense scrub and woodland beside river courses, but sometimes feeds in more open, grassy situations. Most birds winter in Mexico, where species is resident, but a few are found in coastal south Texas. **OBSERVATION TIPS** Easiest to find when fledged young have joined feeding groups, in late summer.

SMOOTH-BILLED ANI

ADULT

GROOVE-BILLED ANI

ADULT

ADULT

Cuculidae

YELLOW-BILLED CUCKOO
Coccyzus americanus L 12–13 in

Unobtrusive, long-tailed woodland bird. Presence often detected by hearing its distinctive call. Feeds on caterpillars, often hairy ones. Sexes are similar. **ADULT** Has dark gray-brown upperparts, least colorful on crown and

MANGROVE CUCKOO

ADULT

darkest through eye. Rufous flight feathers are most obvious in flight. Underparts are otherwise whitish. Tail is long and wedge-shaped when spread; from above, central upper tail is reddish, while rest of tail is black, all feathers having striking white tips; from below, note striking, large white spots (feather tips) to otherwise black tail feathers. Bill is downcurved with yellow base to lower mandible. Note yellow eyering. **JUVENILE** Similar to adult, but less colorful and with less contrasting undertail pattern. **VOICE** Utters a rapid *ke-ke-ke-ke-keeooa-keeooa-keeooa*. **STATUS AND HABITAT** Common summer visitor (mainly May–Sep); winters in South America. Favors dense scrub and woodland, often beside rivers. Usually builds its own nest but occasionally lays eggs in nest of other species, notably Black-billed Cuckoo. **OBSERVATION TIPS** Easiest to see and hear shortly after arrival from migration in late spring. **SIMILAR SPECIES Mangrove Cuckoo** *C. minor* (L 11–12 in), a Florida specialty, is also widespread in Caribbean. Compared to Yellow-billed, note the dark mask, orange-buff wash on belly and undertail coverts, lack of rufous in wings, and different voice (a descending series of *karr-karr-karr...* notes). Favors mangroves.

BLACK-BILLED CUCKOO
Coccyzus erythropthalmus L 11–12 in

Unobtrusive woodland bird. Separable from similar Yellow-billed by differences in bill and eyering colors, tail patterns, and calls. Feeds on hairy caterpillars. Sexes are similar. **ADULT** Has gray-brown upperparts (crown is same color as back) and whitish underparts. Flight feathers are buffy brown (not rufous), and note uniformly dark bill and reddish eyering. Tail is long and wedge-shaped when fanned; upperside is brown with small pale tips to feathers; underside is gray-brown with small white spots (feather tips), defined by subterminal black bands. **JUVENILE** Similar to adult, but duller overall, with grubby-looking underparts and indistinct pattern on undertail. **VOICE** Utters a subdued piping *cu-cu, cu-cu, cu-cu-cu....* **STATUS AND HABITAT** Scarce summer visitor (mainly May–Sep) to temperate, deciduous woodland; winters in northern South America. **OBSERVATION TIPS** Easiest to see on arrival from migration in spring.

GREATER ROADRUNNER
Geococcyx californianus L 23–24 in

Unmistakable ground-dwelling desert bird that runs swiftly from danger or when chasing prey. Powerful bill is used to good effect in catching and killing lizards, insects, and small mammals. In flight (seldom observed), pale primary bases appear as white crescent. Sexes are similar. **ADULT** Has mainly brown plumage, palest and least marked on belly; feathers on rest of body have pale, buff margins or are adorned with buff streaks and spots, creating rather mottled appearance overall. Crest is bushy and erectile. Tail is long, mainly dark brown with pale tips to feathers. **JUVENILE** Similar to adult. **VOICE** "Song" is a descending series of dovelike cooing notes. Utters bill-snapping sounds in alarm. **STATUS AND HABITAT** Scarce resident of deserts with light scrub. **OBSERVATION TIPS** Seen mainly by chance, e.g. crossing a desert track or road. Often sunbathes in early morning hours, sometimes allowing prolonged views from afar.

ADULT

ADULT

BLACK-BILLED CUCKOO

ADULT

YELLOW-BILLED CUCKOO

ADULT

GREATER ROADRUNNER

ADULT

Tytonidae and Strigidae

BARN OWL *Tyto alba* L 16–17 in

Beautiful owl that looks ghostly white when caught in car headlights. Flight is leisurely and slow on broad wings. Sexes are often separable although considerable variation and overlap exists. **ADULT MALE** Has orange-buff upperparts that are speckled with tiny black and white dots. Underparts are whitish overall, but adorned with numerous black spots. White facial disc is heart shaped and bill is yellowish. In flight, underwings are pure white. **ADULT FEMALE** Similar, but underparts (including underwings) are variably flushed with orange-buff. **JUVENILE** Similar to adult. **VOICE** Utters a blood-curdling, screaming call. **STATUS AND HABITAT** Vulnerable and declining. Mainly resident, but northern birds move south in winter. Relies on undisturbed grassland rich in small mammals and is badly affected by habitat loss and degradation, notably from farming. Loss of roosting and nesting sites (tree holes and derelict farm buildings) are also factors in population declines. Installing artificial nest boxes near suitable feeding areas is helping the species. **OBSERVATION TIPS** Usually crepuscular or nocturnal, but in winter and when there are chicks to feed in summer, it sometimes hunts small mammals in late afternoon.

ADULT

SHORT-EARED OWL *Asio flammeus* L 14–15 in

Medium-sized, well-marked owl that often hunts in daylight, mainly for small mammals. Flight is leisurely and slow: glides frequently, and flies holding its long, narrow, and round-tipped wings rather stiffly. Usually quarters ground at low level, but displaying birds sometimes rise to considerable heights. Often sits on fence posts or grassland tussocks. Sexes are similar, but female is larger and often darker than male. **ADULT AND JUVENILE** Buffy brown overall, but heavily spotted and streaked on upperparts, including neck; underparts are paler overall, but heavily streaked. Facial disc is round; note staring yellow eyes and short "ear" tufts. **VOICE** Displaying birds sometimes utter deep hoots. **STATUS AND HABITAT** Declining, but still fairly common across northeastern Canada during breeding season. Favors open habitats—tundra, undisturbed grassland, and prairie. Moves south in fall, range extending to southern U.S. **OBSERVATION TIPS** Partly diurnal habits mean it is fairly easy to see in open grassland habitats.

ADULT

LONG-EARED OWL *Asio otus* L 15–16 in

Nocturnal and secretive owl. When alarmed, sometimes adopts elongated posture with "ear" tufts raised. In flight, could be mistaken for Short-eared, but has orange-buff overall underwing color (whitish in Short-eared) and more extensive, but barred, dark wingtips. Orange-buff upper wing patch is more striking than on Short-eared. Sexes are similar. **ADULT AND JUVENILE** Have dark brown upperparts and paler underparts; however, whole body is heavily streaked. At close range, note rounded, orange-buff facial disc and staring orange eyes. "Ear" tufts are appreciably longer than those of Short-eared. **VOICE** Mostly silent, but series of deep hoots is sometimes heard in spring. **STATUS AND HABITAT** Nests in dense woodland and scrub thickets, usually in vicinity of open country for hunting. Outside breeding season, birds disperse and northern populations migrate south. In winter, roosts communally in dense thickets. **OBSERVATION TIPS** Hard to observe in daytime, although most people's experience will be a partial view at a daytime winter roost.

BARN OWL

ADULT

SHORT-EARED OWL

ADULT

LONG-EARED OWL

ADULT

ADULT

Strigidae

GREAT HORNED OWL *Bubo virginianus* L 22–23 in

Huge and impressive owl with a bulky body, proportionately large head, and striking "ear" tufts that may be raised or flattened. Active mainly at dusk and after dark, has a broad diet, but prefers tackling prey the size of rabbits and hares. Typically scans for prey from lookout perch, then glides down on broad wings, grabbing and killing victim with powerful talons. Several subspecies exist: palest of all is ssp. *subarcticus*, which occurs across Arctic and sub-Arctic North America, but birds in most of range covered by this book, and described here, are a darker, richer brown. Given this variation, sexes are similar, although female is larger than male. **ADULT** Has mostly brown plumage overall, beautifully patterned on upperparts and resembling tree bark; underparts are strongly barred. Head has rounded, orange-brown facial disc and yellow eyes. **JUVENILE** Has fluffy down at first, but by fall acquires adultlike plumage. **VOICE** Territorial "song" (heard in midwinter) comprises a series of tremulous hoots; male's hoot is deeper than female's. **STATUS AND HABITAT** Common but strongly territorial, hence thinly spread. Tolerates a wide range of habitats from forests in north of range to deserts in south. Sometimes also in surprisingly urban settings. **OBSERVATION TIPS** Nests extremely early in season (eggs typically laid Jan–Mar depending on geographical location), so incubating birds are sometimes obvious in leafless winter trees. Otherwise, occasionally glimpsed in car headlights while hunting after dark, or located by tracking small birds mobbing a roosting bird in daytime.

SNOWY OWL *Bubo scandiacus* L 21–26 in

Huge and unmistakable species, which lacks "ear" tufts. Often active during the day, and obliged to be diurnal in Arctic breeding grounds by perpetual summer daylight. Even if resting or roosting, open nature of its favored habitats, and sheer size, make it relatively conspicuous. Feeds on lemmings and voles during summer months; diet in winter range is often more varied. Sexes are dissimilar. **ADULT MALE** Has essentially pure white plumage with small black spots and bars; at close range, feathered feet, black bill, and yellow eyes can be seen. **ADULT FEMALE AND 1ST-WINTER MALE** Mainly white, but note more extensive blackish spots on upperparts and dark barring below. **1ST-WINTER FEMALE** Heavily marked with dark barring on all parts, except head. **VOICE** Mostly silent, although territorial male sometimes utters series of deep hoots. **STATUS AND HABITAT** Fairly common tundra-breeding species within its high Arctic range, although numbers vary considerably from year to year, influenced by abundance or available selection of prey.

JUVENILE

Outside breeding season, most birds move south, the extent to which they travel influenced by severity of winter weather and availability of prey. **OBSERVATION TIPS** Relatively easy to see if you visit its high Arctic breeding grounds in summer. In winter, most observations are by chance. Can turn up almost anywhere across Canada and northern U.S. in suitable habitats—often open grassland or coastal areas. In such situations, white plumage makes it easy to spot.

ADULT

GREAT HORNED OWL

ADULT

MALE

FEMALE

SNOWY OWL

Strigidae

BARRED OWL *Strix varia* L 21–22 in

Northeastern America's most familiar medium-sized woodland owl. Sometimes found perched on tree branch during daytime, with fluffed up body plumage; proportionately large head and rounded facial disc are obvious. Feeds on small mammals, amphibians, and large invertebrates. Nests in tree holes or sometimes in abandoned twig nests of other birds. Sexes are similar. **ADULT** Has brown plumage overall; upperparts are dark brown, but beautifully marked with white spots, flight feathers with dark bars, while underparts are buff-gray with bold, dark streaks. Note short, barred tail, brown concentric rings around eyes, and ruff of brown-barred feathers on throat. Eyes are dark and bill is yellow. **JUVENILE** Has fluffy plumage at first, but acquires adultlike plumage by fall. **VOICE** Utters a series of gruff hooting notes—typically *who-hu-ho-hoo*—mostly after dark, but sometimes during daytime. **STATUS AND HABITAT** Widespread and common, associated with mixed deciduous and coniferous woods and forest and often found near water. Range has expanded north and west in recent decades, but territorial birds are generally rather sedentary. Nests in tree holes or abandoned crow's nests. **OBSERVATION TIPS** Easy to hear in wooded habitats and occasionally flushed from roost in daytime. Amazing daytime views can sometimes be had beside boardwalks through swamp reserves in Florida.

GREAT GRAY OWL *Strix nebulosa* L 27–28 in

Spectacularly huge and beautifully patterned owl with a proportionately long tail, large head, and rounded facial disc marked with dark concentric rings around eyes. Fluffed up body feathers often accentuate bulky appearance. Feeds mainly on small rodents and typically scans for prey while perched overlooking forest clearing or grassland adjacent to trees. Able to detect movements of small mammals through layer of snow and will plunge through, usually feet-first, to capture prey. Mostly nocturnal in winter, but during breeding season, lengthy daylight hours oblige diurnal hunting too. Nests in large, abandoned twig nests or in natural cavities in tree stumps. Sexes are similar. **ADULT** Has mainly gray-brown plumage, upperparts with intricate darker markings; underparts are barred and streaked. Note the staring yellow eyes and yellow bill. **JUVENILE** Fluffy at first, but by fall acquires adultlike plumage. **VOICE** Territorial male's "song" comprises a series of deep *hoo* notes, whose pitch rises at first then falls throughout the series. **STATUS AND HABITAT** Widespread, but nomadic, presence or absence dictated by availability of prey; territories widely spaced and so seldom common. Favors boreal forests across northern part of range, but montane conifer forests further south. Mainly sedentary, but shortage of prey and adverse weather sometimes causes irruptive movements south of usual range in winter. **OBSERVATION TIPS** Male's song is clue to species' presence. Fiercely protective of nest, so do not approach closely or you may be attacked and suffer injury.

ADULT

ADULT

ADULT

BARRED OWL

ADULT

ADULT

GREAT
GRAY OWL

Strigidae

EASTERN SCREECH-OWL *Megascops asio* L 8–9 in
Widespread owl of wooded habitats, including mature suburban gardens. Mostly nocturnal, but sometimes starts feeding at dusk; prey includes small mammals and birds, insects, and other invertebrates. Screeching song and calls are a familiar sound, and this is the only small, "eared" owl you are likely to encounter within range covered by this book. Nests in natural tree holes and old woodpecker holes; readily takes to the provision of nest boxes. Several subspecies occur in North America, and birds also occur in two color morph extremes (gray and rufous) with intermediates. Shows considerable variation in relative proportions of different morphs across range: typically gray predominates in north and west areas, and in Texas, while rufous is commonest in east. Given this variation, sexes are similar. **ADULT** Either reddish brown overall or gray-brown. Upperparts are beautifully patterned with fine dark lines and white spots; feathers on underparts are marked with dark central streak and fine dark barring. Note the staring yellow eyes, pale-tipped yellowish bill, and "ear" tufts that can be raised at will. **JUVENILE** Similar to adult. **VOICE** Typical territorial call comprises a plaintive, descending whistle followed by a rapid series of tremulous, whinnying piping whistles. Other vocalizations include various screeching and hooting calls. **STATUS AND HABITAT** Favors a wide range of wooded and lightly wooded habitats from forests to wooded suburban gardens and parks. **OBSERVATION TIPS** More easily heard than seen, but sometimes tolerant of human observers in suburban settings where it is not disturbed.

FERRUGINOUS PYGMY-OWL
Glaucidium brasilianum L 6.5–7 in
Small and relatively long-tailed owl with rufous plumage overall. Mainly active during daylight hours. **ADULT** Has reddish brown upperparts and tail, with delicate pale streaks on head and nape, and spots on back and wings. Note the false "eyes" on the nape. Underparts are pale with bold rufous streaks. **JUVENILE** Similar to adult, but streaks and spots on upperparts are much less distinct. **VOICE** Male's typical territorial song is a rapid series of *pu-pu-pu* piping notes, recalling a frog or perhaps a smoke alarm. **STATUS AND HABITAT** A mainly Central and South American species whose resident range extends to southern Arizona and southern Texas. Favors desert scrub and riverside woodland. **OBSERVATION TIPS** Listen for the distinctive call.

NORTHERN SAW-WHET OWL
Aegolius acadicus L 7–8 in
Endearing, plump-bodied owl with a large head and short tail. Entirely nocturnal and roosts in dense cover during daytime. Nests in tree holes. Sexes are similar. **ADULT** Has reddish brown plumage overall. Upperparts are beautifully patterned with pale spots, largest on back and wings, finest and densest on head; underparts are whitish, but heavily streaked rufous. Facial disc is more oblong than round, flushed buffy reddish around margins and with white "eyebrows" framing yellow eyes. **JUVENILE** Recalls adult, but has mainly reddish brown upperparts and orange buff underparts with white between the eyes. **VOICE** Male's territorial call (heard in spring) comprises an almost mechanical-sounding, repetitive series of piping whistles, fancifully recalling a saw being sharpened (whetted); a good 21st-century comparison might be an intruder alarm. **STATUS AND HABITAT** Fairly common, but low-density breeding species in conifer and mixed forests. Interior northern populations migrate south for winter and some altitudinal migration is seen in otherwise rather sedentary populations. **OBSERVATION TIPS** Easiest to locate by imitating song (with practice, this is easy to whistle), and listening for response. Otherwise hard to locate, but usually indifferent to observers if discovered.

EASTERN SCREECH-OWL

ADULT, GRAY MORPH

ADULT, RUFOUS MORPH

FERRUGINOUS PYGMY-OWL

ADULT

NORTHERN SAW-WHET OWL

ADULT

Strigidae

BOREAL OWL *Aegolius funereus* L 10–11 in

Plump-bodied owl with short tail and proportionately large head with oblong facial disc. Strictly nocturnal and roosts in dense cover. Sexes are similar. **ADULT** Has rich brown plumage overall. Upperparts are marked with bold white spots, smallest and densest on head; underparts are whitish, but heavily streaked with rufous brown. Facial disc is whitish with dark border; yellow eyes are framed by white "eyebrows." **JUVENILE** Mainly brown with white "eyebrows". **VOICE** Male's territorial call comprises a series of piping hoots that rise and fall in pitch during delivery. **STATUS AND HABITAT** Widespread, but present at low densities in thick boreal and mountain forests with mix of deciduous and coniferous trees. Mainly sedentary, but irruptive southward if prey numbers crash. **OBSERVATION TIPS** Hard to find because of unobtrusive habits and inclination to sit tight while roosting. Presence easiest to detect by call. Alternatively, befriend a birder who has installed nest boxes for the species.

JUVENILES

NORTHERN HAWK-OWL *Surnia ulula* L 15–16 in

Long-tailed appearance is diagnostic. In silhouette, recalls a large falcon, but note large, rounded head and typical owl face. Active during daylight hours, typically perching on prominent lookout, scanning ground for small mammal prey. Nests in tree holes. Sexes are similar. **ADULT** Gray-brown overall. Upperparts are marked with pale spots, smallest and densest on head; underparts are barred, as is long, tapering tail. Eyes and bill are yellow and facial disc is pale and rounded with striking white "eyebrows." **JUVENILE** Similar to adult. **VOICE** Male's territorial call comprises a series of trilling, piping notes that rise and fall in pitch throughout delivery. **STATUS AND HABITAT** Widespread in taiga forest, but never common. Precise distribution and breeding success is dictated by numbers of small mammal prey. **OBSERVATION TIPS** Low density, nomadic habits, and fickle site faithfulness make it tricky to pin down. However, on the plus side, diurnal habits and fondness for perching on treetops allow superb views if you do find one.

BURROWING OWL *Athene cunicularia* L 9.5–10 in

Distinctive owl with a bold nature. Although hunting is mainly nocturnal, often sits or perches conspicuously during daytime, in vicinity of nest or roost burrow. Body is dumpy, head is rounded, and tail is proportionately short. Legs are relatively long and bird often bobs up and down when curious or agitated. Sexes are similar. **ADULT** Gray-brown overall, but upperparts are beautifully patterned with pale spots (smallest on head), while dark breast is adorned with pale spots and underparts are otherwise pale with strong, brown barring. Facial disc is rounded and dark eyerings and white "eyebrows" frame yellow eyes. **JUVENILE** Similar to adult, but underparts are mainly pale and unmarked, except for darker chest. **VOICE** Male's typical song is a piping and repeated *cu-coo, cu-coo....* Birds utter soft, screeching calls when alarmed. **STATUS AND HABITAT** Fairly common in open habitats, including grassland and deserts; has adapted well to modified landscapes such as golf courses. **OBSERVATION TIPS** Arguably the easiest owl to observe and typically tolerant of people, especially in Florida.

ADULT

BOREAL OWL

ADULT

ADULT

NORTHERN HAWK-OWL

ADULT

ADULT

BURROWING OWL

CHUCK-WILL'S-WIDOW
Caprimulgus carolinensis L 12–13 in
Nocturnal species, heard more often than it is seen. Hawks insects after dark, catching prey in its capacious mouth; tail is proportionately longer than that of the otherwise quite similar Whip-poor-will. Beautifully patterned plumage gives it good camouflage when resting on the ground among fallen leaves and branches. Sexes are separable. **ADULT MALE** Reddish brown overall, with intricate pattern of gray and black on upperparts and barring on underparts. Note the whitish collar, dark breast, and pale wing bar. Tail has buffy tips and white inner webs to outer feathers. **ADULT FEMALE** Similar, but white is absent on tail. **JUVENILE** Similar to adult female. **VOICE** Song is *chuck-wee-whidow*. **STATUS AND HABITAT** Summer visitor (mainly May–Aug) favoring mixed woodland. Winters mainly in Central America but some remain in southern Florida. **OBSERVATION TIPS** Listen for the distinctive song.

WHIP-POOR-WILL *Caprimulgus vociferus* L 9–10 in
Long-winged, long-tailed bird with a large head and huge gape, with which it engulfs flying insects. Nocturnal, feeding mainly on moths and beetles. Eyes are large, but hidden by partly-closed eyelids in daytime. Beautifully patterned plumage provides superb camouflage when resting on tree branch or fallen leaves in daytime. Sexes are separable. **ADULT MALE** Has gray-brown plumage overall, but subtle and intricate patterns of black and buff create impression of tree bark. Flight feathers and wing coverts are reddish brown. Note white half collar (sometimes hidden) separating blackish throat from dark brown chest band. Outer tail feathers are extensively white toward tip. **ADULT FEMALE** Similar, but outer tail feathers are tipped buff (not white). **JUVENILE** Similar to adult. **VOICE** Song (delivered after dark) is a liquid *Whip-poo-weel*, the middle syllable slightly stuttering; call is a liquid *quip*. **STATUS AND HABITAT** Common summer visitor (mainly May–Sep) to dry mixed or deciduous forests with clearings. Winters mainly in Central America but also Florida. **OBSERVATION TIPS** Presence is easiest to detect by listening for song.

COMMON NIGHTHAWK *Chordeiles minor* L 9–10 in
Our most familiar nighthawk. Feeds mostly after dark (sometimes at dusk) catching flying insects in huge mouth. Often roosts on tree branch or post. In flight, looks long-winged with white wing patches and long, forked tail. Sexes are separable. **ADULT MALE** Has blackish brown plumage overall. Upperparts are finely marked with fine black and whitish lines (looks like tree bark); throat is white and underparts have dark brown barring on pale background.

Note white band across primaries in resting birds and in flight. Tail has white subterminal band, only obvious in flight. **ADULT FEMALE** Similar, but throat patch is buff, wing patch is less striking and white tail band is typically absent. **JUVENILE** Similar to adult. **VOICE** Male's call is a strangled, rather froglike *we-ert* or *pe-ert*, uttered in flight. **STATUS AND HABITAT** Common summer visitor (mainly May–Sep) to open areas such as forest openings. **OBSERVATION TIPS** Roosting birds often perch conspicuously; sometimes hawks for insects around streetlights. **SIMILAR SPECIES Lesser Nighthawk** *C. acutipennis* (L 8–9.5 in) is smaller with relatively shorter wings and tail. Plumage is more rufous and intricate with square-ended tail. Male's call is a trilling whistle. Summer visitor; mainly western range extends to arid areas of southern Texas.

CHUCK-WILL'S-WIDOW

ADULT

WHIP-POOR-WILL

MALE

FEMALE

MALE

COMMON NIGHTHAWK

JUVENILE

MALE

CHIMNEY SWIFT *Chaetura pelagica* L 5–5.5 in

Small swift and the only one of its kind you are likely to encounter in eastern North America. Recognized by its narrow, pointed wings and cigar-shaped body. Soaring and banking birds fan the tail, but otherwise it is held closed. Active flight is speedy, with frequent changes in direction and style; its wingbeats are shallow and rapid. Catches flying insects on the wing. Breeding birds are typically associated with manmade structures, including chimneys. Presence is often first detected by hearing its twittering calls. Sexes are similar, although males have slightly notched tail. **ADULT** Has dark brown plumage, palest on throat. Spinelike tips to tail feathers are only visible at close range. **JUVENILE** Similar to adult. **VOICE** Utters rapid, chattering twitters. **STATUS AND HABITAT** Common summer visitor (mainly May–Sep) to eastern North America, but range extends to Midwest. Associated mostly with urban areas for breeding; nests and roosts in chimneys and cavities in tall buildings. Winters mainly in Amazonia region of South America. **OBSERVATION TIPS** Easy to see within range during summer months in towns and cities.

RUBY-THROATED HUMMINGBIRD

Archilochus colubris L 3.5–4 in

Unmistakable within range because of its size, shape, and habits, and because it is the only hummingbird likely to be seen in eastern North America. Very similar to Black-chinned (*see below* for description), its southwestern counterpart. Geographical range is best pointer for beginners. Needlelike bill is almost straight. Sexes are dissimilar. **ADULT MALE** Has metallic green upperparts. Throat usually appears black but iridescent ruby gorget is seen at certain angles of direct sunlight. Underparts are whitish, with grubby green feathering on belly. Note white spot behind eye. **ADULT FEMALE** Has green upperparts and mainly whitish underparts, with fine gray streaks on throat and gray-green feathers on flanks. Fanned tail has white feather tips and black subterminal band. **JUVENILE** Similar to adult female. **VOICE** Call is a sharp *chip*. **STATUS AND HABITAT** Widespread and fairly common summer visitor (mainly May–Aug) to eastern North America, favoring gardens and open woodland. **OBSERVATION TIPS** Easy to see in summer range and often visits feeders.

BUFF-BELLIED HUMMINGBIRD

MALE

SIMILAR SPECIES Black-chinned Hummingbird *A. alexandri* (L 3.5–4 in) male has a mostly black throat with a violet lower band seen in good light. Throat color is often hard to discern and separation of both sexes from Ruby-throated counterparts is often best achieved by noting Ruby's longer tail projection beyond wings and slightly tapering (not broad and blunt-ended) primary outline. A southwestern specialty, whose range extends to Texas; present mainly Apr–Aug. **Buff-bellied Hummingbird** *Amazilia yucatanensis* (L 4–4.25 in) is a mainly Mexican hummingbird with a toehold in southern Texas. Adult has a green head, neck, breast, and upper back, and a pale buff belly; lower back, rump, wings, and tail are reddish brown, and bill is long, downcurved, dark-tipped, and reddish. Juvenile is similar but duller. Breeds and occurs year-round in southern Texas in small numbers; most Texan birds migrate south in fall. Easiest to see at feeders.

CHIMNEY SWIFT

ADULT

MALE

RUBY-THROATED HUMMINGBIRD

MALE

BLACK-CHINNED HUMMINGBIRD

MALE

MALE

BLACK-CHINNED HUMMINGBIRD

FEMALE

RUBY-THROATED HUMMINGBIRD

MALE

FEMALE

Alcedinidae

BELTED KINGFISHER *Ceryle alcyon* L 13–14 in

North America's only widespread kingfisher. Typically feeds by diving for fish from perch overlooking water. Alert to danger, and seldom

JUVENILE

tolerant of close human approaches. Nests in riverbank burrows. Sexes are dissimilar. **ADULT MALE** Has blue-gray back, upper wings, and tail, wings in particular are adorned with small white spots. Head, which has shaggy crest, is also blue-gray (but note white spot in front of eye); separated from blue-gray breast band by broad, white collar. Underparts are otherwise white. In flight, note contrast between white coverts and dark flight feathers on underwing, and white wing patch at base of outer flight feathers on upper wing. **ADULT FEMALE** Similar, but note the prominent orange-red band on belly, extending along flanks at base of wing, most obvious in flight. **JUVENILE** Similar to respective sex adult, but with reddish mottling on otherwise blue breast band. **VOICE** Typical call is a distinctive, loud, harsh rattle. **STATUS AND HABITAT** Widespread and generally common close to clear, fish-rich waters, typically rivers and lakes in summer, but also estuaries in winter. Present year-round in southern parts, but northern birds are migratory summer visitors. **OBSERVATION TIPS** Easy to find because it perches prominently near water. Rattling call often attracts attention.

RINGED KINGFISHER *Ceryle torquatus* L 16–17 in

The largest kingfisher in North America. Recalls Belted, but larger size and reddish underparts enable easy recognition. Bill is massive, and daggerlike, with a yellow base and dark tip. Perches on dead branches overhanging water, and dives for fish. Nests in riverbank burrows. Sexes are dissimilar. **ADULT MALE** Has blue back and upper wings, the latter marked with small white spots and dark streaks. Head is blue with a shaggy crest (and small white spot in front of eye); this is separated from back and reddish underparts by white collar. Tail is adorned with white spots above and below. **ADULT FEMALE** Similar, but note the broad blue breast band, separated from reddish underparts by a white chest band. **JUVENILE** Similar to respective adult, but female's chest band has some reddish feathering while male has hint of blue chest band. **VOICE** Utters a loud rattling call, lower pitched than that of Belted. **STATUS AND HABITAT** Widespread in South and Central America but also resident in southern Texas, mainly on Rio Grande. **OBSERVATION TIPS** Often perches prominently.

GREEN KINGFISHER
Chloroceryle americana L 8.5–9 in

Green color and smaller size separate it from larger kingfisher species. Has a dark, daggerlike bill and dives for fish. Flight is fast and low over water. When agitated, bobs body and pumps tail up and down. Sexes are dissimilar. **ADULT MALE** Has green back, wings, and upper tail; wings have white spots and outer tail feathers are white at base, white spotted towards tip. Head is mainly green, separated from green back and reddish orange breast by broad white collar. Underparts are otherwise white with dark spots. **ADULT FEMALE** Similar, but chest band is mottled green. **JUVENILE** Similar to adult female, but many feathers are marked with buff. **VOICE** Utters a staccato series of *tchit-tchit-tchit-tcheirit* notes. **STATUS AND HABITAT** Resident beside small streams and pools in southern Texas. **OBSERVATION TIPS** Often unobtrusive but sometimes perches on exposed dead branch.

BELTED KINGFISHER

FEMALE

MALE

RINGED KINGFISHER

FEMALE

MALE

FEMALE

MALE

GREEN KINGFISHER

Picidae

JUVENILE

RED-BELLIED WOODPECKER
Melanerpes carolinus L 9–9.5 in
Widespread and familiar ladder-backed woodpecker of woodland, parks, and gardens. Most striking
feature is red on head (not on belly). Drums loudly.
Sometimes caches food in crevices in bark. Sexes are
dissimilar. **ADULT MALE** Has finely barred black and
white back and upper wings, white rump, and mainly
pale grayish white underparts with dark chevrons on
flanks. Crown, nape and lores are red. **ADULT FEMALE** Similar, but crown is grayish white with only limited amount of red on loral and
supraloral area at base of upper mandible. **JUVENILE** Resembles adult, but nape
is pale grayish orange. **VOICE** Utters a soft, almost disyllabic, but actually slurred,
chu-urrr, chu-urr, chu-urr.... **STATUS AND HABITAT** Common in eastern North
America and range seems to be expanding north and west. Found in a wide range
of wooded habitats. Mainly resident but some movements among northern birds
occur in response to harsh winter weather. **OBSERVATION TIPS** Easy to see within
range, and sometimes visits feeders in winter.

GOLDEN-FRONTED WOODPECKER
Melanerpes aurifrons L 9–10 in
Well-marked woodpecker that is the southern, arid woodland counterpart of Red-bellied. All birds have bold black and white barring on back
and upper wings, white rump and golden yellow nape. Feeds on insects, seeds,
and fruits, and will visit feeders. Nests in holes excavated in trees such as
pecan. Drums loudly. Sexes are dissimilar. **ADULT MALE** Has grayish white
underparts that show off dark eye and contrast with dark tail. Note the red
crown and yellow feathers above base of upper mandible. **ADULT FEMALE** Similar, but crown is gray, and yellow on nape and above base of bill is paler. **JUVE-
NILE** Similar to respective sex adult but yellow elements of plumage are absent. **VOICE** Calls include
agitated, churring chatters and sharp series of *kek-kek-kek...* notes. **STATUS AND HABITAT** A mainly
Central American species whose range extends to Texas and southern Oklahoma, where it is resident
and locally common. Favors a wide range of wooded habitats. **OBSERVATION TIPS** Easy to see in Lower
Rio Grande Valley.

NORTHERN FLICKER *Colaptes auratus* L 12–13 in
Familiar and well-marked medium-sized woodpecker. Variation
exists in wing color and two forms are recognized and separated
geographically, although hybrid intermediates occur in zone of overlap.
"Yellow-shafted" Flicker (the one seen in range covered by this book) has
yellow flight feather shafts and flush of same color on underwing coverts.
In "Red-shafted," these elements of plumage are reddish pink. Excavates
nest holes in trees and feeds on wood-boring insects and ants, sometimes on
ground. Sexes are dissimilar. **ADULT MALE** Has golden brown back and upper
wing coverts, both with black barring; rump is white and tail is black. Head is
grayish overall with buffish forecrown; "Yellow-shafted" has extensive buff on face, black malar stripe,
and red nape patch ("Red-shafted" has red malar stripe). Note striking black crescent on chest and
dark-spotted whitish underparts. **ADULT FEMALE** Similar, but head lacks malar stripe; "Yellow-shafted"
has red nape patch. **JUVENILE** Similar to respective sex adult. **VOICE** Utters a rapid, raptorlike *kew-kew-
kew....* **STATUS AND HABITAT** "Yellow-shafted" is common in all kinds of wooded habitats; mainly resident but northern populations are migratory. "Red-shafted" is widespread in west. **OBSERVATION TIPS**
Easy to see.

FEMALE

MALE

RED-BELLIED WOODPECKER

FEMALE

MALE

GOLDEN-FRONTED WOODPECKER

FEMALE RED-SHAFTED

MALE RED-SHAFTED

FEMALE YELLOW-SHAFTED

MALE YELLOW-SHAFTED

NORTHERN FLICKER

FEMALE YELLOW-SHAFTED

Picidae

RED-HEADED WOODPECKER
Melanerpes erythrocephalus L 9–9.5 in

Extremely well-marked and distinctive woodpecker, recognized in flight from above by its white rump and wing patches that contrast with otherwise black upper wings and tail. White on underwing is also striking in flight. Nests unobtrusively in excavated holes, mainly in dead trees. Drumming is rapid. Feeds on insects, seeds, and fruits, typically in trees, but will also feed on ground and "fly-catch" on the wing. Sexes are similar. **ADULT** Has mainly black back, tail, and upper wings, with white patch on tertials and rump. Head and neck are bright red and are separated from white underparts by narrow black border. Has a dark eye and rather pale gray and darker tipped bill. **JUVENILE** Has red and black elements of adult's plumage replaced by brown. Underparts are whitish with dark streaks, and pale tertials have brown barring. **VOICE** Call is a harsh *quee-erk*. **STATUS AND HABITAT** Common, mainly resident in eastern North America, but its range also extends west and north in summer, where present mainly May–Sep. Favors a range of lightly wooded habitats, including orchards. **OBSERVATION TIPS** Easy to recognize in flight but can be surprisingly hard to find when feeding unobtrusively. Sometimes visits feeders in winter.

MALE

FEMALE

YELLOW-BELLIED SAPSUCKER
Sphyrapicus varius
L 8–9 in

Colorful and migratory woodpecker that feeds on sap (obtained by drilling holes) and also on insects. Territorial birds drum loudly. Sexes are separable with care. **ADULT MALE** Has mainly black and white body plumage but note barring on back, wings, and tail, and white patch on wings; breast is black and underparts are otherwise grubby pale yellow with streaks and bars on flanks. Head is well marked by a red throat (which is bordered black) and crown, white stripe running below eye and curving around to breast, and white stripe behind eye. **ADULT FEMALE** Similar, but throat is white. **JUVENILE** Has barred brownish plumage overall but with adult's bold, white wing patch. **VOICE** Utters a harsh, mewing *quee-err*. **STATUS AND HABITAT** Common summer visitor (mainly May–Aug) to mixed and deciduous boreal forests, favoring areas where aspen and birch predominate (both are good sources of sap). Winters in similar habitats in southeastern U.S. and Mexico. **OBSERVATION TIPS** Easy to see.

LADDER-BACKED WOODPECKER
Picoides scalaris L 7–7.5 in

Well-marked, mainly black and white desert woodpecker. Feeds on boring insects and cactus fruits. Excavates nest holes in trees and large cacti. Sexes are dissimilar. **ADULT MALE** Has barred black and white pattern on back and wings, and white barring on outer feathers of otherwise black tail. Head has red crown and nape, and black line around ear coverts on otherwise white face. Underparts are grubby white, but with neat black spots on breast and bars on flanks. **ADULT FEMALE** Similar, but crown is black; nasal tufts are grubby white. **JUVENILE** Resembles adult male. **VOICE** Utters a harsh, chattering call and a sharp *pik*. **STATUS AND HABITAT** A mainly Central American species whose resident range extends to southwestern U.S., from Texas to Arizona. Fairly common in arid scrub and in woodland in Texas. **OBSERVATION TIPS** Easy to see in suitable habitats.

JUVENILE

RED-HEADED
WOODPECKER

ADULT

JUVENILE

FEMALE

MALE

YELLOW-BELLIED
SAPSUCKER

MALE

MALE

LADDER-BACKED
WOODPECKER

JUVENILE

Picidae

DOWNY WOODPECKER *Picoides pubescens* L 6–7 in
North America's smallest woodpecker. Often feeds on slender branches, males more so than females. Excavates tree holes for nesting. Sexes are separable. **ADULT MALE** Has mainly black upperparts, but with white spots and barring on wings, white stripe on back, and barred white outer tail feathers. Head has black cap, ear coverts, mustache, and lower nape, with red patch on upper nape. Underparts and rest of head are otherwise white. **ADULT FEMALE** Similar, but nape is entirely black. **JUVENILE** Similar to adult female but with dull red patch on crown. **VOICE** Utters an agitated, chattering *ki-ki-ki-ki* and a sharp *pic*. Drumming is rapid, but slower than that of Hairy. **STATUS AND HABITAT** Common and widespread resident of deciduous woodland, parks, and gardens, and to lesser extent of coniferous forest. **OBSERVATION TIPS** Unobtrusive and rather easy to overlook. Often visits feeders, when it is easy to observe.

HAIRY WOODPECKER *Picoides villosus* L 9–10 in
Similar to Downy, but appreciably larger. Our most widespread woodpecker. Variation exists in size and markings across North America, with many geographically distinct subspecies. Northern birds tend to be largest, with cleaner-looking white areas; ssp. *villosus*, widespread in east, is described here, unless otherwise specified. Sexes are separable with care. **ADULT MALE** Has mainly black upperparts with a white back and white barring and spots on wing. Head has black crown, ear coverts, mustache (linked to black shoulders), and lower nape; upper nape is red. Underparts and rest of face are whitish. Newfoundland ssp. *terranovae* and Florida ssp. *audubonii* have greatly reduced amount of white on back; latter has buff-washed underparts. **ADULT FEMALE** Similar to respective subspecies male, but nape is entirely black. **JUVENILE** Similar to adult female, but crown has reddish patch. **VOICE** Utters a rasping *cheek* and a rattling whinny. Drumming is rapid. **STATUS AND HABITAT** Widespread and fairly common resident of all types of deciduous and coniferous woodland, as well as wooded parks and gardens. **OBSERVATION TIPS** Easy to see in suitable habitats.

AMERICAN THREE-TOED WOODPECKER
Picoides dorsalis L 8–9 in
Stocky, medium-sized woodpecker with three toes—two forward-pointing, one pointing backward (apart from Black-backed, all other North

FEMALE

American woodpeckers have four toes). Not unduly wary, but unobtrusive and easily overlooked. Feeds mainly on wood-boring beetles, located by drilling and bark-stripping. Sexes are separable with care. **ADULT MALE** Has mostly black upperparts with subtle white barring down the center of the back, and on flight feathers and outer tail feather. Face is mainly black but with yellow crown and white stripe behind eye (linking to back) and white facial stripe. Throat and underparts are white with dark barring on flanks. **ADULT FEMALE** Similar, but crown is speckled white (not yellow). **JUVENILE** Similar to adult female, but with some dull yellow on crown. **VOICE** Utters a sharp *wik* or *pik*. **STATUS AND HABITAT** Widespread, but generally rather scarce in old-growth pine and spruce forest. Mostly resident, but nomadic to a degree outside the breeding season in search of food, visiting burned woodland with standing dead trees. **OBSERVATION TIPS** Presence detected by the call, or discovery of fallen bark at base of tree.

DOWNY WOODPECKER

FEMALE

MALE

MALE

HAIRY WOODPECKER

FEMALE

AMERICAN THREE-TOED WOODPECKER

MALE

Picidae

BLACK-BACKED WOODPECKER
Picoides arcticus L 9–10 in

Similar to American Three-toed Woodpecker. Three-toed. Separable using plumage details and (with practice) call, although not especially vocal. Drumming is loud and carries far. Feeds mainly on wood-boring beetles, by drilling and bark-stripping. Sexes are separable with care. **ADULT MALE** Has mostly black upperparts, including tail, but note subtle pale barring on flight feathers. Head has yellow crown and bold white facial stripe. Throat and underparts are white, apart from dark barring on flanks. **ADULT FEMALE** Similar, but crown is black. **JUVENILE** Similar to respective sex adult, although duller and female has a few yellow crown feathers. **VOICE** Utters a chattering *chik* call, sharper than that of American Three-toed. **STATUS AND HABITAT** Widespread, but never common, favoring old-growth pine and spruce forests, but also visiting burned areas with standing trees to feed. **OBSERVATION TIPS** Unobtrusive and easily overlooked. Presence sometimes detected by drumming or discovery of stripped, fallen bark at base of tree.

RED-COCKADED WOODPECKER
Picoides borealis L 8–9 in

Ladder-backed woodpecker that is unhelpfully named, since male's red "cockade" is seldom visible in field. Excavates nest hole in mature pine, lives in family groups, and engages in cooperative breeding. Sexes are similar. **ADULT** Has black back and wings with neat, even, white barring. Tail is mostly black above, barred whitish below. Head has black crown, nape, and malar stripe, and otherwise white plumage including patch at base of bill and behind eye. Underparts are white with distinct black spots and bars on flanks. Male has narrow red spot (the "cockade") at upper rear edge of white "face." **JUVENILE** Similar, but with red forecrown; acquires adult plumage by first fall. **VOICE** Utters a squeaky *quee'up*. **STATUS AND HABITAT** Rare resident of mature southeastern pine forests maintained in part by regular natural fires. Habitat loss and degradation has resulted in forest fragmentation and geographical isolation of some populations; vulnerable to local extinction. Its fate mirrors that of its habitat. **OBSERVATION TIPS** Visit suitable habitats and listen for its distinctive call.

PILEATED WOODPECKER
Dryocopus pileatus L 16–17 in

North America's largest woodpecker. Unmistakable with its mainly black plumage and white and red head markings. Bill is large, pale, and chisel-like. Feeds mainly on carpenter ants and beetle larvae excavated from timber via typically rectangular holes. Drumming is loud and carries far. Sexes are separable. **ADULT MALE** Has mainly black body plumage, except for small white patch at base of primaries on closed wing. In flight, patch is more obvious, and white underwing coverts are striking. Angular-looking head has white throat and white stripes behind eye and extending from base of bill down side of neck. Tufted crown is red; note red malar stripe and pale eye. **ADULT FEMALE** Similar, but only rear of crown is red and malar stripe is black. **JUVENILE** Resembles respective sex adult, but has brownish eyes. **VOICE** Utters a harsh, agitated *ke-ke-ki-ki-ki*.... **STATUS AND HABITAT** Fairly common forest resident. Does best in undisturbed, old-growth forest, but tolerates younger woodland if a few large trees are present for nesting. **OBSERVATION TIPS** Easy to find in suitable habitats.

FEMALE

FEMALE

MALE

FEMALE

BLACK-BACKED WOODPECKER

RED-COCKADED WOODPECKER

FEMALE

MALE

PILEATED WOODPECKER

Tyrannidae

EASTERN KINGBIRD *Tyrannus tyrannus* L 8–9 in

Familiar black and white kingbird. Often perches on roadside wires and usually indifferent to people. Reddish orange concealed crown patch is seldom revealed. Feeds mainly by making aerial sorties after insects from an exposed perch. Sexes are similar. **ADULT** Has neatly defined black hood grading to dark gray back and dark wings, the latter having whitish feather margins. Tail is black with white terminal band. Underparts, including throat, are mostly white, but note subtle pale gray wash on chest. Feet and bill are dark. **JUVENILE** Similar, but cap, back, and wings are tinged brownish. **VOICE** Utters a metallic, rasping *k'dzee-k'dzee...*, sometimes rapid and

WESTERN KINGBIRD

accelerating. **STATUS AND HABITAT** Common summer visitor (mainly May–Aug) to a variety of open habitats. Winters in South America. **OBSERVATION TIPS** Generally easy to find. **SIMILAR SPECIES Western Kingbird** *T. verticalis* (L 8–9.5 in) is a mainly western species whose range sometimes extends east. All birds have a pale gray head (darkest through eye and palest on cheek), pale olive-gray back and dark wings with pale feather margins; chest is pale gray and underparts, including underwing coverts, are otherwise pale lemon yellow. Summer visitor (mainly Apr–Aug) to farmland and open country and often perches in the open, making observation easy.

GRAY KINGBIRD *Tyrannus dominicensis* L 9–9.5 in

Recalls Eastern Kingbird, but larger and longer-tailed, with grayer upperparts and a much stouter, longer bill. Flycatches from exposed perches. Sexes are similar. **ADULT** Has mostly dark gray upperparts, but note the black "mask" through eye, black flight feathers, and pale edges to wing coverts. Throat and underparts are whitish, washed gray on breast and flanks. Bill and legs are dark. **JUVENILE** Similar, but many upperpart feathers have brownish edges. **VOICE** Utters a squeaking trill (can be imitated with bird squeaker). **STATUS AND HABITAT** A mainly Caribbean species that is a local summer visitor (mainly May–Sep) to mangroves and coastal forests in Florida. Winters further south in Caribbean. **OBSERVATION TIPS** Easy to see in coastal Florida.

SCISSOR-TAILED FLYCATCHER

Tyrannus forficatus L 10–15 in

Long, forked tail makes identification of all birds easy, and adult's long tail streamers are unmistakable. All birds feed on insects, typically caught in aerial sorties; often perches on overhead wires. Male performs spectacular courtship display in flight. Sexes are similar, but male's tail streamers are longer than female's. **ADULT** Has very pale gray (nearly white) head, pale gray back and breast. Wings are blackish with white feather margins and tail is deeply forked, the outer feather long and streamerlike. Underparts are whitish, but flushed pinkish orange on belly, undertail, and underwing coverts; note the deep red axillaries ("armpits"). **JUVENILE** Much paler than adult with only faint pinkish flush on underparts. Tail is forked and relatively long, but outer feathers are not so long and streamerlike. **VOICE** Utters a sharp *wip* or more chattering *wip-k'prrr*. **STATUS AND HABITAT** Locally common summer visitor (mainly Apr–Aug) to Texas, Louisiana, and adjacent states. Favors open country and farmland. Winters mainly in Central America. **OBSERVATION TIPS** Easy to see and tolerant of people.

ADULT

EASTERN KINGBIRD

JUVENILE

ADULT

GRAY KINGBIRD

ADULT

SCISSOR-TAILED FLYCATCHER

ADULT

Tyrannidae

GREAT CRESTED FLYCATCHER
Myiarchus crinitus L 8–9 in

Eastern North America's only widespread *Myiarchus* flycatcher. Perches upright. Feeds by flycatching, gleaning insects from foliage and dropping to ground for prey. Sexes are similar. **ADULT** Has dark gray-brown hood and nape grading to olive-brown back. Wings are mainly dark, but note rufous-fringed primaries and white fringes to other feathers, most noticeably on tertials and coverts (wing bars). Face, throat, and breast are dark gray with clear separation from yellowish underparts, creating somewhat dark-hooded appearance. Gray wash extends onto flanks. Tail is mainly rufous. **JUVENILE** Similar, but with duller colors; wing bars and most flight feather fringes are rufous. **VOICE** Utters an upslurred *whu-eep* and a harsh *chrrrt*. **STATUS AND HABITAT** Common summer visitor (mainly Apr–Sep) to wooded habitats. Winters mainly in Central and South America. **OBSERVATION TIPS** Easy to see. **SIMILAR SPECIES Ash-throated Flycatcher** *M. cinerascens* (L 7.5–8.5 in) has pale underparts, grayish white on throat, washed pale lemon on belly. Resident in arid woodland in south Texas, summer visitor further west.

ASH-THROATED FLYCATCHER

ADULT

OLIVE-SIDED FLYCATCHER
Contopus cooperi L 7–8 in

Plump-bodied, rather dark-looking flycatcher. Often perches on exposed dead branches, adopting an upright posture. Flying insects caught in aerial forays. Bill is dark and relatively large, and tail is short. Sexes are similar. **ADULT** Has mostly dark olive-brown upperparts, with indistinct pale eyering. Wings and tail are mostly blackish with faint pale wing bars; white feathers on side of rump sometimes overlap inner wing feathers at rest. Throat is white and color continues down center of breast to belly and undertail. Streaked dark olive-brown flanks look like an unbuttoned vest. **JUVENILE** Similar, but plumage, including wing bars, is warmer buff overall. **VOICE** Utters a liquid *quip-wee-ber* or a rapid *wip-wip-wip*. **STATUS AND HABITAT** Widespread and still locally common summer visitor (mainly May–Aug) to boreal forests and damp, coniferous woodland. Has declined markedly in recent years. Forest loss and degradation here, and in South American winter quarters, are probably to blame. **OBSERVATION TIPS** Easy to observe, but scarcer in recent years.

EASTERN WOOD-PEWEE *Contopus virens* L 6–6.5 in

Slimmer and longer-tailed than Olive-sided Flycatcher, with more striking wing bars and uniform olive-brown breast (without central white line bordered by dark "waistcoat"). Compared to Willow and Alder Flycatchers (*see* p.210), darker overall, with less striking wing bars and relatively longer wings (extend well beyond rump when perched). Legs are dark and bill is mostly dark, but with dull orange base to lower mandible. Makes aerial sorties after flying insects, from perch at mid tree level (lower than Olive-sided Flycatcher). Sexes are similar. **ADULT** Has dark gray-brown upperparts overall. Wings and tail are mostly blackish, but note pale wing bars and pale fringes to secondaries and tertials. Underparts are gray-brown overall, palest on throat and grading to whitish on belly and vent. **JUVENILE** Similar, but brighter-looking with buffy wing bars and fringes to inner flight feathers. **VOICE** Call is a trisyllabic *pee-err-wee*. **STATUS AND HABITAT** Widespread, but declining, summer visitor (mainly May–Sep) to open woodland. Winters in South America. **OBSERVATION TIPS** Easy to see.

JUVENILE

GREAT CRESTED FLYCATCHER

ADULT

OLIVE-SIDED FLYCATCHER

ADULT

ADULT

EASTERN WOOD-PEWEE

ADULT

Tyrannidae

EASTERN PHOEBE *Sayornis phoebe* L 6–7 in

Squat-bodied flycatcher with understated plumage. Perched bird often pumps forked tail up and down, sometimes with a swaying motion. Flycatches insects, usually from a low perch; sometimes hovers. Often associated with manmade habitats, nesting under bridges or on buildings. Sexes are similar. **ADULT** Has mainly gray-brown upperparts, darkest on head. Wings are blackish with two whitish wing bars and pale fringes to secondaries and tertials. Throat and rest of underparts are whitish, but with grayish flanks and variably yellow-buff suffusion on belly, most obvious in freshly molted fall plumage. **JUVENILE** Similar, but with buffy wing bars and subtly more intense yellow wash on belly. **VOICE** Utters a sharp *chip* call; song is a shrill *phee-werr, phee-eer-d'dip*. **STATUS AND HABITAT** Common and widespread summer visitor (mainly Apr–Sep) to woodland, parks, and gardens, across much of eastern North America. Winters in southeastern U.S. and Mexico. **OBSERVATION TIPS** Easy to see, often near water, although frequently unobtrusive; listen for the distinctive song.

LEAST FLYCATCHER *Empidonax minimus* L 5.25–5.5 in

Small, short-winged *Empidonax* flycatcher (collectively, and affectionately, these are known as "empids"). Flycatches actively from low to mid-height perches; also gleans insects from foliage while hovering. Often perches upright and routinely flicks wings and tail in agitated manner. Head is relatively large and large eye is emphasized by whitish eyering. Lower mandible of rather dainty bill is pale orange-buff with a darker tip. Sexes are similar. **ADULT** Has dull olive-gray upperparts overall. Dark wings have pale fringes to inner flight feathers and two white wing bars; tail is dark. Underparts are whitish, palest on throat and belly, with diffuse gray band on chest and faint yellow wash on lower flanks. **JUVENILE** Similar, but in fall has buffy wing bars. **VOICE** Song is a repeated *ch'Wik, ch'Wik...*; call is a sharp *whit*. **STATUS AND HABITAT** Common summer visitor (mainly May–Aug) to open deciduous woodlands. Winters in Central America. **OBSERVATION TIPS** Although it can be very difficult, try using body proportions, voice, and habitat preference to aid separation from similar species.

ACADIAN FLYCATCHER
Empidonax virescens L 5.5–6 in

The most widespread "empid" in eastern and southeastern North America. Feeds by flycatching from mid-level perch, or by gleaning insects

from foliage. Compared to other "empids," note its larger size, rather long primary projection, relatively large bill, flat forehead, rather peaked rear crown, and distinctive call and song. Sexes are similar. **ADULT** Has mostly olive-yellow head, neck, and back. Wings are dark with bold white wing bars. Note the white eyering, pale gray throat, olive-yellow wash on breast, and otherwise whitish underparts. **JUVENILE** Similar to adult, but with buffy wing bars. **VOICE** Song is a loud *per-Pweep*; call is a sharp *pweet*. **STATUS AND HABITAT** Common summer visitor (mainly Apr–Aug) to deciduous forests, especially areas near streams and rivers. Winters mainly in Central and South America. **OBSERVATION TIPS** Easy to see in suitable habitats.

ADULT

EASTERN PHOEBE

JUVENILE

ADULT

LEAST FLYCATCHER

ADULT

ADULT

ACADIAN FLYCATCHER

Tyrannidae

WILLOW FLYCATCHER *Empidonax traillii* L 5.5–6 in

Widespread woodland flycatcher. Best separated from Alder using voice. Occurs as several subspecies: eastern birds (described in detail below) are almost identical to Alder; western ones (outside range covered by this book) are subtly browner and darker. Feeding habits similar to those of Alder: engages in aerial sorties after flying insects from perches near top of trees; also hovers and gleans insects from foliage. Sexes are similar. **ADULT** Has olive-gray upperparts (Alder's upperparts are usually subtly greener). Has faint pale eyering (on average, less distinct than Alder) and pinkish orange lower mandible. Wings are dark with pale fringes to inner flight feathers and two white wing bars; tail is dark (wings and tail slightly longer in Alder). Underparts are pale with pale olive wash on chest. **JUVENILE** Similar to adult, but with buffy wing bars. **VOICE** Song is a harsh, buzzing *fzz'Byew*; call is a sharp *whuit*. **STATUS AND HABITAT** Fairly common summer visitor (mainly May–Aug) to damp woodlands and often associated with its namesake tree. Winters in Central and South America. **OBSERVATION TIPS** Best identified with certainty using voice; fortunately, like Alder, sometimes sings on migration as well as on breeding grounds.

ADULT

ALDER FLYCATCHER
Empidonax alnorum
L 5.5–6 in

Confusingly similar to Willow, and both species favor damp woodland. Best identified by voice; silent birds are often not separable. *See* Willow's entry for discussion of subtle structural differences. Engages in aerial sorties from perches near top of tree after flying insects; also hovers and gleans insects from foliage. Sexes are similar. **ADULT** Has dull olive-green upperparts. Note narrow white eyering and broad-based bill with pinkish orange lower mandible. Wings are dark with pale inner flight feather fringes and two bold white wing bars. Underparts are pale with olive-gray wash on chest. **JUVENILE** Similar to adult, but with buffy wing bars. **VOICE** Song is a harsh, repeated *rrr'BEE-eh*; call is a sharp *piip*. **STATUS AND HABITAT** Common and widespread summer visitor (mainly Jun–Aug) to damp, deciduous woodland with alders and willows. Winters in South America. **OBSERVATION TIPS** Hard to separate from Willow with certainty, unless song is heard; with practice, call is a good clue too.

YELLOW-BELLIED FLYCATCHER
Empidonax flaviventris L 5–5.5 in

Distinctive, but unobtrusive "empid" that favors deep shade; often first detected by its voice. Usually adopts an upright posture when perched. Head looks proportionately large and tail relatively short. Sexes are similar. **ADULT** Has olive-green upperparts; note the whitish eyering and pale pinkish orange lower mandible. Wings are dark with pale fringes to inner flight feathers and two striking white wing bars. Underparts are yellowish, with darker olive wash across breast. **JUVENILE** Similar, but brighter, with buffy yellow wing bars. **VOICE** Song is a sharp, chirping, and disyllabic *ch'Week*; call is a whistling *ch'wee*. **STATUS AND HABITAT** Widespread and common summer visitor (mainly Jun–Aug) to northern forests, favoring areas of dense spruce in particular. Winters in Central and South America. **OBSERVATION TIPS** Easily overlooked and its presence is best detected by its voice.

WILLOW FLYCATCHER

ADULT

ALDER FLYCATCHER

ADULT

ADULT

ADULT

YELLOW-BELLIED
FLYCATCHER

Laniidae

LOGGERHEAD SHRIKE
Lanius ludovicianus L 8.5–9.5 in

Striking gray, black, and white predatory passerine that perches on wires and dead branches. Prey ranges from insects to small birds and mammals. Often impales larger prey on thorns or barbed wire and uses its powerful hooked bill to dismember the victim. Can be confused with larger Northern Shrike, from which it is distinguished by its smaller body and bill, shorter wings and tail, and various subtle plumage differences. Of the two, Loggerhead is the one that is widespread and present year-round across much of southern U.S.; Northern Shrike is a winter visitor. Sexes are similar. **ADULT** Has blue-gray upperparts with white margin to mantle. Dark mask extends around the forehead, above bill line, defined above by narrow white line above, and white cheeks and throat below. Wings are mainly black, but with a small white patch (obvious in flight) at the base of the primaries. Tail is long and wedge-shaped, mainly black but with white outer tips. Underparts pale; whitest on throat, darkest on breast. **JUVENILE** Similar, but has scaly-looking upperparts due to pale feather margins; underparts are faintly barred. **VOICE** Song is a series of repeated, harsh chirping *ch'Wee* phrases; call is a harsh *chakk*. **STATUS AND HABITAT** Widespread, but declining resident, across much of its range, favoring open country such as meadows and farmland with plenty of perches, bushes, and trees. Northernmost populations are migratory, moving south in fall. **OBSERVATION TIPS** Seldom numerous but usually conspicuous when perched on wire fences or bushes.

NORTHERN SHRIKE *Lanius excubitor* L 9.5–10.5 in

Striking and impressive-looking predatory passerine that often perches on a dead branch or overhead wire. Similar to Loggerhead, but bulkier; subtle plumage differences also aid separation of the two species. Captures prey up to the size of small birds and mammals. Has similar habit to Loggerhead of impaling victims on thorns or barbed wire and dismembering them using its powerful, hook-tipped bill. Sexes are similar. **ADULT** Has pale blue-gray upperparts. Black mask extends to bill, but does not continue around forehead. Wings are mainly black, but note white patch at base of primaries (striking in flight and a bit more extensive than in Loggerhead). Tail is long and wedge-shaped, mainly black, but with white outer tips. Underparts are pale gray. **JUVENILE** Has gray and white elements of adult's plumage replaced by light brown or tan; underparts are scaly and mask is absent or very faint. Some birds begin to acquire adult plumage during first winter. **VOICE** Song is a series of harsh phrases; calls include an insistent *kree, kree....* **STATUS AND HABITAT** Breeds across Arctic North America, favoring tundra with scattered trees and open taiga forest; widely scattered and never numerous. Winters across central North America and then favors open country with scattered trees. **OBSERVATION TIPS** Obvious and easy to spot when perched in the open, but stays in cover for long periods, when it is surprisingly unobtrusive and hard to find for such a striking bird.

JUVENILE

JUVENILE

LOGGERHEAD
SHRIKE

ADULT

NORTHERN SHRIKE

ADULT

Vireonidae

WHITE-EYED VIREO *Vireo griseus* L 5–5.5 in

Pale-eyed, secretive vireo that is heard more frequently than it is seen. Feeds mainly on insects and forages in a deliberate manner. Sexes are similar. **ADULT** Has greenish cap, back, and rump. Face, sides of neck, and nape are gray. Eye has pale iris, with dark line in front and is surrounded by yellow "spectacle" and supercilium extending forward. Darkish wings have two white wing bars. Throat is white and underparts are otherwise pale with gray wash on chest and yellow wash on flanks. Bill is stout and legs are blue-gray. **JUVENILE** Similar, but paler, with dark iris and white eyering. Acquires adultlike plumage and pale iris in winter. **VOICE** Song is a series of loud phrases such as *chic, chip-ee-err-cheeo*; call is a harsh *shrrr*. **STATUS AND HABITAT** Common summer visitor (mainly Apr–Sep) to dense, brushy deciduous woodland; widespread in eastern North America. Winters from southeastern U.S. to Mexico. **OBSERVATION TIPS** Easier to hear than to see.

YELLOW-THROATED VIREO
Vireo flavifrons L 5–5.5 in

Striking and colorful vireo, with a disproportionately large head and stout bill. Forages for insects in a deliberate manner and easily overlooked when feeding in dappled foliage. Sexes are similar. **ADULT** Has yellowish green upperparts and bright yellow lores, eyering, throat, and breast; underparts are otherwise white. Dark wings have pale fringes to inner flight feathers and two white wing bars. Legs are blue-gray. **JUVENILE** Similar to adult. **VOICE** Song is a repeated *zse'eret, tchu-et*; calls include harsh *tche* notes. **STATUS AND HABITAT** Common summer visitor (mainly Apr–Aug) to deciduous and mixed woodland in eastern North America. Winters mainly in Central America. **OBSERVATION TIPS** Easy to identify, but often hard to locate in the first instance; learn and listen for the call and song.

ADULT

BELL'S VIREO *Vireo bellii* L 4.5–4.75 in

Active, but highly secretive, warblerlike vireo. Feeds mainly on insects, foraging among dense foliage in a deliberate manner. Western birds (found outside range of this book) are paler and grayer than eastern birds (described in detail below). Sexes are similar. **ADULT** Has greenish upperparts overall; marginally darker wings have two pale wing bars, lower one brighter and more distinct than upper. Dark eye has white supercilium and white "eyelid" below creating incomplete spectacled effect. Underparts are pale overall but washed buffy yellow. **JUVENILE** Similar to adult. **VOICE** Song is a rapid, chattering *chewee-cheweed'de'de'der*; call is a thin *chee*. **STATUS AND HABITAT** Local and generally rather scarce summer visitor (mainly Apr–Aug) to dense, riverine woodland and scrub across the Midwest. Winters in Mexico. **OBSERVATION TIPS** Listen for its distinctive song.

WHITE-EYED VIREO

ADULT

YELLOW-THROATED VIREO

ADULT

BELL'S VIREO

ADULT

Vireonidae

BLUE-HEADED VIREO *Vireo solitarius* L 5–5.5 in

Well-marked male is easy to identify and duller-plumaged female is still distinctive with the striking white wing bars, white "spectacle," and stout bill. Unobtrusive and easily overlooked if silent and foraging for insects in dappled foliage.

ADULT

Sexes are similar. **ADULT** Has olive-green back and blue-gray hood with striking white "spectacles." Dark wings have yellowish fringes to inner flight feathers and two yellowish wing bars. Tail has white outer feathers. Throat is white and underparts are otherwise mostly white with buffy yellow wash on flanks. Male is usually brighter than female. **JUVENILE** Duller than adult female. **VOICE** Song is a series of spaced, thin whistling notes; call is a rasping *tche*. **STATUS AND HABITAT** Common summer visitor (mainly Apr–Sep) to woodland habitats across northern North America, and in mountains further south; winters in southern U.S., Mexico, and Central America. **OBSERVATION TIPS** Easiest to locate by its song.

RED-EYED VIREO *Vireo olivaceus* L 6–6.5 in

Relatively large and well-marked vireo and the most widespread and familiar of its kind in eastern North America. Forages unobtrusively among foliage and gleans insects while hovering. Easily overlooked if silent, but fortunately it is a vocal species and often attracts attention with its incessant song. Sexes are similar. **ADULT** Has olive-gray back and neck. Head has striking pattern of dark gray crown and long, white supercilium, defined above and below by black lines. Note the red iris and rather long bill. Underparts are whitish with dull yellow wash on flanks and undertail. **JUVENILE** Similar, but with dull iris. **VOICE** Song is a varied series of 2-, 3-, and 4-syllable phrases, including *tse-Oo-ee* and *tsee-Ooo*, sometimes sung in triplets; call is a nasal *zz'nrrr*. **STATUS AND HABITAT** Common summer visitor (mainly May–Aug) to temperate woodlands across eastern North America. Winters in South America. **OBSERVATION TIPS** Easy to hear and fairly easy (by vireo standards) to find.

BLACK-WHISKERED VIREO
Vireo altiloquus L 6.25–6.5 in

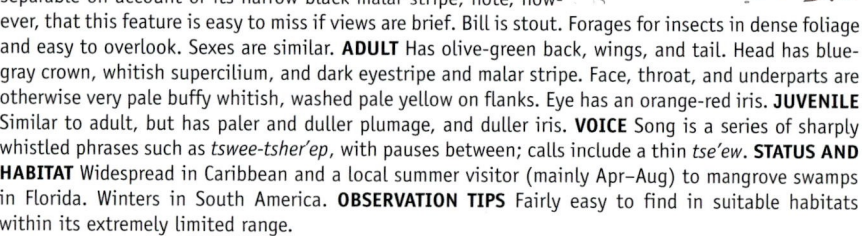

Florida specialty that is superficially similar to Red-eyed Vireo, but separable on account of its narrow black malar stripe; note, however, that this feature is easy to miss if views are brief. Bill is stout. Forages for insects in dense foliage and easy to overlook. Sexes are similar. **ADULT** Has olive-green back, wings, and tail. Head has blue-gray crown, whitish supercilium, and dark eyestripe and malar stripe. Face, throat, and underparts are otherwise very pale buffy whitish, washed pale yellow on flanks. Eye has an orange-red iris. **JUVENILE** Similar to adult, but has paler and duller plumage, and duller iris. **VOICE** Song is a series of sharply whistled phrases such as *tswee-tsher'ep*, with pauses between; calls include a thin *tse'ew*. **STATUS AND HABITAT** Widespread in Caribbean and a local summer visitor (mainly Apr–Aug) to mangrove swamps in Florida. Winters in South America. **OBSERVATION TIPS** Fairly easy to find in suitable habitats within its extremely limited range.

BLUE-HEADED VIREO

ADULT

RED-EYED VIREO

ADULT

BLACK-WHISKERED VIREO

ADULT

Vireonidae

WARBLING VIREO *Vireo gilvus* L 5.5–6 in

Unobtrusive warblerlike vireo with a distinctive song. Observation is often challenging: feeds quietly, searching for insects among foliage, often near tops of trees. Note the relatively large head and stout bill. Western subspecies are subtly smaller, greener, and have shorter bills than widespread eastern ssp. *gilvus* and may be separate species; ssp. *gilvus* is described here. Sexes are similar. **ADULT** Has olive-green upperparts, marginally darkest on forecrown. Has whitish supercilium and lores. Wings lack obvious pale feather fringes or wing bars. Underparts, including face and throat, are pale overall with drab yellow wash on flanks and undertail. **JUVENILE** Similar to adult, but with obvious yellow flush to flanks and undertail. **VOICE** Song comprises bursts of warbling phrases, with pauses between as if bird is catching its breath; call is a nasal *tchrrr*. **STATUS AND HABITAT** Common summer visitor (mainly Apr–Sep) to riverside deciduous woodland. Winters in Central America. **OBSERVATION TIPS** Learn and listen for the distinctive song to detect the species' presence.

PHILADELPHIA VIREO
Vireo philadelphicus L 5.25–5.5 in

Short-billed, short-tailed, warblerlike vireo. Specifically, appearance overall recalls Tennessee Warbler (*see* p.256), from which it is told by its stouter bill, relatively larger head, and stronger plumage patterns. Forages for insects in a more deliberate manner than most warblers. Sexes are similar. **ADULT** Has an olive-green back and neck with a grayish crown, white supercilium, and dark eyestripe with a white line below. Underparts, including throat, variably flushed yellow with least amount of color on belly. **JUVENILE** Similar, but yellow on underparts is more obvious. **VOICE** Song comprises a series of short phrases with pauses in between, rather similar to that of Red-eyed Vireo; call is a nasal *tchrrr*. **STATUS AND HABITAT** Generally rather scarce summer visitor (mainly May–Sep) to new growth deciduous woodland; often in similar habitats to Red-eyed Vireo although the two species' behavior ensures there is little overlap when feeding and nesting. **OBSERVATION TIPS** Easiest to detect by song.

BLACK-CAPPED VIREO *Vireo atricapilla* L 4.5–5 in

Distinctive vireo. Forages among foliage and gleans insects while hovering. Sexes are dissimilar. **ADULT MALE** Has a black hood, and white lores and mask surrounding red eye. Back and rump are greenish, dark wings have two pale wing bars and pale fringes to inner flight feathers, and underparts are whitish, palest on throat with buff wash on flanks. **ADULT FEMALE** Similar, but hood is dark gray. **JUVENILE** Recalls adult female, but has browner plumage overall and dull eye. **VOICE** Song

comprises warbling phrases such as *fzz-ch'ch'ch-chee* with pauses between; calls include a harsh *zrree*. **STATUS AND HABITAT** Local and endangered summer visitor (mainly Apr–Aug) to scrub-covered rocky ground with sumac and oaks in Texas; dense, ungrazed new growth is ideal. Habitat destruction and nest parasitism by Brown-headed Cowbird have aided decline. Winters in Mexico. **OBSERVATION TIPS** Listen for the distinctive song.

ADULT, FEMALE

WARBLING VIREO

ADULT

PHILADELPHIA VIREO

ADULT

ADULT

BLACK-CAPPED VIREO

ADULT, MALE

BLUE JAY *Cyanocitta cristata* L 11–12 in

Familiar and unmistakable, mainly blue bird with a distinct crest. Bold and inquisitive in gardens and parks where it is not persecuted, but otherwise it can be unobtrusive. Opportunistic feeder with varied diet: takes bird-table food as well as eggs and young of songbirds. Sexes are similar. **ADULT** Has bright blue cap, nape, and back. Wings are blue overall with laddered black markings and bold white patches and wing bar. Tail is blue with

ADULT

laddered black and white outer tips. Underparts are pale gray, face and throat with a dark border. **JUVENILE** Similar, but blue elements of plumage are grayer. **VOICE** Calls are varied and include a shrill *jay, jay, jay...* and a whistling *pee'de-de*. A good mimic, especially of raptors. **STATUS AND HABITAT** Common resident in a wide variety of wooded habitats, from forests to parks and gardens. Common in east but range extends westward almost to Rockies. In some years, northern populations are irruptive, or migratory southward in fall in variable numbers; occasionally there are widespread movements involving large flocks. **OBSERVATION TIPS** Easy to observe.

FLORIDA SCRUB-JAY *Aphelocoma coerulescens* L 10–11 in

Florida endemic with slim body, long tail, and stout, but rather slender bill. An opportunistic feeder with an omnivorous diet that includes berries, fruits, insects, and the eggs and young of songbirds. Usually seen in family groups. Sexes are similar. **ADULT** Has a pale gray-brown back, but otherwise mostly dark blue upperparts; note, however, the dark cheeks and eyeline and pale forecrown, extending back as faint supercilium. Throat is whitish and streaked, with discrete demarcation from otherwise grubby pinkish gray underparts. **JUVENILE** Similar, but dull gray on head, back, and wing coverts, with

WESTERN SCRUB-JAY

ADULT, INTERIOR

blue flight feathers and tail. **VOICE** Utters a harsh, nasal *cheerp, cheerp, cheerp...* and other chattering calls. **STATUS AND HABITAT** Common and widespread resident of scrubby woodland and overgrown suburban lots. Has declined markedly due to habitat loss and degradation **OBSERVATION TIPS** Easy to see and often indifferent to people. **SIMILAR SPECIES Western Scrub-jay** *A. californica* (L 11–12 in) is bluer on head but otherwise similar; a mainly western species, resident in Texas.

GRAY JAY *Perisoreus canadensis* L 11.5–12 in

Distinctive, plump-bodied bird with a relatively large, rounded head, short bill, and "fluffy," soft-looking plumage. Usually unobtrusive, but sometimes bold and inquisitive, particularly around campsites and picnic areas. An opportunistic feeder that lives in small groups outside the breeding season. Sexes are similar. **ADULT** Has a dark gray back and rear of crown. Nape, forecrown, and underparts are pale gray. Wings are dark, with pale feather margins in most birds; tail is dark. **JUVENILE** Rather uniformly dark gray overall. **VOICE** Utters a soft, fluty *pheeoo* and a harsh, chattering *chakkk*. **STATUS AND HABITAT** Widespread and fairly common resident in taiga and mountain coniferous forests. **OBSERVATION TIPS** Listen for its distinctive calls. Often easy to see if you camp in an established and well-used site in northern forests within the species' range.

BLUE JAY

JUVENILE

ADULT

ADULT

FLORIDA SCRUB-JAY

ADULT

GRAY JAY

JUVENILE

Corvidae

AMERICAN CROW *Corvus brachyrhynchos* L 15–18 in

Archetypal crow and the yardstick by which to judge other dark-plumaged corvids. Sometimes bold, but becomes more wary where persecuted. An opportunistic feeder with an omnivorous diet that includes carrion, scraps scavenged at garbage dumps, and grain spills, and live prey. Variably gregarious outside breeding season. Sexes are similar. **ADULT** Has glossy, all-black plumage with a relatively long, dark bill and dark legs. In flight, note the rather long, fan-shaped tail. **JUVENILE** Similar, but has a pale iris and an brownish tinge overall to plumage. **VOICE** Utters a familiar, raucous *caaw, caaw*. **STATUS AND HABITAT** Populations have declined markedly due to West Nile Virus in some areas, but still widespread and common, favoring a wide range of habitats, including urban areas. Resident across much of its range, but northern birds migrate south in fall. **OBSERVATION TIPS** Easy to find.

FISH CROW *Corvus ossifragus* L 15–17 in

Southeastern coastal counterpart of American Crow and extremely similar to that species, which is otherwise marginally larger. Crow aficionados can detect Fish Crow's more slender bill, relatively longer wings and tail, and more extensive gloss to plumage; in flight, note the Fish Crow's more pointed wingtips and faster wingbeats. But in most instances specific identification is most reliably based on call; that of Fish Crow is more nasal than American Crow. An opportunistic feeder that is typically found on coasts, but increasingly on margins or lakes and rivers. Sexes are similar. **ADULT** Has glossy, all-black plumage with a relatively long bill. In flight, note the rather long, fan-shaped tail. **JUVENILE** Similar, but has an brown tinge overall to plumage. **VOICE** Utters a weak nasal *cah-hah*. **STATUS AND HABITAT** Widespread resident of coastal southeastern U.S. Seldom seen far from water, typically favoring coastal beaches, lagoons, and estuaries, but increasingly seen further inland on shores of lakes and rivers. **OBSERVATION TIPS** Easy to see, but challenging to identify with absolute certainty until you learn to distinguish its call from that of American Crow.

ADULT

COMMON RAVEN *Corvus corax* L 24–25 in

Large and impressive bird, and North Americs's largest corvid. Appreciably larger than American Crow and easily recognized on the ground by its more massive bill and the shaggy throat that appears most ruffled when the bird is calling. In flight, recognized by the long, thick neck and wedge-shaped tail. Diet is varied and opportunistic, taking eggs and young of smaller birds in season, and carrion at other times. Incredibly aerobatic, tumbling and rolling in midair; often seen in pairs. Sexes are similar. **ADULT** Has mainly black plumage but, in good light, an oily or metallic sheen is discernible. **JUVENILE** Similar, but has paler eye and brownish tinge to plumage. **VOICE** Utters a loud and deep *cronk* call. **STATUS AND HABITAT** Widespread and fairly common resident in a wide range of habitats from tundra, mountains, and farmland, to deserts in southwest. **OBSERVATION TIPS** Size, coloration, and long, wedge-shaped tail usually make identification in flight easy.

ADULT

ADULT

AMERICAN CROW

FISH CROW

ADULT

ADULT

ADULT

COMMON RAVEN

HORNED LARK *Eremophila alpestris* L 7–8 in

Distinctive ground-dwelling songbird that is rather long-bodied and is recognized by its striking black and yellowish facial markings and "horn-like" head feathers; these features are particularly striking in summer males. Many subspecies exist in North America, differing in size, intensity of yellow on face, and shade of brown on upperparts; the ranges of some of these subspecies overlap in winter. Forms flocks outside the breeding season, sometimes mixing with longspurs (*see* p.296). In flight, all birds show pale underwings. Sexes are similar, but females are duller than their respective subspecies

ADULT, PALE SUBSPECIES

male counterparts. Unless otherwise stated, ssp. *alpestris*, widespread in the northeast, is described below. **ADULT** Has black mask, breast band, forecrown, and "horns"; face is otherwise yellowish. Underparts are whitish overall. Upperparts are sandy brown overall with rufous wash on shoulders and nape. Subspecies from interior are paler overall with "colder" sandy brown upperparts and only a hint of yellow wash on pale plumage elements of face. **JUVENILE** Speckled, with a hint of the adult's facial markings. **VOICE** Flight calls include a thin *tsee-titi*; song is a series of tinkling notes, preceded by a few rasping *chrrt* notes. **STATUS AND HABITAT** Common in open, barren habitats ranging from tundra and grassland to deserts. Present year-round, represented by some sedentary subspecies across much of U.S., but northern and tundra-breeding populations (including ssp. *alpestris*) move south for the winter. **OBSERVATION TIPS** Easy to locate and sometimes found in sizeable, mixed-species flocks in winter.

TREE SWALLOW *Tachycineta bicolor* L 5.5–6 in

Distinctive swallow with contrasting, bicolored plumage. Colorful blue-green sheen on adult's dark upperparts is not always obvious in poor light and birds can look distinctly black and white. Catches insects on the wing and sometimes gathers in flocks when feeding is good; will also eat berries in winter months. In flight, note the broad pointed wings and slightly forked tail; narrow wedge of white (sides of rump) is usually visible at side of base of upper tail. Nests in natural tree holes, but will also use manmade nest boxes. Adult sexes are similar. **ADULT** Has blackish upperparts, but in good

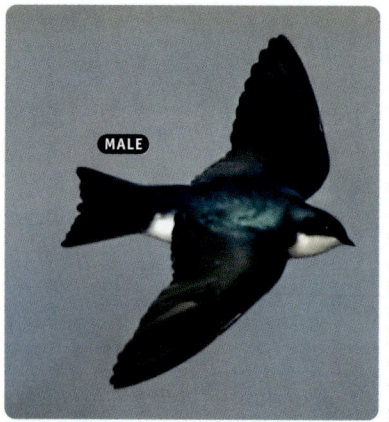

MALE

light note the blue-green sheen on the cap, back, rump, and wing coverts. Dark elements of plumage on head form a complete and discrete cap that extends below the eye. Underparts, including throat, are white. First-year females have browner upperparts, reduced sheen (or none at all) and white tips to tertials. **JUVENILE** Similar to dull adult (i.e. upperparts are brownish and no sheen is visible); often shows a faint gray-brown breast band. **VOICE** Call and song comprise a series of whistling chirps. **STATUS AND HABITAT** Common summer visitor (present mainly Apr–Sep) to a range of open habitats. Often feeds over water, where flying insects are typically abundant, and often nests in the vicinity of marshes and lakes. Winters across southern U.S. and Central America. **OBSERVATION TIPS** Easy to see, especially near freshwater. If you want to encourage this species' presence in your yard, site nest boxes in suitable trees.

HORNED LARK

ADULT

ADULT

TREE SWALLOW

FEMALE

MALE

Hirundinidae

PURPLE MARTIN *Progne subis* L 7–8 in

Well-loved, plump-bodied hirundine; largest of its kind in the region. Readily takes to manmade nest boxes. In flight, broad-based, trian-

MALE

FEMALE

gular wings and relatively slow wingbeats create passing resemblance to European Starling. Sexes are dissimilar. **ADULT MALE** Can look all-dark in poor light, but at close range note glossy bluish purple sheen on body plumage. **ADULT FEMALE** Has gray-brown upperparts overall, with variable hint of bluish sheen on back and cap; note the pale gray collar and forehead. Underparts are mottled gray-brown, palest on belly and often forming a distinct patch. **JUVENILE** Similar to female, but with much paler underparts, clean and whitish on belly and undertail. First-summer male retains many juvenile characters. **VOICE** Song is a series of gurgling, churring notes; calls include whistles and a liquid *chrrr*. **STATUS AND HABITAT** Locally common summer visitor (present mainly Apr–Aug) to open rural and suburban habitats. Widespread in most of eastern North America and attached to human settlement. Winters in South America. **OBSERVATION TIPS** Easy to see. Install nest boxes to encourage the species.

BANK SWALLOW *Riparia riparia* L 5.25–5.5 in

Tiny hirundine and the smallest of its kind in the region. Often seen catching insects in rapid flight, with flicking wingbeats, low over water; often congregates where feeding is good. Typically nests colonially in burrows excavated in vertical sand or gravel banks and cliffs, beside rivers, and in quarries and excavations. Sexes are similar. **ADULT** Has sandy gray-brown upperparts and mainly white underparts, with a striking, well-defined brown

ADULT

breast band. Division between brown cap and white throat is well defined. Tail is relatively long and slightly forked (appears unforked when fully fanned). **JUVENILE** Similar to adult, but with more obvious pale buff fringes to many wing feathers. **VOICE** Utters a buzzing alarm call; song is a series of abrupt, twittering notes. **STATUS AND HABITAT** Widespread and common summer visitor (mainly Apr–Sep) to a wide range of habitats. Winters in South America. **OBSERVATION TIPS** Easy to see, especially near water.

NORTHERN ROUGH-WINGED SWALLOW

Stelgidopteryx serripennis L 5–6 in

Similar to, but slightly larger than, Bank Swallow, separable in all plumages by noting absence of dark breast band; underparts are also grubbier white overall. Nests in crevices and holes in rock faces; either solitarily or in small colonies (not the large colonies sometimes seen in Bank Swallow).

JUVENILE

Catches insects on the wing, often feeding over water. Sexes are similar. **ADULT** Has rather uniform brown upperparts, with pale fringes to inner flight feathers and coverts sometimes visible. Brown on face grades to light brown on throat and breast; underparts are otherwise whitish. Tail appears almost square-ended when fanned in flight. **JUVENILE** Similar, but more rufous overall, with noticeably broad, rufous margins to inner flight feathers and wing coverts; throat is warm buff. **VOICE** Utters a range of buzzing call notes. **STATUS AND HABITAT** Widespread and common summer visitor (mainly Apr–Sep) to a wide range of open habitats. Winters mainly in Central America. **OBSERVATION TIPS** Absence of dark breast band allows separation from Bank Swallow.

FEMALE

PURPLE MARTIN

MALE

FEMALE

BANK SWALLOW

ADULT

ADULT

NORTHERN ROUGH-WINGED SWALLOW

JUVENILE

Hirundinidae

CLIFF SWALLOW
Petrochelidon pyrrhonota L 5.5–6 in

Compact swallow with broad-based, triangular, and relatively short wings. Pale orange-buff rump, obvious in flight, is diagnostic across much of range, but beware of confusion with Cave Swallow (*see below*) within that species' limited North American range. Nests colonially, making mud nests on cliffs and manmade structures. Catches flying insects on the wing. Sexes are similar. **ADULT** Has bluish black cap and white-lined bluish black back. Note the pale collar, reddish orange cheeks, and dark throat; forehead is white in most birds. Rump is buffy and square-ended tail is dark. Underparts are mostly pale with darker spots on undertail coverts. **JUVENILE** Duller than adult, with unmarked back; lacks reddish elements of facial plumage and has paler rump. Throat is dark (cf. juvenile Cave). **VOICE** Utters various soft twittering notes. **STATUS AND HABITAT** Common summer visitor (mainly Apr–Sep) to a wide range of habitats. Winters in South America. **OBSERVATION TIPS** Easy to find.

CAVE SWALLOW *Petrochelidon fulva* L 5.5–6 in

Similar to Cliff Swallow, but separable with care. Reddish orange forehead distinguishes adult from all but southwestern Cliffs (unlikely to be encountered in east), and note paler throat and face generally, showing obvious contrast with dark cap. Juvenile Cave's pale face, throat, and nape are best features for separation from juvenile Cliff. Nests colonially, making mud nests in caves or under bridges. Sexes are similar. **ADULT** Has bluish black cap and white-lined bluish black back. Has pale collar and pale reddish orange cheeks and throat; forehead is reddish orange (more extensive than in southwestern Cliffs). Rump is reddish buff and square-ended tail is dark. Underparts are mostly pale with darker spots on undertail coverts. **JUVENILE** Duller and less colorful than adult, with pale buff forehead and pale buff nape, throat and breast grading to whitish underparts. **VOICE** Utters a sharp *che-wiit* and various twittering notes. **STATUS AND HABITAT** Locally common summer visitor (mainly Mar–Aug), mostly to Texas, but range expanding; often feeds in vicinity of water. A few remain in southern Texas throughout year but most are presumed to winter in Central America. **OBSERVATION TIPS** Beware confusion with Cliff Swallow.

ADULT

BARN SWALLOW *Hirundo rustica* L 6.5–7 in

Familiar and colorful swallow. Flight is dashing and varied as it pursues flying insects; often feeds low over ground or water. Builds mud nest, sometimes in cave or on cliff ledge, but frequently on ledge in barn or outbuilding. Sexes are separable. **ADULT MALE** Has blue cap, nape, and back, with red forehead and throat. Blue breast band separates throat from buffy orange underparts, including underwing coverts. Note the long, deeply forked tail. **ADULT FEMALE** Similar, but has a shorter tail and much paler, buffy white underparts. **JUVENILE** Similar to adult female, but with very short tail streamers and orange-buff (not red) throat and forehead. **VOICE** Song is a series of twittering warbles; calls include a sharp *che-viit*. **STATUS AND HABITAT** Common and widespread summer visitor (mainly Mar–Sep) to open country, including farmland and grassland. Winters mainly in South America. **OBSERVATION TIPS** Easy to see.

JUVENILE

ADULT

ADULT

CLIFF SWALLOW

JUVENILE

CAVE SWALLOW

ADULT

FEMALE

BARN SWALLOW

MALE

Paridae

TUFTED TITMOUSE *Baeolophus bicolor* L 6–6.5 in

Distinctive and endearing bird that is inquisitive and often indifferent to observers. Easily recognized as a titmouse by its tufted

crest and blue-gray plumage. Nests in natural tree holes, but readily uses nest boxes in wooded suburbs. Regularly visits feeders, especially during winter months. Sexes are similar. **ADULT** Has mainly soft blue-gray upperparts with a peaked crest and blackish forehead. Dark eye is emphasized by otherwise pale face and underparts are mainly very pale blue-gray, with orange-buff wash on flanks and whitish undertail coverts. Bill is dark and legs are blue-gray. **JUVENILE** Similar, but has grayish forehead. **VOICE** Song is a disyllabic *peet-oo, peet-oo...*; call is a nasal *zree*. **STATUS AND HABITAT** Common resident of dry, open wood habitats including deciduous woodland, mature gardens, and urban parks. **OBSERVATION TIPS** Easy to find. Encourage it with feeders and nest boxes.

ADULT

BLACK-CAPPED CHICKADEE
Poecile atricapillus L 5.25–5.5 in

Regular visitor to bird feeders and typically indifferent to people, especially ones who provide food. Nests in tree holes, but readily occupies nest boxes. Feeds on invertebrates and seeds, according to season, and joins roving mixed species flocks outside breeding season. Sexes are similar. **ADULT** Has a gray-buff back and mostly dark wings, but with whitish edges to inner flight feathers and greater coverts, forming a pale panel. Head has prominent black cap, extending narrowly down nape, and neatly defined black throat and bib. White on face covers cheeks and extends to sides of nape. Underparts are otherwise pale with buffy pinkish wash to rear of flanks. Tail is dark with pale fringes to feathers. Legs are gray and short, stubby bill is dark. **JUVENILE** Similar to adult. **VOICE** Song is a whistled, disyllabic *fee-bee*; calls its name: *chika-dee-dee-dee*. **STATUS AND HABITAT** Widespread and common resident in a wide range of wooded habitats, including gardens and urban parks. **OBSERVATION TIPS** Usually extremely easy to see.

CAROLINA CHICKADEE
Poecile carolinensis L 4.75–5 in

Very similar to Black-capped. Fortunately, ranges overlap only slightly. Slightly smaller size is of little use in field identification. With experience, Carolina's subtly different proportions (smaller head and shorter tail) and voice can be useful pointers. Visits feeders, uses nest boxes, and joins roving mixed-species flocks of small birds outside breeding season. Sexes are similar. **ADULT** Has "cold" look to plumage compared to Black-capped. Has gray-buff back and darkish wings; pale margins to inner flight feathers and greater coverts are duller and show less contrast than on Black-capped. Black cap, throat, and bib are similar in extent to Black-capped but white on face grades subtly from white cheeks to pale gray on sides of nape (uniformly white in Black-capped). Underparts are grayish overall with faint buff wash on flanks (flanks are warmer buff in Black-capped). Tail is dark, but with pale (not white) fringes. Legs are gray and bill is dark. **JUVENILE** Similar to adult. **VOICE** Song is a four-note whistling *fee-bee fee-bay*; call is a rapid *chika-dee-dee*, higher pitched than that of Black-capped. **STATUS AND HABITAT** Common and widespread resident of deciduous wooded habitats. **OBSERVATION TIPS** Easy to see.

TUFTED TITMOUSE

ADULT

BLACK-CAPPED CHICKADEE

ADULT

CAROLINA CHICKADEE

ADULT

Paridae, Remizidae, and Certhiidae

BOREAL CHICKADEE *Poecile hudsonica* L 5–5.5 in

Hardy Arctic and northern chickadee with "warm" overall look to plumage. Caches seeds as a food resource for winter months. Sexes are similar. **ADULT** Has brown cap, extending narrowly down nape, and brown back. Wings are dark with very indistinct pale feather margins. Neatly defined black throat borders the grayish face, which is whitish only toward the front. Pale underparts are strongly washed orange-buff on flanks. **JUVENILE** Similar to adult. **VOICE** Has a trilling song; calls include a thin *dee* and a *tsika-chay-chay*. **STATUS AND HABITAT** Widespread and fairly common resident of northern and boreal conifer forests. Mostly rather sedentary, but occasionally undertakes irruptive movements south in late fall and winter if food supplies fail. **OBSERVATION TIPS** Usually easy to find, but unobtrusive in breeding season.

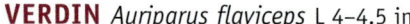

ADULT

VERDIN *Auriparus flaviceps* L 4–4.5 in

Distinctive little desert bird with a rather warblerlike appearance. Forages actively but unobtrusively among foliage for invertebrates, and frequently flicks tail. Sexes are similar, but female is duller than male. **ADULT** Has gray-buff back and nape. Wings are mainly gray-buff, but with darker flight feathers and small reddish patch on "shoulder" (often indistinct or partly hidden). Face is mostly yellow, but with dark lores and eye. Underparts are pale gray, and legs and tiny, pointed bill are dark. **JUVENILE** Plain gray overall, lacking adult's color on face and "shoulders." **VOICE** Has a whistling, trisyllabic song; calls include a sharp *tseip*. **STATUS AND HABITAT** Widespread and fairly common resident of desert scrub and open mesquite woodland in Texas. **OBSERVATION TIPS** Its typically solitary nature outside breeding season can make it tricky to find. Persistent searching usually pays off.

BROWN CREEPER *Certhia americana* L 5–5.25 in

Unmistakable woodland bird, whose well-marked brown plumage is a good match for tree bark. Feeds by climbing tree trunks in a mouse-like manner, probing crevices for small invertebrates with its needlelike, downcurved bill. Spiky tail is used as support and bird typically works its way upwards from base of tree in a spiral manner, then drops to base of adjacent trunk to repeat the process. Sometimes joins roving mixed-species flocks outside the breeding season. Nests in natural crevices under loose tree bark. Several subspecies exist; those from east are described here. Sexes are similar. **ADULT** Has brownish upperparts heavily marked with pale teardrop spots on crown, face, and back; note the bold whitish supercilium. Short wings have buffy barring, and rump and base of tail are rufous. Underparts are whitish overall, with buff wash on flanks and undertail. Variation exists in precise hue of upperparts (ranging from grayish to rufous), even within the same regional populations. **JUVENILE** Similar to adult, but with faint barring on chest. **VOICE** Song is a series of *tsee-see-see* notes; call is a thin *tsee*, recalling that of Golden-crowned Kinglet (*see* p.240). **STATUS AND HABITAT** Widespread and fairly common in forest habitats; resident in parts of northeast, but northern birds migrate south for winter. **OBSERVATION TIPS** Outside breeding season, search roving mixed-species flocks and listen for its high, thin calls. Note, however, people who are hard of hearing may not be able to detect the notes.

BOREAL CHICKADEE

ADULT

BROWN CREEPER

ADULT, MALE

VERDIN

JUVENILE

ADULT

Sittidae

WHITE-BREASTED NUTHATCH
Sitta carolinensis L 5.75–6 in

North America's largest nuthatch. Often joins roving mixed-species flocks outside breeding season and visits bird feeders. Like other nuthatches, often climbs down tree trunks headfirst. Several subspecies exist; eastern birds are described here. Sexes are separable. **ADULT MALE** Has slate-gray back and wings, with dark centers and pale edges to tertials and wing coverts. Nape and crown are black, contrasting with white face, throat, and breast; underparts are otherwise rather pale, with gray wash on flanks, and rufous and white on vent and undertail coverts. **ADULT FEMALE** Similar, but crown and nape are dark gray, not black, and flanks are paler. **JUVENILE** Similar to adult, but wing feathers have buff fringes. **VOICE** Song is a series of nasal, whistling notes; call is a nasal *n'yenk*. **STATUS AND HABITAT** Common resident of mixed and deciduous woodland. Some dispersal occurs outside breeding season, presumably related to food shortages. **OBSERVATION TIPS** Easy to see and identify.

RED-BREASTED NUTHATCH
Sitta canadensis L 4.5–5 in

Colorful and well-marked nuthatch with a compact, plump body and slender, pointed bill. Joins roving mixed-species flocks of small birds outside the breeding season. Sexes are separable with care. **ADULT MALE** Has blue-gray back, wings, and tail. Head is marked with black crown and eyestripe, and white supercilium, cheeks, and chin. Throat and rest of underparts are reddish buff. **ADULT FEMALE** Similar, but black elements of head plumage are paler and underparts are paler orange-buff. **JUVENILE** Similar to respective sex adult, but with brownish wing feathers. **VOICE** Song is a series of nasal *errn* notes, similar to its nasal call, which is reminiscent of a toy trumpet. **STATUS AND HABITAT** Widespread and common in coniferous forests. Present year-round in many areas, but northern populations migrate south in fall and many others periodically undertake irruptive movements (some long distance), presumably in response to food shortages. **OBSERVATION TIPS** Often first detected by its distinctive call.

BROWN-HEADED NUTHATCH
Sitta pusilla L 4.25–4.5 in

Southeastern pine forest specialty. Like other nuthatches, often climbs head-first down tree trunks. Feeds acrobatically, often on slender, outermost branches. Nests in cavities excavated in dead trees. Joins roving mixed-species flocks outside breeding seasons. Sexes are similar. **ADULT** Has blue-gray back and wings with subtly paler fringes to edges of inner flight feathers. Tail is short and blue-gray. Cap is brown and nape is mostly brown, but with a prominent whitish spot at rear. Cheeks and throat are white, and underparts are pale overall, but with a faint buff wash to breast and undertail coverts, and gray wash to flanks. **JUVENILE** Similar to adult, but paler overall and with buff wash to upperpart feathers. **VOICE** Call is distinctive and almost humorous, being reminiscent of a child's squeaky toy. **STATUS AND HABITAT** Locally fairly common resident of pine forests in southeastern U.S. Population is declining overall, in part due to inappropriate land management, for example, suppression of natural fires. **OBSERVATION TIPS** Fairly easy to see in suitable pine forests within range.

FEMALE

MALE

WHITE-BREASTED NUTHATCH

FEMALE

RED-BREASTED NUTHATCH

MALE

BROWN-HEADED NUTHATCH

ADULT

Troglodytidae

HOUSE WREN *Troglodytes aedon* L 4.75–5 in

Tiny bird with typical wren proportions: rounded body and short wings. Tail is often cocked straight-up. Has a needlelike bill and relatively short legs. Forages in vegetation for insects and spiders. Nests in tree holes, but readily uses nest boxes and cavities and crevices in buildings. Sexes are similar, but regional subspecies variation exists; eastern ssp. *aedon* is described here. **ADULT** Has brown plumage overall, darkest on upperparts with barring on wings and tail. Face and throat are buffy, and otherwise mostly pale buff underparts show rufous wash and barring on flanks. **JUVENILE** Similar to adult, but averages more rufous above with scaly appearance to paler face and throat. **VOICE** Song is an accelerating series of sweet, raspy trilling notes, ending in a flourish; call is a raspy *tche-tche*. **STATUS AND HABITAT** Widespread and common summer visitor (mainly May–Aug) favoring gardens, woodland, and scrub, across northern part of its range. Winters from southeastern U.S. to Mexico. **OBSERVATION TIPS** Often first detected by song or call.

WINTER WREN *Troglodytes troglodytes* L 4–4.5 in

Smaller than House Wren; much shorter tail is often cocked. Unobtrusive and looks rather mouselike as it creeps through low vegetation after insects. Flies on whirring wingbeats, usually from one patch of cover to another. Extremely vocal and unseen birds are often detected by their distinctive call. Sexes are similar, but show subtle regional variation; eastern ssp. *hiemalis* is described here. (It is likely that the eastern and western subspecies will be given full species status in the near future.) **ADULT** Has reddish brown upperparts, with barring on wings and tail; note the pale buff supercilium. Underparts are buffy brown, with barring on the flanks. Bill is needlelike and legs are reddish orange in all birds. **JUVENILE** Similar to adult, but with subtly less distinct barring. **VOICE** Unusually loud for a little bird. Song is variable and warbling, often ending in a trill; call is a sharp *chip-chip*. **STATUS AND HABITAT** Present year-round in parts of northeast, but mainly a locally common summer visitor (mainly Apr–Aug), migrating mainly to southeastern U.S. for winter. Favors dense, damp woodland and scrub. **OBSERVATION TIPS** Easy to overlook. Listen for the call or loud song.

CAROLINA WREN
Thryothorus ludovicianus L 5.25–5.5 in

Vocal and familiar garden bird and a colorful, well-marked wren. Where range overlaps with similar Bewick's Wren (*see* p.238), separated by warmer colors overall, uniformly barred, brown tail (without white outer tips), and delicate white-spotted wing bars. Indifferent to, or sometimes curious about, human observers. Sexes are similar. **ADULT** Has rich brown upperparts, with faint dark barring on wings and tail, and a striking white supercilium. Face is speckled grayish buff and underparts are warm buff. Bill is downcurved, and legs are orangeish. **JUVENILE** Similar to adult. **VOICE** Song is a rapid series of fluty whistles; call is a harsh, agitated *tchee-tchee-tchee....* **STATUS AND HABITAT** Widespread and common resident in gardens, scrub, and dense woodland. Mainly sedentary, and northern populations suffer badly in harsh winters. **OBSERVATION TIPS** Easy to see and hear around houses and in gardens.

HOUSE WREN

ADULT

WINTER WREN

ADULT

CAROLINA WREN

ADULT

Troglodytidae

BEWICK'S WREN *Thryomanes bewickii* L 5.25–5.5 in

Well-marked wren with a striking pale supercilium. Rather long tail has white outer tips and is often cocked. Forages for insects and spiders among foliage and on ground, as well as in dense cover. Regional variation exists in plumage (palest and grayest in southwestern birds, outside range of this book) and variation also occurs within populations in same area; eastern ssp. *bewickii* is described here. Sexes are not separable. **ADULT** Has brown upperparts overall, unmarked except on tail, which is barred and has white outer tips. Underparts are grayish white, palest on throat and with rufous wash on rear of flanks. **JUVENILE** Similar to adult. **VOICE** Song comprises a series of wheezy, rasping notes, ending in a trill; calls include various harsh, raspy notes. **STATUS AND HABITAT** Mostly a fairly common, but declining, resident of woods with clearings and thickets, and mature gardens; northern birds move south in winter. **OBSERVATION TIPS** Listen for the song.

MARSH WREN *Cistothorus palustris* L 5–5.25 in

Vocal but secretive wren that is easier to hear than see. In flight (between one patch of cover and another), note the whirring, rounded wings and rounded tail. Perched birds often cock tail. Sexes are similar. **ADULT** Has reddish brown upperparts overall, with subtle barring on wings and tail, white streaks on back, and striking, pale supercilium. Face is gray-buff, palest on throat and with speckling on face. Underparts are pale, but with warm orange-buff wash on flanks. **JUVENILE** Similar, but with grayer face and less distinct supercilium. **VOICE** Song is extremely variable, but typically includes fluty warbling notes; calls include an agitated *tchut*. **STATUS AND HABITAT** Locally common summer visitor (mainly May–Aug) to cattail marshes; winters from southern U.S. to Mexico. Present year-round in some coastal districts. **OBSERVATION TIPS** Easy to hear, but a challenge to see. Patient watching usually pays off.

SEDGE WREN *Cistothorus platensis* L 4.5–4.75 in

Superficially similar to Marsh Wren, but separated by voice, habitat preference, and subtle plumage differences: Sedge has paler, warmer buff plumage overall, with more conspicuous barring on wings and more extensively streaked back. Like many other wrens (including Marsh), male builds several "dummy" nests that are not used. Sexes are similar. **ADULT** Has reddish buff upperparts overall, with subtle dark barring on tail, more striking dark and pale barring on wings, bold dark and pale streaks on back, and a streaked crown; supercilium is buffy. Underparts are buffy brown overall, but palest and whitish on throat. **JUVENILE** Similar to adult, but colors and markings are duller overall. **VOICE** Song is a dry rattle preceded by a couple of sharp *chip, chip* notes; call is a sharp *chip*. **STATUS AND HABITAT** Locally common summer visitor (mainly May–Sep) to wet meadows and marshes where sedges predominate. Winters in similar habitats (plus coastal marshes) in southeastern U.S. **OBSERVATION TIPS** Easiest to find when vocal on breeding grounds.

BEWICK'S WREN

ADULT

MARSH WREN

ADULT

ADULT

SEDGE WREN

ADULT

GOLDEN-CROWNED KINGLET
Regulus satrapa L 3.75–4 in

Tiny and extremely active songbird with a thin, needlelike bill. Superficially warblerlike overall, but recognized by rather dumpy proportions and extremely small size. Distinctive head markings allow separation from similarly sized Ruby-crowned. Forages continuously for small insects and spiders, searching along twigs, buds, and among needles, and sometimes hovering to glean prey from otherwise inaccessible spots. Sometimes found in small flocks, and joins roving mixed-species flocks of other small birds outside breeding season. People with good hearing often locate hidden feeding birds by their thin calls. Sexes are dissimilar. **ADULT MALE** Has mostly gray olive-green upperparts, but note the striking markings on the wings with two white wing bars, the lower and bolder of the two emphasized by black at the base of the secondaries. Face is adorned with long, white supercilium, emphasized below by dark eyestripe and above by black margin to golden yellow crown; bright orange center to crown is revealed only when bird is displaying. Face is otherwise olive-gray and underparts are pale gray-buff. Legs are black and feet are yellowish. **ADULT FEMALE** Similar to male, but with a more yellow crown that

MALE, DISPLAYING

lacks the orange center. **JUVENILE** Similar to adult female, but lacks yellow on crown. **VOICE** Song is a sweet *tswee, tswee, tswoo, tswit-tswit-tswit*; call is a thin *twsee*. **STATUS AND HABITAT** Widespread and common summer visitor (mainly Apr–Sep) to northern coniferous forests. Found year-round in coniferous and mixed forests further south, including increasingly in spruce plantations (less frequently in deciduous woodland); winter migrants favor similar habitats. **OBSERVATION TIPS** Can be hard to follow when foraging actively high in foliage. However, migrants in particular, will often forage much lower and are typically indifferent to human observers.

RUBY-CROWNED KINGLET
Regulus calendula L 4–4.25 in

Marginally larger than Golden-crowned Kinglet, from which it is readily distinguished by its relatively plain face, unmarked except for the broken white patch that surrounds and emphasizes the beady black eye. Forages actively and tirelessly for insects and spiders, caught with its needlelike bill. Often hovers to glean insects in manner of Golden-crowned Kinglet and also flicks its wings in an agitated manner. Sexes are separable. **ADULT MALE** Has mainly grayish olive-green upperparts, but note the dark wings and two white wing bars; lower one is more pronounced than upper one. Ruby crown

MALE, DISPLAYING

patch is only exposed in displaying or agitated birds and is otherwise hidden by grayish olive crown feathers. Underparts are pale olive-gray. **ADULT FEMALE** Similar to male, but lacks ruby crown patch. **JUVENILE** Similar to adult female. **VOICE** Song comprises chattering and warbling notes, preceded by thin *tsee-tsee-tsee* notes; call is a raspy *d'dit*. **STATUS AND HABITAT** Widespread and common summer visitor (present mainly May–Sep) to northern coniferous forests. Winters from southern U.S. to Central America, favoring a range of wooded habitats. **OBSERVATION TIPS** Easy to see in suitable habitats. The high-pitched calls and songs of both kinglets are inaudible to many people.

FEMALE

GOLDEN-CROWNED KINGLET

MALE

RUBY-CROWNED KINGLET

ADULT

Sylviidae and Turdidae

BLUE-GRAY GNATCATCHER
Polioptila caerulea L 4.25–4.5 in

Distinctive little songbird and eastern North America's only gnatcatcher. It looks rather warblerlike overall, with its thin bill and slim body.
But note the very long tail, which is often cocked upright or flicked from side-
to-side. Forages actively in foliage for insects, often near the outermost
branches of shrubs and trees, and sometimes hovers to glean prey from a leaf.
Often seen in pairs. Sexes are dissimilar. **ADULT MALE BREEDING** Has blue-gray
upperparts, except for the blackish wings that have contrasting white tertial
edges. Tail, from above, is mainly black, but with contrasting and striking white

ADULT, NONBREEDING

outer feathers; from below, tail is mostly white. Note
the white eyering and black on forehead extending
to above eye. Underparts are pale gray. **ADULT MALE
NONBREEDING** Similar, but it has a gray, not black,
forehead. **ADULT FEMALE** Similar to nonbreeding
male. **JUVENILE** Similar to adult female, but sometimes has a subtle brownish wash on back. **VOICE**
Song consists of a series of thin notes, and often contains some mimicry of other songsters in the vicinity; call is a soft, grating *zwe'oe*. **STATUS AND
HABITAT** Widespread and common summer visitor
(present mainly Apr–Aug) to deciduous wooded habitats. Present year-round in southeastern U.S. and
winters from there to Central America. **OBSERVATION
TIPS** Easy to see in most suitable habitats.

EASTERN BLUEBIRD *Sialia sialis* L 7–7.25 in

One of eastern North America's most familiar and best-loved birds.
An extremely colorful species that perches conspicuously on wires
and branches, scanning for insect prey on ground below onto which it then
drops. Also flycatches and gleans insects from foliage while hovering; berries
are an important part of its diet in fall and winter in particular. Nests in tree
holes and readily takes to nest boxes. Forms sizeable flocks outside the breeding season, sometimes mixing with other species. Sexes are dissimilar. **ADULT
MALE** Has mainly deep blue upperparts, including scapulars; on the head the
color forms a distinct cap. Throat, sides of neck, breast, and flanks are orange-
red while belly and undertail are white. **ADULT FEMALE** Has mostly gray-brown upperparts with blue
flight feathers and tail, and orange wash on underparts. **JUVENILE** Brown overall with pale spots
on upperparts and scaly-looking underparts. **VOICE** Song is a rapid series of twittering warbling notes;

JUVENILE

call is a sharp *tch'ree*. **STATUS AND HABITAT** Has
declined markedly in recent decades, but still common overall and widespread as a summer visitor
(present mainly Apr–Sep) across the north of its
range; present year-round further south and winter
range extends to northeastern Mexico. Favors lightly wooded terrain including regenerating woodland
and large gardens. Reasons for decline include habitat destruction and degradation, but nest competition from European Starlings and House Sparrows
has also contributed. Nest box schemes are helping
to restore many local populations. **OBSERVATION
TIPS** Easy to see within range; to encourage the
species' presence and reproductive success install
suitable nest boxes in your garden.

BLUE-GRAY GNATCATCHER

MALE, BREEDING

FEMALE

MALE

EASTERN BLUEBIRD

Turdidae

WOOD THRUSH *Hylocichla mustelina* L 7.25–7.75 in

Relatively large, plump-bodied thrush with well-marked plumage. Its wonderful, fluty song is indicative of unspoilt woodland habitat. Feeds mainly by foraging for invertebrates in leaf litter on the woodland floor,

ADULT

but also hunts more actively for insects among foliage and eats berries in season. Sexes are similar. **ADULT** Has mostly rich orange-brown upperparts, brightest on nape. Face is pale, but marked with dense, dark streaks, and underparts are otherwise whitish with well-defined and distinct black spots. Note the white eyering. Legs are pink and bill is pink and dark-tipped. **JUVENILE** Brown and spotted but by first fall it recalls adult. **VOICE** Song is a series of rich, fluty notes and ends in a vibrating trill; call is a rapid, agitated *ptt'ptt'ptt*. **STATUS AND HABITAT** Locally common, but declining summer visitor (present mainly May–Sep) to deciduous woodland; winters in Central America. **OBSERVATION TIPS** Well worth visiting suitable woodland just to hear its song. Feeding birds are unobtrusive and easily overlooked.

VEERY *Catharus fuscescens* L 7–7.3 in

Secretive thrush. Forages in leaf litter for invertebrates. Plumage markings are understated; ironically, this helps with separation

ADULT

from other *Catharus* species (it is the least spotted). Sexes are similar. **ADULT** Has mainly reddish brown upperparts. Face is gray-brown and faintly marked, and pale buff throat is bordered by brown line. Breast is yellow-buff with brown spots, grading to grayish white on rest of underparts, with gray-washed flanks and faint gray spots on lower breast and flanks. **JUVENILE** Brown and spotted, but first-fall bird resembles adult, but with buff tips to wing coverts. **VOICE** Song is a whistled *vee, v'didi, v'didi, veer, veer*, descending stepwise in tone; call is a sharp *veer*. **STATUS AND HABITAT** Common summer visitor (mainly May–Aug) to damp, deciduous woodland, especially thickets of willow. Winters in South America. **OBSERVATION TIPS** Easiest to detect by song.

SWAINSON'S THRUSH
Catharus ustulatus L 7–7.5 in

Similar to other *Catharus* thrushes, but separable with care. Pale buff "spectacles" (eyering and line continuing to base of bill) are reliable features. Compared to Veery, note "cold"-looking olive (not "warm" reddish brown) upperparts, dark line bordering side of throat and more distinct spotting on breast; compared to Hermit Thrush, note lack of contrast between back color and tail (tail is contrastingly reddish in Hermit Thrush); "spectacles" and buff (not gray) cheeks allow separation from Gray-cheeked. Sexes are similar. **ADULT** Has olive-brown upperparts overall. Pale buff throat is bordered by dark line and face and ear coverts are also buff. Underparts are pale with yellow-buff wash and dark spots on breast, subtle gray spots on lower breast, and olive-gray flanks. **JUVENILE** Olive-brown and spotted, but first-fall bird resembles adult with buff tips to wing coverts. **VOICE** Song is a series of fluty whistles; tone rises and intensity diminishes throughout sequence. Call is a sharp *quiirp*. **STATUS AND HABITAT** Common summer visitor (present mainly May–Sep) to coniferous forests. Winters in South America. **OBSERVATION TIPS** Learn and listen for its song.

WOOD THRUSH

ADULT

VEERY

ADULT

ADULT

SWAINSON'S THRUSH

Turdidae

GRAY-CHEEKED THRUSH
Catharus minimus L 7.25–7.5 in

Similar to Swainson's: features to focus on include gray (not buff) cheeks and absence of buff "spectacles." Forages in leaf litter. Sexes are similar. **ADULT** Has mostly gray-brown upperparts, with tail same color as back. Has grayish face and cheeks with subtle pale gray eyering. Whitish throat is bordered by dark line that defines pale malar stripe. Breast is washed yellow-buff and marked with dark spots; underparts are otherwise pale, except for pale gray spots on lower breast and gray flanks. **JUVENILE** Gray-brown and spotted, but first-winter plumage is similar to adult, but with pale tips to wing

BICKNELL'S THRUSH

ADULT

coverts. **VOICE** Song is a series of fluty, whistling notes, often ending in a downslurred, trilling flourish; call is a nasal *piuup*. **STATUS AND HABITAT** Common summer visitor (mainly May–Aug) to wet, northern forests (coniferous and deciduous). Winters in northern South America. **OBSERVATION TIPS** Easiest to detect by listening for song and call. **SIMILAR SPECIES Bicknell's Thrush** *C. bicknelli* (L 6.75–7.25 in) is hard to separate (away from breeding grounds, which are separated geographically) unless you know Gray-cheeked well. Shorter-winged than Gray-cheeked, with warmer upperparts (tail redder than back) and subtle reddish panel on primaries. Scarce summer visitor to montane coniferous forests.

HERMIT THRUSH *Catharus guttatus* L 6.75–7 in

Well-marked *Catharus* thrush. The only member of the genus to winter in our region. Most striking feature is contrast between buffy brown back and more rufous tail. Forages on forest floor for invertebrates; flicks wings and cocks tail. Sexes are similar. **ADULT** Has brown upperparts overall; note rufous panel on primaries. Has a white eyering; white throat is bordered by black lateral line. Underparts are whitish, with yellow wash and black spots on breast; undertail coverts are buffy. **JUVENILE** Spotted, but first-fall bird resembles adult but has pale tips to wing coverts. **VOICE** Song is a series of fluty whistles, with a pause between each phrase; call is a muted *tchuck-tchuck*. **STATUS AND HABITAT** Common summer visitor (mainly May–Aug) to coniferous forests; winters from southern U.S. to Central America. **OBSERVATION TIPS** Easy to see.

AMERICAN ROBIN *Turdus migratorius* L 10–11 in

Our most familiar thrush. Feeds mainly on invertebrates, particularly earthworms. Forms flocks in winter. Sexes are separable. **ADULT MALE** Has gray-brown back, rump, and wings, grading to blackish on head and neck. Note striking white "eyelids"; throat white with black streaks. Tail dark brown and underparts are mostly brick-red to orange-red, but white on belly and undertail. In flight, note reddish underwing coverts. Legs dark; bill yellowish. **ADULT FEMALE** Similar, but with paler gray-brown upperparts, paler throat, and less colorful underparts with pale feather fringes creating slightly scaly look. **JUVENILE** Recalls pale adult female, with bold white teardrop spots on back and dark spots on otherwise washed-out underparts. **VOICE** Song has rich, whistling phrases, with pauses between phrases; calls include a sharp *puup*; flight call is a high, sibilant *wee-wheep*. **STATUS AND HABITAT** Common summer visitor (mainly Apr–Sep) to Canada and northern U.S., favoring a wide range of habitats. Present year-round (numbers boosted in winter) across much of southern U.S. **OBSERVATION TIPS** Easy to see. **SIMILAR SPECIES Clay-colored Thrush** *T. grayi* (L 10 in) Mainly Central American species, now regular in southern Texas. Has mainly gray-brown plumage, warmest and palest on underparts; throat subtly paler with dark streaks. Song recalls American Robin; calls include a slurred whistle. Favors wooded parks.

ADULT

CLAY-COLORED THRUSH

ADULT

1ST-WINTER

ADULT

GRAY-CHEEKED THRUSH

JUVENILE

HERMIT THRUSH

ADULT

AMERICAN ROBIN

MALE

FEMALE

JUVENILE

Mimidae

GRAY CATBIRD *Dumetella carolinensis* L 8.5–9 in

Unmistakable bird if seen well. Retiring habits mean it is easily over-looked, but the distinctive meowing call after which it is named, often alerts observers to its otherwise hidden presence in deep cover. Tail is long and often cocked. Forages for insects and other invertebrates on the ground in leaf litter and also among foliage; also feeds, seasonally, on berries. Sexes are similar. **ADULT** Has mainly deep blue-gray body plumage, but with a striking black cap, dark eye, and brick-red undertail coverts. Tail is blackish and legs and bill are dark. **JUVENILE** Similar to adult. **VOICE** Song is series of harsh, abrupt, and rather chattering whistles and squeaks, often with elements of mimicry; unlike rather similar songs of Northern Mockingbird and Brown Thrasher, each phrase of Catbird's song is not repeated (typically repeated several times in those other species). Song is usually delivered from dense cover. Call is a loud *mew*. **STATUS AND HABITAT** Widespread and common summer visitor (mainly May–Aug) to densely vegetated wooded habitats, including mature parks and gardens. Winters from southeastern U.S. to Mexico and Caribbean. **OBSERVATION TIPS** Easier to hear than to see, but persistent observation usually pays off.

NORTHERN MOCKINGBIRD
Mimus polyglottos L 10–10.5 in

Familiar, long-tailed bird and accomplished songster. Often perches conspicuously. Varied diet includes insects and berries. White flashes are striking when wings are spread in display. Sexes are similar. **ADULT** Has mainly gray upperparts, but note the blackish wings with striking white wing bars and white patch (larger in males) at base of primaries. Tail is mainly black, but with contrasting white outer feathers. Dark line emphasizes the beady yellow eye. Underparts are pale gray-buff, palest on throat and undertail. Bill is dark and slightly downcurved and legs are

JUVENILE

dark. **JUVENILE** Recalls adult, but has paler upperparts, while underparts are warmer buff and heavily spotted on throat and breast. **VOICE** Song consists of rich, warbling phrases, each repeated several times; often sings after dark, especially in artificially lit suburbs. A very good mimic. Call is a sharp *tchek*. **STATUS AND HABITAT** Common in a wide range of habitats with scattered trees and scrub; mostly resident, but northernmost populations move south in fall. **OBSERVATION TIPS** Easy to see and hear.

BROWN THRASHER *Toxostoma rufum* L 11–11.5 in

Well-marked, long-tailed, slim-bodied bird with a longish, downcurved bill. Forages mainly on the ground for insects and other invertebrates, but also feeds on berries and seeds. Rather skulking generally, but retiring habits abandoned by territorial singing birds. Sexes are similar. **ADULT** Has mainly rich reddish brown upperparts, including tail. Wings have two black and white wing bars, face is grayish, and note the beady yellow eye. Underparts are creamy white, but with bold dark streaks on all parts except undertail. **JUVENILE** Similar to adult, but with dark eyes. **VOICE** Song is a series of rich, fluty, whistling phrases, each typically repeated a couple of times; calls including a tongue-smacking *stutt* and a softer *chrrr*. **STATUS AND HABITAT** Fairly common summer visitor (mainly May–Aug) to northern U.S. and Canada; favors dense thickets and scrub. Present year-round in southeastern U.S., where numbers are boosted by migrants from further north. **OBSERVATION TIPS** Easiest to see when singing.

CATBIRD, MOCKINGBIRDS, and THRASHERS

GRAY CATBIRD

ADULT

NORTHERN MOCKINGBIRD

ADULT

BROWN THRASHER

ADULT

Sturnidae and Motacillidae

ADULT, WINTER

JUVENILE

EUROPEAN STARLING

Sturnus vulgaris L 8.5–9 in

Introduced, but now familiar bird of urban and rural areas. Forms sizeable flocks outside breeding season. Walks with a characteristic swagger. Flight is rather undulating and wings look pointed and triangular in outline. Sexes are separable with care in summer. **ADULT MALE SUMMER** Has mostly dark plumage with green and violet iridescence. Legs are reddish orange and bill is yellow with bluish base to lower mandible. **ADULT FEMALE SUMMER** Similar, but has a few pale spots on underparts; base of lower mandible is pale yellow. **WINTER ADULT** (both sexes) Has numerous white spots adorning dark plumage. Bill is dark. **JUVENILE** Gray-brown, palest on throat, and with dark bill. First-winter, similar to adult, but often retains gray-brown head and neck into fall. **VOICE** Highly vocal and an accomplished mimic. Song includes repertoire of clicks, whistles, and elements of mimicking other birds and manmade sounds, such as car alarms; calls include chatters and drawn-out whistles. **STATUS AND HABITAT** Abundant; all birds are descendants of 100 individuals released in Central Park, NYC, in 1890s. Found in a wide range of habitats; northern populations move south in winter. **OBSERVATION TIPS** Hard to miss.

AMERICAN PIPIT *Anthus rubescens* L 6.25–6.5 in

Slim-looking pipit that forms large flocks in winter. Often bobs tail. Plumage varies throughout year and across geographical range, and Arctic breeders are described below. Sexes are similar. **ADULT SUMMER** Has grayish upperparts with faint streaking on back; darkish wings show two whitish wing bars and pale margins to tertials. Underparts are buffy and heavily streaked, also note the dark malar stripe and buff supercilium. Legs are typically dark. **ADULT WINTER** Has more heavily streaked gray back with a pale throat and supercilium; heavily streaked underparts have buff wash confined mostly to flanks. **JUVENILE** More heavily marked than adult. **VOICE** Song (often given in flight) is a slightly accelerating series of tinkling *tlee-tlee-tlee...* notes; call is a thin *p'peet*. **STATUS AND HABITAT** Common summer visitor (mainly May–Aug) to tundra and bare mountaintops. Winters in southern U.S. and Mexico, favoring arable fields and open country. **OBSERVATION TIPS** Easiest to see in winter.

SPRAGUE'S PIPIT *Anthus spragueii* L 6.5–6.75 in

Prairie specialist. Secretive and far easier to hear (in spring at least) than to see: male performs aerial song display for long periods. Otherwise, skulks in short grasses and hard to flush. Does not bob tail. Sexes are similar. **ADULT** Has heavily streaked brown upperparts and two white wing bars. Dark eye is emphasized by pale buffy face; note the whitish throat, lores, and supercilium. Underparts are pale, flushed buff on flanks and breast and mostly unmarked, except for streaking on breast. Legs are pale pinkish. **JUVENILE** Similar to adult, but with more striking wing bars and scaly-looking back. **VOICE** Song is a descending series of breezy whistles; call is a thin *squeet*. **STATUS AND HABITAT** Rare and declining species, favoring short-grass prairies for nesting (present mainly May–Sep); winters from southern U.S. (mainly Texas) south to Mexico, and favors rough grassland with more bare ground at this time. **OBSERVATION TIPS** Striking white outer tail feathers (seen in flight) aid identification.

ADULT, SUMMER

ADULT, WINTER

EUROPEAN STARLING

ADULT, SUMMER

ADULT, WINTER

AMERICAN PIPIT

ADULT

ADULT

SPRAGUE'S PIPIT

Bombycillidae

CEDAR WAXWING *Bombycilla cedrorum* L 7.25–7.5 in

Delightful bird whose distinctive crest and soft-looking orange-buff plumage make it easy to recognize, although confusion with scarcer and much less widespread (in east) Bohemian Waxwing is always a possibility. Use differences in structure and plumage color to distinguish between the two: Cedar's plumage is warmer looking overall (orange-buff, not pinkish and so gray), undertail coverts are white (not chestnut), and its dark wings are almost unmarked. Forms roving flocks outside breeding season that search for berry trees and bushes and strip them before moving on to the next source of food. In flight, silhouette resembles a Starling. Sexes are similar. **ADULT** Has orange-buff plumage overall, palest on underparts and white on undertail. Wings are dark, except for white inner edge to tertials and red, waxlike feather projections. Rump is gray and dark tail has a broad yellow terminal band. Note the prominent crest; dark mask through eye is defined above and below by white line (more striking above than in Bohemian). **JUVENILE** Gray-buff overall; differs from juvenile Bohemian in having unmarked dark wings, except for pale inner margin to tertials. First-winter is similar to adult, but lacks red, waxy wing projections. **VOICE** Song comprises a series of piercing *tzeee* call notes. **STATUS AND HABITAT** Common in open woodland. Present year-round in much of northern U.S.; summer visitor further north and a winter visitor south to Mexico. **OBSERVATION TIPS** Easiest to find outside breeding season when sizeable flocks (sometimes hundreds strong) live nomadic lives in search of berry-laden bushes and shrubs.

JUVENILE

BOHEMIAN WAXWING
Bombycilla garrulus L 8–8.25 in

Plump-bodied bird with an obvious crest; confusion is possibly only with more widespread (in east) Cedar Waxwing (*see above* for detailed distinctions). Winter flocks are often tame, giving superb views. In flight, silhouette is rather similar to a Starling. Sexes are separable with care. **ADULT MALE** Has mainly pinkish buff plumage, palest on belly. Has a crest, black throat, and black mask through eye. Rump is gray, undertail is chestnut, and dark tail has a broad yellow terminal band. Primaries have white and yellow margins; wings also show red, waxlike projections and white bar at base of primary coverts. **ADULT FEMALE** Similar, but has narrower yellow tip to tail, shorter waxy wing projections, and narrower dark throat. **JUVENILE** Gray-buff, streaked, and blotchy-looking overall; first-winter is similar to adult, but white margins to primaries are absent, as are red, waxlike projections. **VOICE** Utters a trilling call and does not sing. **STATUS AND HABITAT** Summer breeding range lies mainly outside area covered by this book and present there mainly Apr–Sep; favors boreal coniferous forests. Present year-round further south and moves still further south and east in winter (into range covered by this book), with flocks roving after berry-laden bushes. Precise winter range is unpredictable, but in some years small flocks reach Atlantic coasts. **OBSERVATION TIPS** Easiest to see in winter, but finding a flock is a matter of luck.

1ST-WINTER

ADULT

MALE

CEDAR WAXWING

BOHEMIAN WAXWING

FEMALE

ADULT

Parulidae

WOOD-WARBLERS can often daunt the novice birder, with many species exhibiting striking plumage differences between the sexes, and at different times of year. Becoming familiar with their songs and calls can be a great aid. In the field, concentrate on features such as the presence or absence of wingbars, and throat and rump color. Behavior and habitat preference are also important identification pointers.

PROTHONOTARY WARBLER
Protonotaria citrea L 5.25–5.5 in
Stunningly colorful and relatively large wood-warbler with a rather long bill. The only one of its kind in the east to nest in natural tree holes and sometimes nest boxes. Sexes are separable. **ADULT MALE** Has bright yellow head, neck, and underparts. Back is olive-yellow and wings are bluish gray with pale feather margins. Dark tail is marked with striking white spots. Legs and bill are dark. **ADULT FEMALE** Similar, but plumage is duller and less colorful overall, and spots on tail are smaller. **JUVENILE** Similar to adult female. **VOICE** Song is a distinctive series of rich, liquid notes: *swiip-swiip-swiip-swiip-swiip*; call is a sharp *tchip*. **STATUS AND HABITAT** Fairly common, but declining summer visitor (mainly May–Aug) to wet woodland, often beside rivers. Winters from Central America to northern South America where it favors coastal mangroves. Species is threatened by loss of specific wintering habitat as well as loss and degradation of breeding habitat. **OBSERVATION TIPS** Easiest to detect by song and call.

BLUE-WINGED WARBLER
Vermivora pinus L 4.5–4.75 in
Colorful wood-warbler. Forages unobtrusively for insects, and silent birds are easy to overlook. Almost unmistakable but, confusingly, hybridizes with Golden-winged; two distinct hybrid forms occur ("Brewster's" and "Lawrence's" Warblers), males of which are fairly easy to recognize. Sexes are dissimilar. **ADULT MALE** Has yellow head and underparts, with black stripe through eye. Nape and back are olive-yellow and wings are bluish with two striking white wing bars. Male "Brewster's" has mostly pale, whitish head and underparts with yellow restricted to forehead and breast. Male "Lawrence's" recalls

ADULT, BREWSTER'S

dull male Blue-winged but with a dark throat and patch through eye. **ADULT FEMALE** Less colorful than male with less distinct wing bars. Hybrid females have duller plumage than their hybrid male counterparts. **IMMATURE** Duller than adult female. **VOICE** Song is a high-pitched buzzing trill, in two parts with different tones; call is a sharp *tsik*. **STATUS AND HABITAT** Locally common summer visitor (mainly May–Aug) to scrub and secondary woodland; population may be increasing. **OBSERVATION TIPS** Easiest to detect by hearing song.

GOLDEN-WINGED WARBLER
Vermivora chrysoptera L 4.5–4.75 in
Well marked wood-warbler, male of which is stunningly attractive. Forages for insects in foliage of shrubs and trees. Hybridizes with Blue-winged Warbler (*see above* for details). Sexes are dissimilar. **ADULT MALE** Has a blue-gray back, nape, and rear of crown, and yellow forecrown. Wings are gray with a bright yellow panel. Has a whitish supercilium, and black "mask" and throat are separated by white malar stripe. Underparts are whitish, with blue-gray wash on flanks. **ADULT FEMALE** Similar, but black elements of head pattern are paler gray. **IMMATURE** Duller and less colorful than respective sex adult. **VOICE** Song is a high-pitched buzz, higher in pitch than Golden-winged; call is a thin *tsip*. **STATUS AND HABITAT** Declining, but still a locally common summer visitor (mainly May–Aug) to neglected meadows in the first stages of colonization by scrub; winters mainly in Central America and Caribbean. **OBSERVATION TIPS** Easiest to detect in first instance by hearing call or song.

PROTHONOTARY WARBLER

FEMALE

MALE

BLUE-WINGED WARBLER

FEMALE

MALE

FEMALE

MALE

GOLDEN-WINGED WARBLER

Parulidae

TENNESSEE WARBLER
Vermivora peregrina L 4.5–4.75 in

Active wood-warbler with plain, clean-looking plumage and dark legs. Probes flowers for nectar and insects and searches among foliage for other invertebrates, notably Spruce Budworm. Sexes are dissimilar. **MALE** In spring, has olive-green back and tail and subtly darker wings with very faint pale wing bars. Head is grayish, with dark line through eye and whitish supercilium and throat; underparts are otherwise whitish, with gray wash on flanks. **FEMALE** In spring recalls male, but is duller with yellowish wash to head and neck. **FALL ADULT** Similar to respective sex in spring, but with less colorful upperparts. **IMMATURE** Yellowish green overall, with discrete pale wing bars and pale supercilium; undertail coverts are usually whitish, but even when washed faint yellow they are much paler than rest of underparts. **VOICE** Song is a three-part series of short notes, the last part the fastest: *sip-sip-sip-sip, si-si-si-si, si'si'si'si'si*; call is a tongue-smacking *tchht*. **STATUS AND HABITAT** Fairly common summer visitor (mainly May–Jul) to boreal coniferous forests, particularly wet spruce woods. Winters in Central and South America. **OBSERVATION TIPS** Easy to see.

ORANGE-CROWNED WARBLER
Vermivora celata L 5–5.25 in

Widespread and relatively long-tailed wood-warbler whose plumage varies across range; northern subspecies, the dullest, is the one seen in the east and described below. Orange crown patch is usually indistinct and not useful in field identification. Immature bird resembles immature Tennessee Warbler; its duller colors, darker underparts, yellowish (not white) undertail coverts, and shorter wing projection are useful features to look for. Sexes are dissimilar. **ADULT MALE** Dull yellow-green overall with a gray wash to face and back; note the indistinct pale eyering and pale supercilium. Underparts are faint-

ADULT, YELLOW FORM

ly streaked and undertail coverts are yellow-buff. **ADULT FEMALE** Similar, but grayer overall and duller. **IMMATURE** Similar to adult female; yellow undertail coverts are usually striking. **VOICE** Song is a vibrating trill, whose pitch drops from start to finish; call is a sparrowlike *tik*. **STATUS AND HABITAT** Common summer visitor (mainly May–Sep) to deciduous woodland edges and weedy clearings. Winters in southern U.S. and Mexico. **OBSERVATION TIPS** Voice, color of underparts, and face pattern are clues to identification. First impressions of face are useful in immatures: if pale broken eyering is most obvious feature, then Orange-crowned is likely; if pale supercilium strikes you then Tennessee is best contender.

NASHVILLE WARBLER
Vermivora ruficapilla L 4.5–4.75 in

Active wood-warbler that is hard to confuse within range covered by this book. Sexes are separable. **ADULT MALE** Has mainly olive-green back, with darker flight feathers and tail. Head and neck are mostly blue-gray, but note rufous crown patch and white eyering; throat and underparts are bright yellow. Legs are dark. **ADULT FEMALE** Similar to male, but less colorful, with dull underparts, browner head, and reduced crown patch. **IMMATURE** Similar to adult female, but even paler, with whitish throat and belly and no crown patch. **VOICE** Song is in two parts, first bouncy and whistling, second rapid and trilling: *t'se-t'se-t'se-t'se, se'se'se'se'se*; call is a thin *tsip*. **STATUS AND HABITAT** Common summer visitor (mainly May–Aug) to deciduous and mixed, brushy woods; often in secondary growth. Winters in Central America. **OBSERVATION TIPS** Easy to see.

TENNESSEE WARBLER

FEMALE

MALE

IMMATURE

ORANGE-CROWNED WARBLER

ADULT

ADULT

IMMATURE

NASHVILLE WARBLER

FEMALE

MALE

Parulidae

NORTHERN PARULA *Parula americana* L 4.25–4.5 in

Colorful and distinctive wood-warbler. An active species that often forages high in treetops; this can make getting prolonged views

FEMALE, IMMATURE

MALE, IMMATURE

a challenge. Sexes are separable. **ADULT MALE** Has mainly blue upperparts with greenish patch on back; note the bold white wing bars and white "eyelids." Underparts are mostly yellow, with blue and orange breast band, and grading to white on undertail. Lower mandible is yellow and legs are dull orange. **ADULT FEMALE** Similar to male but less colorful and without breast band. **IMMATURE** Similar to female, but less colorful. **VOICE** Song is a buzzing, squeaky trill; call is a sharp *tzip*. **STATUS AND HABITAT** Common summer visitor (mainly Apr–Aug) to deciduous, coniferous, and mixed forests; favors woodlands of sufficient maturity to have a good growth of epiphytic plants. Winters in Central America. **OBSERVATION TIPS** Easy to see. Singing birds provide the best opportunities for prolonged observation.

BLACK-THROATED BLUE WARBLER
Dendroica caerulescens L 5–5.25 in

Plump-bodied wood-warbler, the sexes of which have remarkably different plumages. Male is striking and unmistakable; although female's plumage is understated and her colors muted, an absence of wing bars and presence of wing patch, pale undertail coverts, and whitish supercilium are good features to look for. Forages mainly for insects, but also takes berries and fruit in season. Sexes are dissimilar. **ADULT MALE** Has mostly dark blue upperparts with darker flight feathers and a striking white patch at the base of the primaries. Tail is dark overall, but in flight note the bold white patches on outer feathers. Face, throat, and flanks are black with neat cut-off from otherwise pure white underparts. **ADULT FEMALE** Has mostly buffy brown upperparts and paler, buff-yellow underparts, except for whitish undertail coverts. Note the white patch at base of primaries, pale supercilium and lower "eyelid." **IMMATURE** Similar to adult female, but pale wing patch is usually absent and pale markings on head are less distinct. **VOICE** Song is a shrill, squeaky *zee-zerr-zhree*, with something of the quality of a bird squeaker about it; call is a sharp *tuuk*. **STATUS AND HABITAT** Locally common summer visitor (mainly May–Aug) to dense understory of upland deciduous or mixed forests; winters around the Caribbean. **OBSERVATION TIPS** Listen for its distinctive song in breeding range; migrants are seen near coasts.

BLACK-AND-WHITE WARBLER
Mniotilta varia L 5–5.25 in

Striking and aptly named black and white wood-warbler. Its legs are dark and the bill is relatively long and slightly downcurved. Forages for insects in a more deliberate manner than most other wood-warblers, often moving slowly along branches, investigating nooks and crannies all the while. Sexes are separable. **ADULT MALE** Striped black and white overall, palest on underparts, with two white wing bars. Throat is black in spring, white in fall; ear coverts black in spring, gray in fall. **ADULT FEMALE** In spring is similar to fall male; often has buff-washed underparts in fall. **IMMATURE** Recalls fall adult of respective sex, male with white cheeks. **VOICE** Song is a thin *seesa-seesa...*; call is a sharp *tchak*. **STATUS AND HABITAT** Common summer visitor (present mainly May–Aug) to a wide range of wooded habitats. Winters mainly in West Indies, Mexico, and Central America. **OBSERVATION TIPS** Easy to see.

FEMALE

MALE

NORTHERN PARULA

MALE

MALE

BLACK-THROATED BLUE WARBLER

BLACK-AND-WHITE WARBLER

FEMALE

FEMALE

BLACK-THROATED BLUE WARBLER

BLACK-AND-WHITE WARBLER

IMMATURE

FEMALE, IMMATURE

Parulidae

CERULEAN WARBLER *Dendroica cerulea* L 4.5–4.75 in

Endangered, colorful warbler. Favored treetop haunts make it hard to see. Sexes are similar. **ADULT MALE** Mostly bright blue above and white below, with a clear divide between the two. Note the two white wing bars, white throat, and dark streaks on flanks. **ADULT FEMALE** Has blue elements of male's plumage mostly replaced by greenish blue; wings are rather dark, but with two bold white wing bars. Underparts, including face, are pale, flushed yellowish on face, throat,

MALE, 1ST-SUMMER

and flanks, and faintly streaked on flanks too. Note the pale supercilium. **IMMATURE** Similar to adult female, but immature female is more yellow overall. **VOICE** Song is a series of thin whistles, ending in an upslurred trill; call is a soft *tsup*. **STATUS AND HABITAT** Rare and declining summer visitor (mainly May–Sep) to mature, undisturbed mixed deciduous forests with a dense canopy and limited understory; winters in South America. Badly affected by habitat destruction and degradation, here and in its Andean winter quarters. **OBSERVATION TIPS** Best located by song.

BLACKBURNIAN WARBLER
Dendroica fusca L 4.75–5 in

Active warbler that forages for insects high in treetops. Male's orange throat is diagnostic among warblers. Sexes are separable. **ADULT MALE BREEDING** Has mostly black upperparts, including crown, with white lines on back, pale edges to flight feathers, and broad white patch on wing. Face is flushed orange with black patch through eye to ear coverts, continuing as line to side of breast. Breast is flushed yellowish and underparts are otherwise white with black streaks on flanks. Outer tail feathers have extensive white patches.

FEMALE, FALL

ADULT FEMALE BREEDING Recalls adult male, but black elements of plumage are gray and face is flushed yellow, not orange. **ADULT NONBREEDING** Similar to breeding female, but duller and paler. **IMMATURE** Recalls fall adult, but paler overall. **VOICE** Song is a series of thin, high-pitched notes or a series of lower-pitched squeaky *tsi'tu-tsi'tu-tsi'tu* notes; call is a sharp *tsik*. **STATUS AND HABITAT** Common summer visitor (mainly May–Aug) to northern mature mixed coniferous forests and upland forests further south; winters in South America. **OBSERVATION TIPS** Easy to see.

CHESTNUT-SIDED WARBLER
Dendroica pensylvanica L 4.75–5 in

Active little warbler. Adult male is unmistakable and slightly less colorful female is hard to confuse. Sexes are separable. **ADULT MALE BREED-ING** Has streaked black and white back and nape, and blackish wings with pale feather edges and two bold white wing bars. Crown is yellowish and face is white, but with broad, blackish line through eye and blackish "mustache" line. Underparts are mostly white, but has striking chestnut band along flanks. **ADULT FEMALE BREEDING** Similar, but duller and less colorful overall, with streaked crown and less extensive chestnut on flanks. **ADULT NONBREEDING** (seen in fall) Retains some chestnut on flanks and striking wing bars, but has yellowish green upperparts and gray face and throat, grading to otherwise whitish underparts. Note the white eyering. **IMMATURE** Similar to fall adult, but lacks chestnut on flanks. **VOICE** Song is a descending series of sweet whistles, *si-si-si-si, tsi, tsi, tsuu*; call is a tongue-smacking *tchhup*. **STATUS AND HABITAT** Locally common summer visitor (mainly Apr–Aug) to secondary woodland; winters in Central America. **OBSERVATION TIPS** Often forages at low levels in bushes.

FEMALE

MALE

MALE

CERULEAN WARBLER

BLACKBURNIAN WARBLER

FEMALE, BREEDING

MALE, BREEDING

MALE, BREEDING

IMMATURE

CHESTNUT-SIDED WARBLER

FEMALE

Parulidae

CAPE MAY WARBLER *Dendroica tigrina* L 4.75–5 in

Well-marked wood-warbler. Often feeds high in foliage. Pale yellow patch on side of neck is a useful field mark (combined with other plumage features); least obvious in immatures. Sexes are dissimilar. **SPRING MALE** Has olive-yellow upperparts (except side of neck), palest on rump; note the white wing patch (greater coverts). Face is yellowish overall, but with chestnut ear coverts and yellow supercilium. Underparts are mostly yellowish, with bold dark streaks; grades to white on undertail. **SPRING FEMALE** Recalls adult male, but less colorful with olive ear coverts, and two white wing bars. **FALL ADULT** Duller than spring counterparts, male typically without chestnut ear coverts. **IMMATURES** Recall fall adults of respective sex, but with yellow elements of plumage even duller; female is grayish overall. **VOICE** Song is a piping: *peeoo-peeoo-peeoo...*; call is a sharp *tzip*. **STATUS AND HABITAT** Common summer visitor (mainly May–Aug) to boreal forests. Winters in Caribbean. **OBSERVATION TIPS** Easy to see.

MAGNOLIA WARBLER

Dendroica magnolia L 4.75–5 in

Colorful wood-warbler with diagnostic tail underside: white with broad, dark tip. Often feeds at low levels. Sexes are dissimilar. **SPRING MALE** Has blackish back and wings, except for broad, white wing panel. Rump is yellow and dark tail has white marginal band towards middle. Blackish nape links to mask above which is white supercilium and blue-gray crown. Underparts are mostly bright yellow with black chest band and streaks from chest band to flanks; undertail coverts are white. **SPRING FEMALE** Similar, but black elements of body plumage are gray or much duller black. **FALL ADULT** Recalls spring female, but lacks white supercilium; has two white wing bars. **IMMATURE** Less colorful than fall adult, unstreaked below. **VOICE** Song is a whistled *swee-swee-swee-sweep*; call is a thin *tzic*. **STATUS AND HABITAT** Fairly common summer visitor (mainly Jun–Aug) to northern mixed coniferous forests. Winters in Central America. **OBSERVATION TIPS** Easy to see.

AUDUBON'S WARBLER
MALE, BREEDING
MALE, NON-BREEDING
FEMALE, BREEDING
1ST-WINTER

YELLOW-RUMPED WARBLER

Dendroica coronata L 5.25–5.5 in

Widespread wood-warbler. Plumage varies across range: "Myrtle Warbler" occurs in north and east and is described below unless otherwise stated; western "Audubon's Warbler" occurs mostly outside range of this book. Yellow rump and yellow flank patch are seen in all birds. Sexes are dissimilar. **SPRING MALE** "Myrtle" has dark gray upperparts, streaked on back, with two white wing bars and yellow crown stripe. Throat is white and has narrow white supercilium. Breast is blackish and underparts are white with dark streaks and yellow flank patch. "Audubon's" is similar, but has yellow throat and white wing patch. **SPRING FEMALE** Similar to respective male, but paler, with indistinct crown patch. **FALL ADULT** Duller than spring counterpart. **IMMATURE** Recalls dull, buffish fall female without crown patch; note yellow rump and flank patch, and white wing bars. "Myrtle" has white throat and narrow supercilium; "Audubon's" has buff throat. **VOICE** Song is a trilling series of whistles; call is a soft *chep*. **STATUS AND HABITAT** Common summer visitor (mainly May–Aug) to a variety of mixed woods and open, brushy areas, as well as coniferous forests. Winters in southern U.S. and Central America. **OBSERVATION TIPS** Hard to miss.

FEMALE

FEMALE, IMMATURE

MALE

CAPE MAY WARBLER

FEMALE

MALE

MAGNOLIA WARBLER

IMMATURE

FEMALE MYRTLE, DULL SPRING

YELLOW-RUMPED WARBLER

ADULT MYRTLE, NONBREEDING

MALE MYRTLE, BREEDING

Parulidae

BLACK-THROATED GREEN WARBLER
Dendroica virens L 4.75–5 in

Well-marked, black-throated wood-warbler. Forages actively in vegetation and sometimes gleans insects while hovering. Sexes are separable.
ADULT MALE Has olive-green back, extending up nape to crown. Tail is white
from below and dark, with white outer feathers, from above. Wings are blackish with two striking white wing bars. Face is bright yellow, with olive ear
coverts. Throat and chest are black, while underparts are otherwise mostly
white, with black streaks on flanks and yellow wash on lower chest and rear

FEMALE

of flanks. **ADULT FEMALE** Simi-
lar, but throat is whitish or mottled pale yellow. **IMMA-
TURE** Similar to adult female, but black elements of
plumage on underparts are greatly reduced, consisting
mainly of grayish streaks on flanks. **VOICE** Song is a
buzzing *tzur-zee-tzur-tzur-zee* or *zee-zee-zee-tzur-zee*; call
is a soft *t'sip*. **STATUS AND HABITAT** Widespread summer
visitor (mainly May–Jul) to mixed and coniferous
forests; breeding range is mainly northern but extends
into uplands further south. Winters around Caribbean.
OBSERVATION TIPS Most widespread in northern forests.

YELLOW-THROATED WARBLER
Dendroica dominica L 5.25–5.5 in

Smart-looking, long-billed warbler. Combination of bright yellow
throat and mostly black face with pale supercilium, white lower "eyelid," and
white patch on side of neck, are diagnostic. Forages in a deliberate manner
for insects, carefully scrutinizing leaves, needles, and crevices as it goes.
Sexes are similar, but separable. **ADULT MALE** Has mostly blue-gray upperparts including nape and rear of crown; grades to black on forecrown. Has dark
wings overall and two striking white wing bars. Face is mostly black, with white
lower "eyelid" and patch on side of neck; supercilium is either pure white (western subspecies) or mostly white, but tinged yellow in front of eye (eastern sub-

FEMALE

species). Throat and chest are yellow and underparts are
otherwise white with blue-gray streaks on flanks. **ADULT
FEMALE** Similar to male but with grayer forecrown and less
striking stripes on flanks. **IMMATURE** Similar to adult female
but with grubby wash on flanks. **VOICE** Song is descending
series of shrill whistles *tsi, tsi, tsi, tsi, tsu-tsu-tsu*; call is a
sharp *t'swit*. **STATUS AND HABITAT** Common summer visitor
(mainly Apr–Aug) to southeastern pine and broadleaved
woodlands, usually near water; winters from southern U.S.
to Central America. **OBSERVATION TIPS** Easy to see.

KIRTLAND'S WARBLER *Dendroica kirtlandii* L 5.5–5.75 in

Endangered warbler that "pumps" tail up and down while feeding. Sexes are
separable. **ADULT MALE** Mostly blue-gray above, streaked on back with two
white wing bars; color on head forms a distinct hood; note the broken white
eyering. Throat and underparts are mostly yellow grading to white on vent and
undertail coverts; has dark streaks on flanks. **ADULT FEMALE** Similar, but paler
and less colorful overall. **IMMATURE** Recalls adult female, but plumage is paler
and less colorful with buff gray wash to upperparts and less distinct eyering.
VOICE Song is a rich, accelerating *wich-tchew-tchew-tchew-tchwe-wee*; call is a
soft *tchh*. **STATUS AND HABITAT** Rare summer visitor (mainly May–Aug) to young
Jack Pine forests in Michigan; fire prevention (fire is essential for forest regrowth) was a major factor
in species' decline. Winters in Bahamas. **OBSERVATION TIPS** Join a U.S. Forest Service guided tour.

BLACK-THROATED GREEN WARBLER

IMMATURE

MALE

YELLOW-THROATED WARBLER

MALE

MALE

FEMALE

KIRTLAND'S WARBLER

PRAIRIE WARBLER
Dendroica discolor L 4.5–4.75 in

Brightly colored warbler with a striking facial pattern. Pumps its tail up and down while foraging for insects. Common name is inappropriate: favors scrub and young secondary growth woodland rather than grassland. Sexes are separable. **ADULT MALE** Has mostly olive-yellow upperparts, including nape and crown, with rufous streaks on back and two rather indistinct yellowish wing bars. Face is mostly bright yellow, but note dark eyestripe linked to dark crescent below eye. Throat and underparts are mostly bright yellow (palest and whitest on undertail coverts) with black streaks on flanks and side of neck. **ADULT FEMALE** Recalls adult male but face is duller and lacks male's striking black pattern. **IMMATURE** Much duller and paler than respective sex adult. **VOICE** Song is an accelerating series of notes, *tsu, tsu, tsu, tsi'si'si'si*, rising in pitch throughout delivery; call is a sharp *tchip*. **STATUS AND HABITAT** Locally common summer visitor (mainly May–Aug) to overgrown fields and colonizing scrub and woodland; winters in mangroves in Florida and around Caribbean. **OBSERVATION TIPS** Easy to see.

BAY-BREASTED WARBLER
Dendroica castanea L 5.25–5.5 in

Adult male is colorful and striking. Sexes are dissimilar. **SPRING MALE** Has streaked, dark gray back and nape, and blackish wings with two white wing bars. Side of head is creamy white toward the rear, face is mainly black, while crown, throat, chest, and flanks are chestnut; underparts are otherwise creamy white. Upperside to mostly dark tail has only limited white tips. Legs are dark. **SPRING FEMALE** Recalls male, except that back, head, neck, and breast are yellowish green, heavily streaked above. **FALL ADULT**

MALE, IMMATURE

Similar to spring female, but less heavily streaked. **IMMATURE** Dull olive-yellow overall with only subtle streaking on back and buff wash on underparts, including undertail coverts; dark wings have two white wing bars. Very similar to immature Blackpoll; note the dark (not orange) legs. *See* that species' description for further distinctions. **VOICE** Song is a rapid series of five or so piercing whistles; call is a thin *tssip*. **STATUS AND HABITAT** Common summer visitor (mainly May–Aug) to mature spruce forests; breeding success influenced by Spruce Budworm numbers. Winters mainly in Central America. **OBSERVATION TIPS** Easy to see.

BLACKPOLL WARBLER
Dendroica striata L 5.25–5.5 in

Striking wood-warbler in spring (especially male), more tricky to identify in fall: immature is similar to other warbler species, notably Bay-breasted. Sexes are dissimilar. **SPRING MALE** Has olive-gray, dark-streaked back and nape, with black cap and white cheek, defined below by black malar stripe. Underparts are white, with bold black streaks on flanks. Legs and feet

are orange-yellow. **SPRING FEMALE** Recalls male, but head is mostly streaked olive-gray, except for whitish throat and dark malar stripe. **FALL ADULT** Similar to spring female. **IMMATURE** Recalls fall adult, but has olive-yellow wash to upperparts and brighter yellow face and underparts. Compared to immature Bay-breasted, note orange legs and feet and white (not buff) undertail coverts. **VOICE** Song is a short series of high-pitched, thin notes; call is a sharp *chip*. **STATUS AND HABITAT** Common summer visitor (Jun–Aug) to boreal, particularly spruce, forests; winters in northern South America. **OBSERVATION TIPS** Easy to see.

MALE, NONBREEDING

FEMALE

PRAIRIE WARBLER

IMMATURE

MALE

FEMALE, DULL SPRING

BAY-BREASTED WARBLER

FEMALE

MALE

BLACKPOLL WARBLER

FEMALE

IMMATURE

MALE

Parulidae

PINE WARBLER *Dendroica pinus* L 5.25–5.5 in

Familiar eastern wood-warbler that is invariably associated with pines. Sexes are similar, but separable with care. **ADULT MALE** Has mostly olive-yellow upperparts with darker wings that show pale feather edges and two white wing bars. On the head, note the broken yellow eyering and yellow loral spot. Throat, breast, and flanks are yellowish, grading to white on belly and undertail coverts; shows faint dark streaks on side of breast. **ADULT FEMALE** Similar, but paler and less colorful overall, with less distinct streaks on flanks. **IMMATURE** Duller and less colorful than respective-sex adult, immature female being gray-buff overall. **VOICE** Song is a rapid, vibrating trill; call is soft *tchip*. **STATUS AND HABITAT** Common summer visitor (mainly Apr–Sep) to pine forests across north of region; present year-round further south and winter range is mainly in southeastern U.S. **OBSERVATION TIPS** Easy to see in suitable habitats.

PALM WARBLER *Dendroica palmarum* L 5.75–5.5 in

Often feeds on ground and pumps tail. Male is subtly brighter than female. Geographical variation exists in plumage: eastern breeders are brighter and yellower than their western counterparts. **SPRING ADULT** Eastern breeder has mostly olive-buff upperparts with faint streaking on back and two very faint, pale wing bars. Head has extensive chestnut crown, yellow supercilium, olive cheeks, and yellow throat with dark malar stripe; underparts are otherwise bright yellow, with rufous streaks on flanks. Western breeder has grayer back and wings; yellow is restricted to throat and undertail coverts. **FALL ADULT AND IMMATURE** Less colorful than their respective spring adult counterparts, lack rufous crown and streaks on flanks, are only lightly streaked above and have faint buff wing bars. Eastern breeder has yellowish supercilium and yellow wash to underparts; western breeder has white supercilium and gray underparts except for yellow undertail coverts. **VOICE** Song is a buzzing trill; call is a sharp *tchik*. **STATUS AND HABITAT** Common summer visitor (May–Aug) to boreal forests, particularly spruce bogs; eastern breeders occur in northeastern Canada and New England, western breeders nest across central Canada. Birds from all areas winter in southeastern U.S. and Caribbean. **OBSERVATION TIPS** Easy to see.

YELLOW WARBLER
Dendroica petechia L 4.75–5 in

Colorful and familiar wood-warbler showing subtle regional plumage variation; northern birds are typically darker than southern ones. Often forages at relatively low levels and easy to observe. Sexes are separable, but all adults are slightly brighter in spring than fall. **ADULT MALE** Bright yellow overall, darkest on back and with two subtle pale wing bars. Breast and flanks are marked with bold reddish streaks. Caribbean subspecies (seen in Florida) is similar, but has a subtly darker crown and more intense streaks on underparts. **ADULT FEMALE** Recalls respective regional male, but is more uniformly yellow overall and with little or no streaking below. **IMMATURE** Recalls adult female with washed out colors; many individuals are olive-gray overall. **VOICE** Song is a whistling *swee'swee'swee'swee-swit-su-su*; call is a sharp *tchup*. **STATUS AND HABITAT** Common summer visitor (mainly Apr–Aug) to wet thickets (especially willow) and secondary woodland edges. Winters in Central and South America. **OBSERVATION TIPS** Easy to see.

PINE WARBLER

FEMALE

MALE

PALM WARBLER

IMMATURE

MALE

YELLOW WARBLER

FEMALE

IMMATURE

MALE

Parulidae

MOURNING WARBLER
Oporornis philadelphia L 5–5.25 in

Shy and rather secretive, plump-bodied wood-warbler that usually feeds on, or near, the ground. Sexes are separable. **ADULT MALE** Has olive-green back, wings, and tail. Has a blue-gray hood (head and neck), lower margin of which is defined by black, scaled-looking bib. Lores are often darkish. Note virtual absence of pale eyering (cf. Connecticut). Underparts are otherwise bright yellow, with olive wash on flanks, and legs are pinkish. **ADULT**

FEMALE, 1ST-FALL

FEMALE Similar, but hood is uniformly pale gray (without black bib and lores). **IMMATURE** Recalls adult female, but has mostly olive-gray head and neck, with indistinct pale eyering, yellowish throat, and darker, incomplete breast band (corresponding to lower margin of adult's hood). **VOICE** Song is a rich *chrr-chrr-chrr-chrr chu'chu*; call is a thin *tchit*. **STATUS AND HABITAT** Fairly common summer visitor (mainly Jun–Aug) to scrub thickets and dense, secondary woodland. Winters in Central and South America. **OBSERVATION TIPS** Presence easiest to detect by sound. Patient observation is needed to obtain good, prolonged views.

CONNECTICUT WARBLER
Oporornis agilis L 5.5–5.75 in

Robust, but relatively sleek-looking terrestrial wood-warbler. Furtive behavior and largely inaccessible breeding habitat make it a challenge to see. Complete white eyering is a reliable feature in all birds. Sexes are separable. **ADULT MALE** Has olive-green back, wings, and tail. Has a gray hood, palest on throat and darkest on lower margin. Note the striking white eyering. Underparts are otherwise bright yellow, with olive wash on flanks. Legs are pinkish. **ADULT FEMALE** Similar, but with duller, browner hood. **IMMATURE** Recalls adult female, but hood and upperparts are warmer buff-brown. **VOICE** Song is a rich, chirpy *wee-chup'chup, wee-chup'chup, wee-chup'chup, wee-chup'chup, wee*; buzzing call is seldom heard. **STATUS AND HABITAT** Scarce summer visitor (mainly May–Aug) to boggy terrain with thick brush in boreal forests. Winters in South America. **OBSERVATION TIPS** To find this elusive species, learn the song from recordings and visit suitable habitats in spring.

KENTUCKY WARBLER *Oporornis formosus* L 5–5.25 in

Secretive, plump, and short-tailed warbler that is easier to hear than to observe. Once seen, however, distinctive appearance makes identification straightforward. Sexes are similar, but separable. **ADULT MALE** Has mostly olive-green upperparts, including nape and rear of crown, grading to speckled black on forecrown. Black markings on face ("mask" and border to throat) are emphasized by broad yellow supercilium and area just behind and partially below eye ("broken spectacles" effect) and yellow throat; rest of underparts are also yellow. Legs are pink. **ADULT FEMALE** Similar, but black elements of head pattern are paler and less extensive. **IMMATURE** Recalls adult female, but blackish elements of head pattern are almost entirely replaced by dark olive. **VOICE** Song is a series of rich, shrill whistles: *tsee'up, tsee'up, tsee'up, tsee'up*; call is a soft *tchup*. **STATUS AND HABITAT** Locally fairly common summer visitor (mainly May–Aug) to waterside deciduous forests; winters in Central and South America. **OBSERVATION TIPS** A challenge to see, given its furtive nature and relative inaccessibility of its favored breeding habitat.

MALE

MALE

MOURNING WARBLER

CONNECTICUT WARBLER

ADULT

FEMALE, IMMATURE

FEMALE

MALE

KENTUCKY WARBLER

CANADA WARBLER *Wilsonia canadensis* L 5–5.25 in

Colorful, well-marked, relatively long-tailed wood-warbler. Searches for insects among foliage, but also flycatches. Sexes are separable. **ADULT MALE** Has deep blue-gray upperparts, darkest on wings, forehead, and ear coverts. Note the spectacled effect (top, front of white eyering continuing as curved yellow line to base of bill). Underparts, including throat, are mostly bright yellow, but with blackish streaked breast band forming a char-

IMMATURE

acteristic "necklace." Legs are pinkish. **ADULT FEMALE** Recalls adult male, but upperparts are paler and "necklace" is paler and much less distinct. **IMMATURE** Similar to adult female, but with paler forehead and even less distinct "necklace." **VOICE** Song is a short, sweet *chut'tti, chuwee, tchwee-sheree*; call is a sharp *ti'up*. **STATUS AND HABITAT** Common, but declining, summer visitor (mainly Jun–Jul) to damp conifer and mixed forests with a dense shrub layer; often found near water. Winters in northern South America. **OBSERVATION TIPS** Fairly easy to see within range, but present only briefly in our region.

WILSON'S WARBLER *Wilsonia pusilla* L 4.75–5 in

Small, plump-bodied wood-warbler with a dainty bill. Forages actively for insects and spiders, and sometimes flycatches. Sexes are separable. **ADULT MALE** Has mostly olive-yellow upperparts, darkest on wings. Black eye and middle crown are emphasized by mostly yellow face, including forehead. Underparts, including throat, are bright yellow. Legs are pinkish. **ADULT FEMALE** Similar to adult male, but crown is variably dark olive, mottled black at the front (i.e. not entirely black). **IMMATURE** Similar to adult female, but crown is entirely olive-brown (no black). **VOICE** Song is a sweet, whistling rattle *wee che'che'che'che'che'che*; call is a tongue-smacking *tchep*. **STATUS AND HABITAT** Common summer visitor (mainly May–Aug) to damp woodland with a dense understory of shrubs. Winters mainly in Central America. **OBSERVATION TIPS** Easy to see, although hard to follow, given its high activity levels.

HOODED WARBLER *Wilsonia citrina* L 5–5.25 in

Colorful and strikingly marked wood-warbler. Forages actively for insects and usually feeds at fairly low levels in foliage; sometimes flycatches. Often flicks its relatively long tail and reveals extensive white on outer feathers. Sexes are separable. **ADULT MALE** Has mostly olive-green upperparts, although wings are subtly darker. Face is bright yellow and framed by black surrounding area from rear of crown, nape, and sides of neck to throat.

FEMALE, IMMATURE

Underparts are bright yellow and legs are pink. **ADULT FEMALE** Similar, but black elements of male's head pattern are much reduced in extent and intensity. **IMMATURE** Recalls adult female (with pale yellow face), but black elements of head pattern are entirely olive. **VOICE** Song is a rapid series of sweet whistles: *wee'tu-wee'tu-wee'tu-wee-tee-tu*; call is a sharp *chip*. **STATUS AND HABITAT** Locally common summer visitor (mainly May–Aug) to broadleaved forests with a dense understory; often close to water; winters in South America. **OBSERVATION TIPS** Presence is easiest to detect in first instance by listening for its song.

CANADA WARBLER

MALE

FEMALE

FEMALE

WILSON'S WARBLER

FEMALE

MALE

FEMALE

HOODED WARBLER

MALE

Parulidae

WORM-EATING WARBLER
Helmitheros vermivorum L 5–5.25 in

Unobtrusive, stocky, and relatively long-billed wood-warbler with understated body plumage, but rather striking markings on head. Forages among foliage for insects, particularly caterpillars, often searching carefully among hanging tangles of dead leaves. Sexes are similar. **ADULT** Has mostly buff-brown upperparts, including wings and tail. Head is buffy overall, but with long black eyestripe (reaching back to nape) and equally long and parallel dark line on side of crown. Throat and underparts are warm buff, flushed peachy orange on breast. Legs are pale pink. **IMMATURE** Very similar to adult. **VOICE** Song is a rapid, almost insectlike trilling rattle; call is a sharp *tsip*. **STATUS AND HABITAT** Locally common summer visitor (present mainly May–Aug) to dense mixed or deciduous forests; often associated with steep hillsides. Winters mainly in Central America. **OBSERVATION TIPS** Easy to overlook, so learn and listen for its song to detect its presence in suitable habitat.

SWAINSON'S WARBLER
Limnothlypis swainsonii L 5.25–5.5 in

Plump-bodied, short-tailed wood-warbler with mostly terrestrial habits: typically forages on forest floor, turning leaves in search of invertebrates. Wary and sometimes positively furtive, making observation a real challenge. Sexes are similar. **ADULT** Has mostly gray-brown upperparts, including nape, grading to rufous tinge on the crown. Dark buff eyeline and cheeks emphasize the long, pale supercilium. Throat and underparts are pale and unmarked with grayish wash on flanks. **IMMATURE** Similar to adult. **VOICE** Song is a whistled *tsee-tswee-tse-tsu-swe-su*; call is an abrupt *tswe'*. **STATUS AND HABITAT** Scarce summer visitor (present mainly Apr–Sep) to rhododendron woodland in Appalachians but inundated valley-bottom forests in southeastern U.S. Winters in Central America and around Caribbean. **OBSERVATION TIPS** A challenge to find, so learn and listen for its song and be sure to visit suitable habitats.

OVENBIRD *Seiurus aurocapilla* L 5.5–6 in

Plump, mainly terrestrial wood-warbler. Appearance and some of its habits recall those of thrushes. Forages among leaf litter on forest floor for invertebrates. Combination of crown pattern and proportionately large eye (emphasized by striking white eyering) are diagnostic. Species is named after its domed nest that is sited on the ground. Sexes are similar. **ADULT** Has mostly olive-brown upperparts and wings. Has a striking black-

1ST-FALL

bordered, orange crown. Face is olive-brown, with white eyering surrounding the dark eye. Throat is white with black malar stripe; under-parts are otherwise mostly white with bold black spots and streaks, concentrated mainly on the breast and flanks. Legs are pinkish. **IMMATURE** Similar to adult, but has two subtly pale wing bars; crown color is marginally less intense. **VOICE** Song is a vibrant, whistling *ke'Chee ke'Chee ke'Chee ke'Chee*; call is a sharp *tsik*. **STATUS AND HABITAT** Common summer visitor (mainly May–Aug) to mature deciduous and mixed forests; least numerous in west of range. Winters mainly in Central America but to limited extent also in southern U.S. **OBSERVATION TIPS** Listen for the distinctive song, and look for birds foraging unobtrusively on forest floor.

WORM-EATING WARBLER

ADULT

ADULT

ADULT

SWAINSON'S WARBLER

OVENBIRD

ADULT

Parulidae

NORTHERN WATERTHRUSH
Seiurus noveboracensis L 5.75–6 in

Well-marked, rather atypical warbler. Often found near water, typically foraging along muddy margins, constantly pumping tail up and down.
Similar to Louisiana, but see that species' description for separation details.
Sexes are similar. **ADULT AND IMMATURE** Have mostly dark olive-brown
upperparts, including wings and tail. Note the long, bold supercilium that is
an even width and buffy along its entire length. Underparts are whitish overall, with a yellow wash (variable in intensity); has bold dark streaks on throat
and all areas of underparts, except undertail coverts. Legs are stout and dull pink.
VOICE Song is a rich *tu'et-tu'et-tu'et-tu'et tchu-tchu-tchu-tchu*; call is a thin, sharp *tzip*. **STATUS AND
HABITAT** Common summer visitor (mainly May–Aug) to wet habitats (bogs, streams, and rivers) in wooded regions. Winters in Central and northern South America. **OBSERVATION TIPS** Unobtrusive but fairly
easy to see. Found in waterside habitats, even on migration.

LOUISIANA WATERTHRUSH
Seiurus motacilla L 5.75–6 in

Similar to Northern Waterthrush, but marginally larger and longer billed. Voice
and subtle plumage differences (mainly supercilium and throat) are best features for separating the species on migration; breeding ranges barely overlap in
region covered by this book. Habits and habitat preferences are similar to those

ADULT

of Northern. Sexes are similar. **ADULT AND IMMATURE** Have
mostly dark olive-brown upperparts, including wings and tail.
Note the long, bold supercilium that becomes wider above and
behind the eye and is more buff in front of eye, white behind
(even width and uniformly buffish in Northern). Underparts are
whitish overall, with a buff wash on rear of flanks and bold dark
streaks on all areas except throat and undertail coverts (throat
is streaked in Northern). Legs are stout and bright pink. **VOICE**
Song is a resonant, whistling *ti' tsiu tsiu tchew tchew*; call is a
grating *tchtt*. **STATUS AND HABITAT** Common summer visitor
(mainly Apr–Aug) to wet wooded habitats in southeastern
U.S.; winters mainly in Central America and around Caribbean.
OBSERVATION TIPS Presence easiest to detect by song.

COMMON YELLOWTHROAT
Geothlypis trichas L 5–5.25 in

Secretive wood-warbler, easier to hear than to see. Black mask makes
male unmistakable. Sexes are dissimilar. **ADULT MALE** Has olive-brown nape,
back, wings, and tail. Head has broad, black mask, bordered above by a broad,
grayish band, and below by bright yellow throat. Most eastern birds have
bright yellow undertail coverts and grayish flanks; flanks of Gulf coast birds
are usually buffish brown; western birds (outside range covered by this book)
have uniformly bright yellow underparts. Legs are pink in all birds. **ADULT
FEMALE** Lacks male's striking head
markings (face is olive-brown), but is otherwise similar, given
regional variation; yellow throat and undertail coverts are
striking in all birds. **IMMATURE** Similar to adult female, but
throat is less colorful. **VOICE** Song is a vibrant, whistled *wee-
ter, wee-chertee, wee-chertee, wee*; call is a tongue-smacking
tchet. **STATUS AND HABITAT** Common summer visitor (mainly
Apr–Aug) to grassy and brushy marsh habitats, often near
water. Winters from southern U.S. through Central America.
OBSERVATION TIPS Learn the song and call.

FEMALE,
IMMATURE, FALL

NORTHERN WATERTHRUSH

ADULT

LOUISIANA WATERTHRUSH

ADULT

FEMALE

MALE

COMMON YELLOWTHROAT

Parulidae

YELLOW-BREASTED CHAT
Icteria virens L 7.25–7.5 in

Another secretive and furtive wood-warbler, the observation of which is made all the more challenging by the dense nature of its preferred habitat and the near impossibility of exploring it without causing disturbance. Once seen, the species is distinctive on account of its striking plumage, relatively large size, thick bill, and long tail. Sexes are separable with care, although opportunities seldom occur for direct comparison. **ADULT MALE** Has gray-olive back, wings, and tail (with a warmer brownish tint in western birds than eastern ones). Face is grayish overall, but dark eye is emphasized by broken white eyering and upper part leading to base of upper mandible; has black lores. White malar stripe defines margin of yellow throat; yellow breast and flanks; belly and undertail coverts are white. Legs are dark. **ADULT FEMALE** Similar, but markings on head show less contrast. **IMMATURE** Similar to adult female, but duller overall. **VOICE** Song is varied and includes a wide range of harsh chatters and fluty notes (sometimes repeated three or so times) and shrill whistles; call is a harsh *chew*. **STATUS AND HABITAT** Local summer visitor (present mainly May–Aug) to dense shrubby habitats, especially areas where secondary vegetation colonizes damp ground. Winters mainly in Central America. **OBSERVATION TIPS** Learn to recognize the species' song and then patient, quiet observation may pay off. Until you are familiar with the species' habitat requirements it is hard to know if you are in a suitable location if birds are silent.

AMERICAN REDSTART
Setophaga ruticilla L 5–5.25 in

Familiar and well-marked wood-warbler, male of which is stunning. All birds forage actively, often fanning tail to reveal colorful patches at base (orange in adult male, yellow in other plumages); this behavior may startle insect prey allowing easier detection. Sexes are dissimilar. **ADULT MALE** Has mostly black upperparts, but with striking orange patches on wings and base of tail. Head, neck, and chest are black, with orange on sides of breast and flanks, and otherwise white underparts. **ADULT FEMALE** Has greenish gray back, wings, and tail, grayish head, and grayish white underparts; orange elements of male's plumage are yellow. **IMMATURE** Similar to adult female, although some (probably females) have only indistinct yellow color on wings and some males show orange tone to color on flanks and side of breast. First-spring females like adult females; first-spring males show some adult feather details. Full adult plumage is acquired with subsequent molt. **VOICE** Song is a thin, sweet *see-see-see-see-shweer*; call is a thin *chip*. **STATUS AND HABITAT** Very common summer visitor (present mainly May–Aug) to a wide range of wooded habitats, including mature gardens and secondary woodland; range extends across much of the region. Winters mainly in Central and South America, but a few linger in southern Florida. **OBSERVATION TIPS** Easy to see, fun to watch, and usually not especially bothered by people.

MALE, 1ST-SUMMER

YELLOW-BREASTED CHAT

ADULT

MALE

AMERICAN REDSTART

FEMALE

Thraupidae and Emberizidae

SCARLET TANAGER *Piranga olivacea* L 7–7.5 in

Wonderfully colorful, but easy to overlook when perched in dappled foliage, and because it often favors tree canopy for feeding. Combination of bright red body plumage and black wings and tail make male unmistakable. Sexes are dissimilar. **ADULT MALE BREEDING** Has bright red body plumage with black wings and tail. Bill is relatively stout and color varies from pink to gray. **ADULT MALE NONBREEDING** (sometimes seen in fall) Recalls breeding male, but red elements of plumage become yellowish green. **ADULT FEMALE** Has yellowish green plumage overall, with darker wings and tail. **IMMATURE** Recalls adult female, but wings and tail of immature male are much darker than those of immature female. **VOICE** Song is a series of five or six shrill, whistled phrases; call is a tongue-smacking *tchh-brrr*. **STATUS AND HABITAT** Common summer visitor (mainly May–Aug) to deciduous woodland; winters mainly in South America. **OBSERVATION TIPS** Easy to overlook, so listen for its song.

SUMMER TANAGER *Piranga rubra* L 7.5–7.75 in

Male is stunningly colorful, but surprisingly easy to overlook when perched unobtrusively in dappled foliage. Diet includes berries and fruit, but also insects including bees and wasps; stingers are removed by rubbing prey on bark. All birds have a slightly peaked crown. Sexes are dissimilar. **ADULT MALE** Has bright red plumage overall, darkest on wings and tail. **ADULT FEMALE** Usually rather uniformly buff-yellow overall, darkest on wings, back, and tail. Some individuals are mottled with red. **IMMATURE** Recalls adult female at first, but by first spring, male has acquired blotchy red elements to plumage on head, neck, and back. **VOICE** Song is a series of fluty, whistling phrases, mostly disyllabic and with a robinlike quality; call is a rattling *pik-tuk'tuk*. **STATUS AND HABITAT** Common summer visitor (mainly May–Aug) to mixed and deciduous woodland. Winters in Central America. **OBSERVATION TIPS** Fairly easy to see in suitable habitats.

EASTERN TOWHEE
Pipilo erythropthalmus L 7.5–8.5 in

Colorful, long-tailed bird. Scratches ground with both feet together, to expose seeds and insects. Sexes are dissimilar. **ADULT MALE** Has blackish hood, upperparts, and tail, with white edges to tertials and flight feathers, and white at base of primaries. Flanks are reddish orange, undertail coverts are buff, and underparts are otherwise white. Northern birds are larger than southern ones. Most birds have beady red eyes but those from Florida have a pale iris; intermediate eye colors are seen in some southern areas. **ADULT FEMALE** Recalls male, but black elements of plumage are brown. **JUVENILE** Brown and heavily streaked, with two buff wing bars. **VOICE** Song is whistled *sweet-too*, followed by a buzzing trill. **STATUS AND HABITAT** Summer visitor to north of range but present year-round in south; favors dense scrub and brush. **OBSERVATION TIPS** Listen for rustle of feeding birds scratching through leaf litter. Singing males are often conspicuous. **SIMILAR SPECIES Spotted Towhee** *P. maculatus* (L 7.5–8.5 in) is similar, but has white spots on back and two white wing bars; a mainly western species whose range overlaps with Eastern in winter in west of range covered by this book.

MALE

SPOTTED TOWHEE

JUVENILE

TANAGERS and TOWHEES

SCARLET TANAGER

MALE

FEMALE

SUMMER TANAGER

FEMALE

MALE, 1ST-SUMMER

MALE

EASTERN TOWHEE

MALE

FEMALE

MALE, JUVENILE

Emberizidae

GRASSHOPPER SPARROW
Ammodramus savannarum L 5–5.25 in

Secretive, grassland sparrow; seldom willingly leaves cover of its favored meadow habitats. Feeds mainly on insects, but seeds are also eaten. Like other *Ammodramus* species, has relatively large head, long bill, and short tail. Sexes are similar, but subtle subspecies differences are recognized across range. **ADULT** Has dark brown upperparts overall, but feathers on back and tertials, in particular, have rufous margins. Dark crown has white central stripe and note broad, pale supercilium, grayish behind eye, but buffy in front with color extending onto lores. Has a white eyering and buffy face with a dark spot on ear coverts. Underparts are pale and unmarked, with buff wash on breast and flanks that is more pronounced in fall than spring. **JUVENILE** Recalls adult, but is heavily streaked on breast and flanks. **VOICE** Song is a high-pitched, insectlike buzzing trill preceded by a short *tik* or *tik-tok* notes; call is a sharp *tsip*. **STATUS AND HABITAT** Locally common summer visitor (mainly Apr–Sep) to tall and dense grassy habitats, from prairies to hay meadows. **OBSERVATION TIPS** Easiest to see well in spring when males sing from relatively exposed position.

HENSLOW'S SPARROW
Ammodramus henslowii L 5–5.25 in

Scarce and secretive grassland sparrow with a relatively large head. Always a real challenge to find: typically creeps away from observer through matted grasses and is extremely hard to flush. Feeds mainly on insects. Sexes are similar. **ADULT** Has rich brown upperparts overall, but pale edges to back feathers align to create lengthways lines. Tertials and wing coverts have rufous edges, creating panels of color. Crown is brown with dark marginal line, and buffy face is dark on ear coverts with dark malar and mustachial stripes. Underparts are pale, washed buff and dark-streaked on breast and flanks. **JUVENILE** Similar, but paler overall, with less intense streaking. **VOICE** Song is a sharp *t'silik*, easy to overlook amid rustling grass, and because species is most vocal at dawn and dusk; call is a thin *tsic*. **STATUS AND HABITAT** Scarce and local summer visitor to weedy grassland, present within breeding range mainly May–Sep; winters in southeastern U.S., favoring similar grassy areas with matted vegetation. **OBSERVATION TIPS** Count yourself lucky if you see this species. Learn and listen for its song to improve your chances.

LE CONTE'S SPARROW
Ammodramus leconteii L 5–5.25 in

Secretive sparrow that prefers to scurry from danger rather than fly, often through and under flattened grass tussocks. Color and pattern on face are distinctive. Sexes are similar. **ADULT** Has warm buffy brown upperparts overall, but alignment of dark-centered, buff-edged back feathers creates lengthways lines. Face looks buff-orange overall, but note dark crown with white central stripe, and blue-gray ear coverts with two dark spots. Pale throat is defined laterally by thin dark stripes and lightly streaked breast is flushed buff-yellow; underparts are otherwise whitish, with dark streaks and buffy wash on flanks. **JUVENILE** Similar, but patterns and colors on head are muted. **VOICE** Song is a strangled-sounding buzzing trill; call is a thin *tzeet*. **STATUS AND HABITAT** Locally common summer visitor (mainly May–Sep) to marshes and wet grassland. Winters in southeastern U.S. **OBSERVATION TIPS** Easiest to see in spring.

HENSLOW'S SPARROW

ADULT

ADULT

GRASSHOPPER
SPARROW

ADULT

ADULT

ADULT

LE CONTE'S SPARROW

Emberizidae

SALTMARSH SHARP-TAILED SPARROW
Ammodramus caudacutus L 5–5.25 in

Secretive, habitat-specific sparrow whose cryptic plumage (notably lines on back) is a good match for dead stems of salt-marsh grasses. Similar to Nelson's; ranges and habitat overlap in winter. Note Saltmarsh's longer bill, dull streaking on supercilium behind eye (unmarked in Nelson's), and bolder dark streaks on underparts. Sexes are similar. **ADULT** Has brown upperparts overall with white margins on back feathers aligning to form lengthways lines. Has blue-gray on nape and cheeks, and streaked dark crown with a blue-gray central line; face is otherwise mostly orange-buff with a dark line behind the eye and a whitish throat. Underparts are whitish with dark streaks on breast and flanks, and buff wash to side of breast and flanks. **JUVENILE** Recalls adult, but shows less contrast in plumage overall and has a more extensive orange-buff wash to underparts. **VOICE** Song is a vibrating, hissing trill; call is a sharp *tssic*. **STATUS AND HABITAT** Very common locally, but entirely restricted to coastal salt marsh and adjacent grassy marshes. Summer breeding range extends north to Maine, winter range extends south to Florida. Threatened by habitat loss and degradation. **OBSERVATION TIPS** Easiest to find in spring.

NELSON'S SHARP-TAILED SPARROW
Ammodramus nelsoni L 4.75–5 in

Secretive sparrow that runs from danger and is very hard to flush. Plumage markings provide good camouflage. Feeds on invertebrates and seeds. Sexes are similar; interior-breeding birds are brighter than birds from Arctic or east. **ADULT** Has rich brown back and wings; pale margins to back feathers align to form lines (white in interior birds, duller gray in birds from elsewhere in species' range.). Head has dark-bordered gray crown and yellowish buff face, with dark line behind eye and blue-gray ear coverts; nape is also blue-gray. Throat is pale and unmarked, breast and flanks are streaked and flushed yellow-buff; underparts are otherwise white. **JUVENILE** Recalls adult, but is bright yellow-buff overall with little streaking on underparts. **VOICE** Song is a vibrating, hissing trill; call is a sharp *tssic*. **STATUS AND HABITAT** Locally common summer visitor (mainly Jun–Sep) to grassy freshwater marshes in interior; Arctic and eastern birds favor salt marshes. Winters on coastal Atlantic salt marshes. **OBSERVATION TIPS** Least tricky to find in spring.

SEASIDE SPARROW *Ammodramus maritimus* L 5.75–6 in

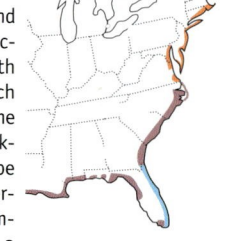

Long-billed salt-marsh sparrow with rather dark plumage. Feeds on seeds and salt-marsh invertebrates. Sexes are similar, but three distinct groups are recognized. **ADULT** "Atlantic coast" form has gray-brown plumage overall, with rufous on wings; white throat is bordered by dark malar stripe above, which is pale, and yellow-washed submustachial stripe; note also the yellow line above and in front of eye. "Gulf Coast" form is similar, but with more striking black markings on head and blackish streaks on back and breast. "Cape Sable" (Florida) form has less rufous on wings and cleaner-looking underparts (not visible in this picture): whitish with black streaks. **JUVENILE** Similar to respective regional adult, but warmer buff overall. **VOICE** Song is a wheezy *t'zup-bree'erzz*; call is a soft *t'zup*. **STATUS AND HABITAT** Restricted to grassy salt marshes and generally scarce, threatened by loss and degradation of habitat. Present year-round in many parts, but northern breeders move south in winter. **OBSERVATION TIPS** Less tricky to see than other coastal *Ammodramus* sparrows.

SALTMARSH SHARP-TAILED SPARROW

NELSON'S SHARP-TAILED SPARROW

ADULT

ADULT

SEASIDE SPARROW

ADULT

ADULT, CAPE SABLE

ADULT, GULF COAST

VESPER SPARROW *Pooecetes gramineus* L 6.25–6.5 in

Not unduly shy and often feeds on ground in the open. Uses poles and isolated trees as song posts. Sometimes mixes in small flocks with other sparrow species. Sexes are similar. **ADULT** Has brown, streaked back; mostly dark tail has white outer feathers (striking in flight). Wing feathers have mostly dark centers and pale margins, but note chestnut lesser coverts (often hidden by body feathers) and two subtle pale wing bars. Dark-streaked crown has pale central stripe. Has a white eyering, dark line behind eye, and dark margins to ear coverts. Whitish throat is bordered by dark stripe and pale underparts are streaked on breast and flanks. **JUVENILE** Similar, but warmer buff overall. **VOICE** Song (sometimes sung at dusk) comprises two or three drawn-out whistles, followed by a chattering trill; call is a sharp *tchip*. **STATUS AND HABITAT** Rather scarce summer visitor (mainly Apr–Sep) to arid grassland and sagebrush; declining due to changes in farming. Winters in southern U.S. and Mexico. **OBSERVATION TIPS** Sometimes feeds beside roads.

SAVANNAH SPARROW
Passerculus sandwichensis L 5.5–5.75 in

Well-marked sparrow. Unobtrusive, but sometimes perches in bush if flushed and then easy to see, albeit briefly. Shows geographical variation in

ADULT

ADULT, IPSWICH

size, color, and bill size. Given this variation, sexes are similar. **ADULT** From most of range covered by this book is brown overall, with bold dark streaking on back. Inner flight feathers and greater coverts look reddish brown in most birds; note also two subtle pale wing bars. Tail is brownish. Darkish crown has indistinct pale central stripe; note dark line behind eye and yellowish supercilium. Pale "mustache" and throat are separated by dark malar stripe. Underparts are pale, but with reddish streaks on breast and flanks. "Ipswich Sparrow" ssp. *princeps* is much paler overall, with sandy buff upperparts. **JUVENILE** Similar to respective subspecies adult. **VOICE** Song is a two-part, buzzing trill (*bzzzrt-tzeee*), preceded by two or three *chip* notes; call is a thin *stip*. **STATUS AND HABITAT** Summer visitor (mainly Apr–Sep) to open grassy habitats. Most birds winter from southern U.S. south. "Ipswich Sparrow" breeds on Sable Island, Nova Scotia and winters on Atlantic coast, favoring dunes. **OBSERVATION TIPS** Easy to see.

SONG SPARROW *Melospiza melodia* L 6–7 in

Familiar, rather long-tailed songster. Central breast spot (not always obvious) is a useful field mark, but not exclusive to this species. Mixes with other sparrows in winter and visits feeders. Shows plumage and size variation across its range with numerous subspecies recognized; eastern birds are fairly uniform and are described below. Sexes are similar. **ADULT** Has streaked brown back, reddish brown wings and tail, and two pale wing bars. Crown is brown with pale central stripe. Face is gray overall; dark eyeline emphasizes the pale supercilium. Has a pale malar stripe and dark border to whitish throat. Breast and flanks are brown and streaked. Underparts are otherwise mostly whitish, but undertail coverts are streaked. Overall, most eastern (described previously) and southwestern birds are warmer brown than most western birds. **JUVENILE** Similar to adult, but more buff overall. **VOICE** Song comprises three or four whistles followed by a trill and variable rich, fluty notes; call is a flat *cheerp*. **STATUS AND HABITAT** Common in open habitats; widespread resident, but a summer visitor to interior north. **OBSERVATION TIPS** Easy to see.

SPARROWS

VESPER SPARROW

ADULT

SAVANNAH SPARROW

ADULT

ADULT

SONG SPARROW

ADULT

ADULT

ADULT, FALL

LINCOLN'S SPARROW
Melospiza lincolnii L 5.75–6 in

Plump-bodied sparrow with understated, but subtly attractive plumage. Smaller and shorter-tailed overall than Song Sparrow. Peaked crown is often raised when agitated. Sexes are similar. **ADULT** Has streaked brown back and reddish brown wings, with two indistinct pale wing bars, and reddish brown tail. Head is marked with brown crown and pale central stripe, and broad, gray supercilium, defined below by dark line through eye. Cheeks are grayish and has buff malar stripe and dark line bordering faintly streaked whitish throat. Breast and flanks are washed buff and heavily streaked; under-parts are otherwise whitish. **JUVENILE** Similar, but more buff overall and with more distinct wing bars. **VOICE** Song starts with a breezy *zee-err*, followed by a delightful series of jingling trills, each on a differ-ent pitch; call is a soft *tchup*. **STATUS AND HABITAT** Common summer visitor (mainly Apr–Sep) to weedy, brushy fields and other open habitats, often close to water; winters from southern U.S. to Central America. **OBSERVATION TIPS** Easy to see.

SWAMP SPARROW *Melospiza georgiana* L 5.75–6 in

Dumpy looking sparrow; similar to Lincoln's, but with much more rufous wings, tail, and (when breeding) crown. Calls of two species are also different. Sexes are similar. **ADULT SUMMER** Has streaked brown back and rufous wings and tail. Crown is rufous and face is gray overall, with dark eyestripe, and dark lower edge to ear coverts bordering the buffy malar

ADULT

stripe. Dark line borders unstreaked white throat and underparts are other-wise mostly unmarked gray, but with rufous wash on flanks. **ADULT WINTER AND IMMATURE** Similar, but crown is dull brown with pale central stripe; breast and flanks are streaked. **JUVENILE** Similar to winter adult, but browner overall and more heavily streaked. **VOICE** Song is a sweet, musical rattle, about 2–3 seconds in duration; call is a sharp *tchip*. **STATUS AND HABITAT** Common summer visitor (mainly Apr–Sep) to shrubby wetlands; winters from southeastern U.S. to Central America. **OBSERVATION TIPS** Fairly easy to see. Like many other sparrows, responds to "pishing."

LARK SPARROW
Chondestes grammacus L 6.25–6.5 in

Large, well-marked sparrow. Often feeds on relatively open ground, hence easy to see. Forms small flocks outside breeding season. In flight, note the long, rounded, and mostly dark tail with striking white edges; pattern also used in display. Sexes are similar. **ADULT** Has streaked, gray-brown back and brown wings with faint pale wing bars. Head is boldly patterned: chest-nut crown with pale central stripe, white supercilium, dark-framed chestnut ear coverts, and black malar stripe bordering white "mustache" and throat. Underparts are otherwise whitish, with striking dark central breast spot. **JUVENILE** Similar, but duller and much more streaked. **VOICE** Song is a series of musical trills, buzzing phrases and whistling notes; call is a thin *tsit*. **STATUS AND HABITAT** Fairly common summer visitor (mainly Apr–Aug) to bare, grassy ground, open woodland, and prairies with scattered bushes and trees. Winters in southern U.S. and Mexico. **OBSERVATION TIPS** Easy to see in suitable habitats, but usually fairly thinly scattered.

LINCOLN'S SPARROW

ADULT

SWAMP SPARROW

ADULT

LARK SPARROW

ADULT

Emberizidae

BACHMAN'S SPARROW *Aimophila aestivalis* L 6–6.25 in

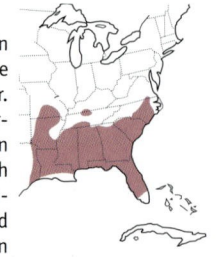

Southeastern specialty that is endemic to U.S. Presence is easy to detect in spring when singing, but otherwise it is secretive and hard to flush. Subtle regional variation exists in plumage. Given this variation, sexes are similar. **ADULT** From west or northeast of range, has reddish brown and gray upperparts overall, colors align to form lengthways stripes on back. Reddish brown crown has pale central stripe; note the gray supercilium and face with reddish brown eyestripe. Underparts are pale, flushed buffy brown on breast. Southeastern subspecies is darker overall and has buff elements of plumage replaced by gray. **JUVENILE** Similar to respective adult, but with bolder head pattern and more pronounced streaking below. **VOICE** Song is a sweet, tuneful rattle, preceded by a thin "inhaled" whistle; call is a sharp *t'zip*. **STATUS AND HABITAT** Scarce in open grassy and brushy areas within pine forests; present year-round in many locations, but breeding range extends north in spring. Threatened by habitat loss and degradation. **OBSERVATION TIPS** Fairly easy to see when singing, but otherwise a real challenge to find.

AMERICAN TREE SPARROW
Spizella arborea L 6–6.25 in

Distinctive sparrow. Combination of bicolored bill (dark upper mandible, yellowish lower one), subtle rufous eyestripe, and dark breast spot, are good identification features. Forms flocks outside breeding season. Birds are brightest in breeding season and sexes are similar. **ADULT** Has dark-streaked rufous back and rufous wings with two pale wing bars. Face is gray overall, but with rufous crown and stripe behind eye, and subtle dark stripe bordering gray throat. Underparts are otherwise pale gray, with rufous wash on flanks and dark breast spot. **JUVENILE** Recalls adult, but is heavily streaked.
VOICE Song is a descending series of rather piercing notes, ending with a trilling flourish; call is a thin *tseeup*. **STATUS AND HABITAT** Locally common summer visitor (mainly Apr–Sep) to shrubs and trees at northern edge of boreal forest; winters in weedy, grassy habitats adjacent to trees and shrubs across much of U.S. except south. **OBSERVATION TIPS** Easy to see in suitable habitats.

FIELD SPARROW *Spizella pusilla* L 5.75–6 in

Superficially similar to American Tree Sparrow, but distinguished by its uniformly pinkish (not bicolored) bill and absence of breast spot. Chipping Sparrow (*see* p.292) has a different face pattern: dark eyestripe and white supercilium. Forms flocks outside breeding season. Eastern birds are marginally warmer brown overall than western birds. Sexes are similar. **ADULT** Has a dark-streaked reddish brown back and wings with two white wing bars. Face is gray overall, but has a rufous crown and eyestripe. Underparts are washed rufous on breast and flanks. **JUVENILE** Similar to adult, but heavily streaked below. **VOICE** Song is a series of rich, whistling, disyllabic *tee-oo* phrases, ending in an accelerating trill; call is a sharp *tik*. **STATUS AND HABITAT** Common summer visitor (mainly Apr–Aug) to grassy, weedy fields with nearby scrub; found year-round in much of southeast and winter range extends to Mexico. **OBSERVATION TIPS** Easy to see. Sometimes perches in bushes when disturbed.

BACHMAN'S SPARROW

ADULT, WESTERN

ADULT, SOUTHEASTERN

ADULT

FIELD SPARROW

AMERICAN TREE SPARROW

MALE

JUVENILE

Emberizidae

CHIPPING SPARROW *Spizella passerina* L 5.5–5.75 in

Familiar, well-marked sparrow. Forms flocks outside breeding season and often rather tame in suburban parks and gardens. Sexes are similar, but plumage varies seasonally. **ADULT BREEDING** Has dark-streaked buffy brown back and buffy brown wings with two whitish wing bars. Paler, grayer rump is sometimes observed in flight. Plumage is otherwise mostly gray, but note the chestnut crown, white supercilium, and dark eyestripe. Also has whitish throat. **ADULT NONBREEDING** Similar, but has brown crown with pale central stripe and buff supercilium. **JUVENILE** Recalls nonbreeding adult, but is heavily streaked. First winter recalls nonbreeding adult, but brown elements of plumage are buffy. It is the only sparrow to migrate in its juvenile plumage. **VOICE** Song is a rapid, rattling trill with a rather inanimate quality; call is a thin *tzip*. **STATUS AND HABITAT** Common summer visitor (mainly May–Sep) to a range of open wooded habitats, including parks and mature gardens. **OBSERVATION TIPS** Easy to see.

CLAY-COLORED SPARROW
Spizella pallida L 5.5–5.75 in

Fairly distinctive when breeding, but nonbreeding birds are similar to Chipping Sparrow. At that time, Chipping has richer brown upperparts, with more contrasting face pattern: darker eyestripe, paler supercilium, and more rufous crown. Forms flocks outside breeding season. Sexes are similar. **ADULT BREEDING** Has heavily dark-streaked brown back and brown wings with two white wing bars; note the buffy brown rump. Nape is gray, crown is brown, and has whitish supercilium; brown ear coverts are defined above by dark eyestripe and below by dark malar stripe, and note white "mustache" and throat. Underparts are otherwise gray-buff. **ADULT NONBREEDING** Paler and more buff overall, most noticeably on underparts and supercilium. **JUVENILE** Similar to nonbreeding adult, but heavily streaked below. **VOICE** Song is a series of breezy, vibrating, buzzing trills, vaguely cricketlike; call is a thin *tzip*. **STATUS AND HABITAT** Fairly common summer visitor (mainly May–Aug) to grassland and prairies; winters in similar habitats, mainly in Mexico (scarce in southern Texas). **OBSERVATION TIPS** Fairly easy to see on breeding grounds.

WHITE-THROATED SPARROW
Zonotrichia albicollis L 6.5–6.75 in

Woodland sparrow. Forms flocks outside breeding season. Sexes are similar, but two colour morphs occur. **ADULT** Has dark-streaked brown back and reddish brown wings with two white wing bars; rump and tail are gray-brown. Has dark crown; "White-striped" form has pale central stripe and broad supercilium (white behind eye, yellow-buff in front); "Tan-striped" form has yellow-buff central stripe and supercilium. All birds have white throat and gray cheeks and underparts, palest on belly and undertail coverts.

ADULT, TAN-STRIPED FORM

JUVENILE Recalls adult, but is heavily streaked below; head markings are indistinct. First-winter recalls "Tan-striped" adult, but duller overall. **VOICE** Song is a piercing, whistling *see-tsee-chrr-ch'd'd-ch'd'd*; call is a sharp *cheenk*. **STATUS AND HABITAT** Common summer visitor (mainly Apr–Aug) to northern mixed and deciduous forests; winters in dense wooded and brushy habitats, mainly in southeastern U.S. Present year-round in parts of northeast. **OBSERVATION TIPS** Often visits feeders.

ADULT, NONBREEDING

CHIPPING SPARROW

JUVENILE

ADULT, BREEDING

ADULT, BREEDING

ADULT, NONBREEDING

CLAY-COLORED SPARROW

WHITE-THROATED SPARROW

ADULT

ADULT

Emberizidae

WHITE-CROWNED SPARROW
Zonotrichia leucophrys L 7–7.5 in

Distinctive sparrow that is widespread and familiar in winter, when it forms large flocks. Subtle subspecies variation exists across range; taiga breeders are described here. Sexes are similar. **ADULT** Has dark-streaked brown back and reddish brown wings with two white wing bars; tail and rump are gray-brown, and has black eyestripe and black crown with bright white central stripe. Supercilium is very broad and white behind eye and plumage is otherwise mostly gray with limited brown on flanks. Bill is dull pink. **JUVENILE** Immature and first-winter recalls adult, but is heavily streaked above and below. First-winter recalls adult, but black elements of head pattern are brown. **VOICE** Song comprises a couple of piercing whistles followed by several bird-squeakerlike grating chirps; call is a sharp *pink*. **STATUS AND HABITAT** Generally common summer visitor (mainly May–Aug) to weedy and brushy areas, sometimes seen in taiga woodland. Winters from southeastern U.S. to Mexico. **OBSERVATION TIPS** Easy to see.

HARRIS'S SPARROW
Zonotrichia querula L 7.5–8 in

Large, plump, and distinctive sparrow. All birds have a pink bill. Endemic to Canada as a breeding species. Forms flocks outside the breeding season and mixes with other sparrow species. Sexes are similar, although typically male has larger bib than female and bib increases in size with age. **ADULT BREEDING** Has streaked reddish brown back and reddish brown wings with two white wing bars. Head has largely gray cheeks with black crown, face, throat, and bib, and ear covert margins. Underparts are whitish gray, with dark streaks on flanks. **ADULT NONBREEDING** is similar, but gray ele-

ADULT, NONBREEDING

ments of head plumage are buffish brown and dark crown is speckled. **JUVENILE** Lacks black on face and has streaked breast and flanks. First-winter has hint of adult's black face markings, but a white throat and dark streaking on breast. **VOICE** Song comprises long, drawn-out and penetrating whistles; call is a sharp *tchink*. **STATUS AND HABITAT** Locally common summer visitor (mainly May–Sep) to stunted boreal forests on brushy fringes of tundra; in winter, favors open woodland and scrub in central Great Plains. **OBSERVATION TIPS** Note species' restricted breeding and winter ranges.

FOX SPARROW *Passerella iliaca* L 7–7.25 in

Large, plump-bodied sparrow whose plumage markings and bill size vary across its vast geographical range. Darker and grayer western subspecies are not covered here and the descriptions below relate to taiga-breeding "Red" birds. In all birds, streaks and spots on breast often coalesce to form a central spot or patch of dense spots. Sexes are similar. **ADULT** Has gray and reddish back and wings, with two indistinct wing bars, and striking red and gray pattern on face. Underparts are boldly streaked reddish brown. Bill is pinkish orange. **JUVENILE** Similar to adult. **VOICE** Song is a sweet, whistled *swee too-wee, see tchet-tchu-tchu ee*; call is a sharp *tch'tup*. **STATUS AND HABITAT** Common summer visitor (present mainly May–Aug) to taiga woodland, especially with willows and alders. Winters from southeastern U.S. to Mexico. **OBSERVATION TIPS** Often visits feeding stations, but otherwise rather unobtrusive outside breeding season.

WHITE-CROWNED SPARROW

IMMATURE

ADULT

HARRIS'S SPARROW

ADULT, BREEDING

FOX SPARROW

ADULT

Emberizidae

DARK-EYED JUNCO *Junco hyemalis* L 6.25–6.5 in

Confusingly variable across its huge geographical range, represent-ed by several different-looking subspecies "groups." Only "Slate-colored" birds are widespread in range covered by this book; descriptions below refer to these birds unless otherwise stated. Forms flocks outside breeding season. All birds have white outer tail feathers and a dark eye. **ADULT MALE** "Slate-colored" has mostly slate-gray plumage, except for white belly and undertail coverts; bill is pink. "Oregon" birds (whose Midwest winter range comes close to that covered by this book) have a black hood, reddish brown upperparts, and white underparts with a reddish wash on the flanks. **ADULT FEMALE** Recalls male of respective subspecies group, but in "Slate-colored" gray elements of plumage are tinged rufous, especially on crown and wings. "Oregon" females are paler overall than their male counterparts. **JUVENILE** Recalls adult female, but is browner and heavily streaked. **VOICE** Song is a rapid, trilling *tu'tu'tu'tu'tu*; call is a tongue-smacking *tchht*. **STATUS AND HABITAT** Common in coniferous and mixed forests. Present year-round in central parts of range but common in summer (mainly May–Aug) to northern boreal forests, wintering throughout U.S. in scrub and woodland. **OBSERVATION TIPS** Easy to see.

LAPLAND LONGSPUR

Calcarius lapponicus L 6–6.25 in

Colorful longspur. All birds have striking reddish brown greater coverts. Forms flocks outside breeding season. Sexes are separable. **ADULT BREEDING MALE** Has buff, brown, and black streaks on back, and brown wings with reddish brown greater coverts and tertial edges. Broad pale stripe (most-ly white, but yellowish behind eye) runs from base of wings, framing the ear coverts to the eye; breast, face, and crown are black, and nape is reddish brown. Underparts are otherwise mostly white, but streaked black on flanks. **ADULT NONBREEDING MALE**

1ST-WINTER

Similar, but paler overall and black elements of plumage are mostly brown, but with dark-framed buff ear patch, white throat, and dark breast. **ADULT FEMALE** Recalls nonbreeding male, but is paler overall. **JUVENILE** Recalls adult female, but is heavily streaked. **VOICE** Song is a short series of scratchy whistles; call is a rattle. **STATUS AND HABITAT** Common summer visitor (mainly Apr–Aug) to northern tundra; winters in bare, grassy habitats. **OBSERVATION TIPS** Easy to see in suitable habitats.

SMITH'S LONGSPUR *Calcarius pictus* L 6–6.25 in

Breeding male is distinctive. All birds have noticeably "warm" buff plumage. Forms flocks outside breeding season, when easy to overlook in favored grassland habitats. Bill is narrower than in Lapland Longspur. Sexes are dissimilar. **ADULT BREEDING MALE** Has streaked brown back and brown wings with two white wing bars and white "shoulder" patch. Head has dark cap with white supercilium and eye surround, and white spot on ear coverts. Underparts and neck are orange-buff. **ALL OTHER PLUMAGES** Recall breeding male, but are duller overall, lack white "shoulder" patch, but have streaked back and nape; black elements of head pattern are replaced by streaked brown, white elements are replaced by buff. **VOICE** Song is a sweet whistling trill; call is a dry rattle. **STATUS AND HABITAT** Local summer visitor (mainly Jun–Aug) to northern tundra; winters in grassland in south-central U.S., from Texas to Iowa. **OBSERVATION TIPS** Note its limited range.

DARK-EYED JUNCO

ADULT, SLATE-COLORED

JUVENILE

MALE, WINTER

LAPLAND LONGSPUR

MALE, BREEDING

SMITH'S LONGSPUR

JUVENILE

MALE, BREEDING

Emberizidae and Cardinalidae

SNOW BUNTING *Plectrophenax nivalis* L 6.75–7 in

Plump-bodied bunting with "fluffy"-looking plumage and a stubby bill. In flight, note the extensive areas of white on the inner wing. Forms flocks outside breeding season. Sexes are separable and there is distinct seasonal variation in adult plumage. **ADULT BREEDING MALE** Has mainly white plumage, except for the black back, outer flight feathers, patch on leading edge of wing and tail center. Legs and bill are black. **ADULT NON-BREEDING MALE** Recalls breeding male, but back has orange-buff feather fringes, and similar color is seen on tertial margins and on fringes of feathers of crown, nape, ear coverts, and

1ST-WINTER

flanks. Orange-buff fringes wear during winter, revealing black and white plumage by spring. Bill is yellow during the winter months. **ADULT FEMALE** Recalls a dull male in respective seasonal plumage, but in summer the white elements of the plumage are grubby while the black feathers are fringed brown. **JUVENILE** Streaked and brownish overall. By first winter, it recalls respective sex winter adult, but with more extensive orange-buff on face and underparts. **VOICE** Song is a tinkling series of twittering whistles; calls include a soft *tiu*. **STATUS AND HABITAT** Common summer visitor (May–Sep) to barren northern tundra, from northern Canada and Greenland west; winters widely across southern Canada and northern U.S. in grassy fields; occasionally seen on beaches. **OBSERVATION TIPS** Fairly easy to find if you visit the high Arctic in spring. In winter, its precise occurrence is unpredictable and flocks soon abandon previously favored sites if food supply is exhausted.

ROSE-BREASTED GROSBEAK
Pheucticus ludovicianus L 8–8.25 in

Large-billed and distinctively marked songbird. Often feeds unobtrusively in cover and can be surprisingly hard to spot in dappled foliage. Diet includes insects and seeds in spring and summer, but feasts on fruits prior to fall migration. Sexes are dissimilar. **ADULT BREEDING MALE** Has black hood and back (with white rump), and black wings with white "shoulder" patch, wing bar, and base to primaries; latter seen as broad patch in flight when bright red underwing coverts are also noticed. Breast is bright red and underparts otherwise mostly white. First-summer male like adult male, but has some female-like elements in plumage. **ADULT NONBREEDING MALE** (plumage acquired before fall migration) Similar, but black elements of plumage are mottled brown. **ADULT FEMALE** Has mostly streaked brown upperparts with two white wing bars and white base to primaries. Has broad, pale supercilium, and underparts are pale overall but with bold dark streaking. Underwing coverts are yellowish and bill is pink. **JUVENILE** Like heavily streaked female; by first fall, male has hint of red breast. **VOICE** Song is a series of rich, fluty whistles, recalling that of American Robin; call is a sharp *piik*. **STATUS AND HABITAT** Common summer visitor (mainly May–Aug) to open, deciduous woodland; winters in Central America. **OBSERVATION TIPS** Easy to see.

MALE, BREEDING

SNOW BUNTING

1ST-WINTER

MALE, NONBREEDING

ROSE-BREASTED GROSBEAK

MALE, BREEDING

FEMALE

MALE, 1ST-FALL

NORTHERN CARDINAL
Cardinalis cardinalis L 8.75–9 in

Arguably North America's most instantly recognizable bird with its erectile peaked crest, long tail, and male's stunningly colorful plumage. Often visits feeders in winter. Sexes are dissimilar. **ADULT MALE** Mostly bright red except for well-defined black face. Bill is bright red. **ADULT FEMALE** Has mostly gray-buff body plumage with red tail, red tinge on wings, and red tip to crest. Has a limited amount of black on face and subdued red bill. In flight, note the red underwing coverts (underwing is entirely red in male). **JUVENILE** Recalls adult female, but is dull brown overall, with reddish flush to breast and tail in particular. Bill is dark. **VOICE** Song is an insistent series of rich, fluty whistles, typically either *tiu-tiu-tiu-tiu* or *p'dee-p'dee-p'dee-p'dee*; call is a sharp *tik*. **STATUS AND HABITAT** Common resident of wooded habitats, parks, and gardens. **OBSERVATION TIPS** Easy to see in most parks and gardens within its range.

BOBOLINK *Dolichonyx oryzivorus* L 7–7.25 in

Well-marked grassland bird. Often perches conspicuously and forms flocks outside breeding season. Male performs song flight in spring. Sexes are dissimilar. **ADULT BREEDING MALE** Has mostly black plumage, but with buff nape, white rump, and white "shoulder" patch (scapulars); edges of tertials and greater coverts are edged white. **ADULT BREEDING FEMALE** Has buffy brown plumage overall, with dark streaking on back, and

FALL BIRD

with dark centers and buff margins to covert feathers and tertials. Head has dark stripe behind eye and dark crown with pale central stripe. Throat is pale and underparts are otherwise pale buff, with dark streaking on flanks. **ALL OTHER PLUMAGES** Similar to breeding female, but warmer buff overall. **VOICE** Song (given in flight) is a fluty and vaguely onomatopoeic *b'bob-o-lii'ink* followed by various chattering notes; call is a melodious *pink*. **STATUS AND HABITAT** Common summer visitor (mainly May–Aug) to tall-grass prairies and weedy meadows. Winters in central South American grassland. **OBSERVATION TIPS** Easy to see.

DICKCISSEL *Spiza americana* L 6.25–6.5 in

Sparrow-like grassland bird with a proportionately large bill. Forms huge flocks outside breeding season and prior to migration. Sexes are dissimilar. **ADULT MALE** Has a dark-striped, gray-brown back, reddish brown wings, and gray tail and nape. Head is gray overall, but with striking yellow supercilium and eye surround, yellow malar stripe and black bib surrounding white throat patch. Underparts are flushed yellow on breast, grading to grayish white on belly; undertail coverts are white. Colors are subdued in nonbreeding plumage and black bib is obscured by pale feather fringes. **ADULT FEMALE** Recalls a dull, washed-out male with no black bib and more extensive white throat. **JUVENILE** Recalls plain adult female with hint of adults' face pattern. **VOICE** Song is a repeated, vaguely onomatopoeic *dik-dik-dik, ciss-sess-sel*; call is a buzzing *fzzppt*. **STATUS AND HABITAT** Common summer visitor (mainly May–Aug) to Midwest prairies and farmland; numbers and breeding locations affected by factors such as rainfall. Winters mainly in Venezuelan llanos, where subject to persecution in agricultural areas. **OBSERVATION TIPS** Easy to see in Midwest.

NORTHERN CARDINAL

FEMALE

MALE

FEMALE

MALE, BREEDING

BOBOLINK

DICKCISSEL

FEMALE

MALE

Cardinalidae

BLUE GROSBEAK *Passerina caerulea* L 6.75–7 in

Plump-bodied bird with a large, conical bill. Bill size allows separation of colorful male from superficially similar Indigo Bunting; female's plain, unstreaked plumage allows separation from female Rose-breasted Grosbeak, which has similarly large bill. Feeds unobtrusively in brush, but sometimes sings from exposed perch. Sexes are dissimilar. **ADULT MALE** Stunning, with mainly blue plumage; note the two reddish brown wing bars, buffy tertial edges, and black face. **ADULT FEMALE** Has brown plumage overall, darker above than below and with two reddish brown wing bars and pale throat. **JUVENILE** Recalls adult female, and by first winter has warmer reddish brown plumage overall. By first spring, male acquires blue color on head, rump, and tail. **VOICE** Song is a burst of bright, chirping whistles; call is a sharp *pink*. **STATUS AND HABITAT** Common summer visitor (mainly May–Aug) to brushy areas and neglected, overgrown grassland; winters in Central America. **OBSERVATION TIPS** Easy to see.

INDIGO BUNTING *Passerina cyanea* L 5.5–5.75 in

Familiar roadside bird in many areas, and stunning male sometimes perches on fence wires, twitching tail in an agitated manner. Forms flocks outside breeding season. Sexes are dissimilar. **ADULT BREEDING MALE** Has mostly uniformly bright blue plumage, darkest and grayest on flight feathers; bill is silvery gray and conical. **ADULT NONBREEDING MALE** Has blotchy brown and blue plumage (caused by brown feather edges); resplendent again by spring. **ADULT FEMALE** Has brown plumage overall, darker above than below and with two faint wing bars and faint streaking on underparts. **JUVENILE** Recalls adult female; by first spring, male acquires some blue elements of adult's plumage, but still looks blotchy. **VOICE** Song is a slightly descending series of chirpy, slurred whistles, ending in a trilling flourish; call is a sharp *stik*. **STATUS AND HABITAT** Common summer visitor (mainly May–Sep) to weedy fields, scrubby margins to deciduous woods, and similar habitats, often found in the vicinity of water. Winters mainly in Central America. **OBSERVATION TIPS** Easy to see.

PAINTED BUNTING *Passerina ciris* L 5.5–5.75 in

Male is flamboyantly colorful and color combination might be considered vulgar if employed in fashion! Rather secretive nature and unobtrusive habits (often feeds in deep cover) can make it hard to spot. Sexes are dissimilar. **ADULT MALE** Has mostly blue hood, with narrow bright red center to throat; underparts and rump are also bright red. Back is bright yellowish green and wings are brown with green feather margins. **ADULT FEMALE** Has mostly bright yellowish green upperparts including tail and hood, and mostly paler yellow underparts including narrow throat. **JUVENILE** Recalls plain, gray-buff version of adult female, with only hint of green on upperparts; by first spring, male has acquired some of adult's blue and red feathering. **VOICE** Song is a sweet series of warbling whistles; call is a sharp *tchip*. **STATUS AND HABITAT** Locally common summer visitor (mainly May–Sep) to dense undergrowth and thickets bordering woods and streams; winters mainly in Central America, but also southern Florida. **OBSERVATION TIPS** Often a challenge to find, despite its bright colors.

FEMALE

MALE, 1ST-SPRING

BLUE GROSBEAK

MALE

FEMALE

MALE, 1ST-SPRING

INDIGO BUNTING

MALE

FEMALE

PAINTED BUNTING

MALE

Icteridae

EASTERN MEADOWLARK
Sturnella magna L 9.5–10 in
Long-billed grassland bird that often sings from roadside posts. Easily recognized as a meadowlark and recognition as such is straightforward across most of its eastern range where it is the only meadowlark species present. But, specific identification is tricky where range overlaps with Western Meadowlark. Note Eastern's white malar stripe bordering the yellow throat, and the greater extent of white in its outer tail. Also, flank markings tend to look streaky in Eastern, but spotty in Western. Subspecies plumage variation exists across range; Southwestern "Lilian's" (*lilianae*) is palest and most similar to sympatric Westerns. Sexes are similar. **ADULT** Has marbled brown upperparts. Head has buff cheeks, dark stripe behind eye, and dark crown. Pale supercilium is yellow in front of eye and yellow throat is bordered by white malar stripe and defined below by "V"-shaped black chest band. Underparts are flushed yellow on breast, grading to white on belly and with dark spots on flanks. In winter, black "V" is obscured by pale feather tips. **JUVENILE** Similar to winter adult. **VOICE** Song is a whistled *tsee'oo'ee tseeuu*; call is a rattle. **STATUS AND HABITAT** Common and widespread in grassland; largely resident, but northern birds migrate south in fall. **OBSERVATION TIPS** Easy to see.

ADULT, NONBREEDING

WESTERN MEADOWLARK
Sturnella neglecta L 9.5–10 in
Very similar to Eastern Meadowlark and also found in similar grassy habitats, perching on fence posts and the like. In areas of overlap, usually found in drier habitats. Specific identification can be a challenge: note differences in voice; Western Meadowlark's fuller yellow throat (yellow extends onto malar stripe while Eastern Meadowlark has a more distinct white malar stripe bordering its yellow throat); and extent of white in the outer tail—in Western Meadowlark outer two feathers are white, third-in having limited white (Eastern Meadowlark has three white outer tail feathers, fourth-in having limited white). To add to the confusion, northern birds are darker than southern ones; given this variation, sexes are similar. **ADULT** Has marbled brown upperparts including wings. Head has buff cheeks, dark stripe behind eye, and dark crown. Pale supercilium is yellow in front of eye and yellow throat is defined below by "V"-shaped black chest band. Underparts are flushed yellow on breast, grading to white on belly and with dark spots on flanks. In winter, black "V" is obscured by pale feather tips. **JUVENILE** Similar to winter adult. **VOICE** Song is a short burst of fluty whistles *tu'lu Tee te'oo tliu'oo-tu*; call is a dull *tchuup*. **STATUS AND HABITAT** Common and widespread in grassland and on farmland; resident in center of its range, but northern birds migrate south in fall and winter range extends to Texas. **OBSERVATION TIPS** Easy to see.

ADULT, NONBREEDING

ADULT

EASTERN MEADOWLARK

ADULT

WESTERN MEADOWLARK

ADULT

Icteridae

YELLOW-HEADED BLACKBIRD
Xanthocephalus xanthocephalus L 9.5–9.75 in
Stocky wetland bird. Male is unmistakable. Forms flocks outside breeding season. Sexes are dissimilar and male is larger than female. **ADULT MALE** Has bright yellow hood and breast (with black eye surround), and otherwise mostly black plumage, except for striking white wing patch (primary coverts). **ADULT FEMALE** Has a yellowish buff face and breast (palest on throat, malar stripe, and supercilium) and otherwise rather uniform and unstreaked dark brown plumage. **JUVENILE** Yellow-buff overall, darker above than below, with two white wing bars; first-winter female is similar to adult female; first-winter male is similar to adult female, but has hint of adult white wing patch, plus dark lores and more intense yellow suffusion on head. **VOICE** Song comprises harsh, grating and chattering screeches; call is a dry *k'duk*. **STATUS AND HABITAT** Common summer visitor (mainly May–Aug) to marshy habitats; winters mainly in Mexico. **OBSERVATION TIPS** Easy to see.

RED-WINGED BLACKBIRD
Agelaius phoeniceus L 8.75–9 in
Widespread and familiar bird. Forms huge foraging and roosting flocks outside breeding season. Sexes are dissimilar. **ADULT MALE** Has mostly black plumage with red colorful "shoulder." In winter, black elements of plumage have subtle brown edges. **ADULT FEMALE** Brown overall and heavily streaked on back and underparts; plumage is palest on throat (sometimes washed pinkish buff) and has a pale supercilium. **IMMATURE MALE** Similar to winter adult, but with more extensive brown edging to feathers. **IMMATURE FEMALE** Recalls adult female, but lacks pinkish buff wash to throat. **VOICE** Song is harsh, grating and screechy; call is a sharp *tchik*. **STATUS AND HABITAT** Contender for North America's most abundant bird; favors farmland and wetlands. Present year-round across much of central and southern U.S., and summer range extends to fringe of Arctic. Northern birds move south in fall and winter range extends to Central America. **OBSERVATION TIPS** Hard to miss, even in suburbs.

RUSTY BLACKBIRD *Euphagus carolinus* L 9–9.25 in
Pale-eyed blackbird with a slender bill. Named after rusty feather margins seen in fall and early winter. Sexes are dissimilar. **ADULT BREEDING MALE** Has blackish plumage overall with a green sheen in good light. **ADULT NONBREEDING MALE** Has rusty brown feather edges over much of body, which slowly wear away such that plumage is usually pristine black by late winter. **ADULT BREEDING FEMALE** Dark gray-brown overall, darkest on wings and tail. **ADULT NONBREEDING FEMALE** Has rusty brown edges to many feathers; color is particularly striking on head (where supercilium contrasts with darker eyestripe), back, and tertials. **IMMATURES** Similar to respective-sex

FEMALE, SUMMER

winter adults. **VOICE** Song is a series of gurgling chatters (recalling a distant flock of European Starlings) followed by a breezy whistle; call is a soft *tchuk*. **STATUS AND HABITAT** A wet woodland species. Favors northern and taiga forests for breeding (present there mainly May–Sep). Winters in southeastern U.S. Formerly common, but now threatened: numbers have declined catastrophically in recent decades. **OBSERVATION TIPS** Breeding grounds are hard to access, so easiest to see in winter.

YELLOW-HEADED BLACKBIRD

FEMALE

MALE

RED-WINGED BLACKBIRD

FEMALE

MALE

MALE, BREEDING

ADULT, NONBREEDING

RUSTY BLACKBIRD

Icteridae

BREWER'S BLACKBIRD
Euphagus cyanocephalus L 9–9.25 in
Widespread and familiar colonially nesting bird. Often bold in subur-
ban locations. Sexes are dissimilar. **ADULT BREEDING MALE** Has black
plumage overall; in good light, has purple sheen on head and blue-green
sheen to back, wings, and breast. Note the pale iris. **ADULT NONBREEDING
MALE** Duller, due to brownish feather edges, which gradually wear off.
ADULT FEMALE Rather uniform dark gray-brown, darkest on wings and tail.
Iris is dark in most birds. **IMMATURES** Similar to respective sex winter adults.
VOICE Song is a piercing, squeaky whistle, sometimes followed by call-like *tchak*
notes. **STATUS AND HABITAT** Commoner west of range covered by this book, but still a widespread sum-
mer visitor to farmland and other open habitats. Migrates south in fall and winters in southeastern U.S.
Range has expanded overall due to human alteration of natural environment. **OBSERVATION TIPS** Easy
to see and often tame in suburban parks and gardens.

BROWN-HEADED COWBIRD
Molothrus ater L 7.5–7.75 in
Widespread and familiar open country bird, reviled in some quarters
because of the impact its nest-parasitizing lifestyle has on songbirds. Effect
on certain endangered species is undeniable but, as with most things in natural world, the story behind many species' decline is seldom clear-cut. Sexes
are dissimilar. **ADULT MALE** Has a dark brown hood and otherwise blackish
plumage, with a green sheen in good light. **ADULT FEMALE** Plain brown overall, darkest on wings and tail; note the subtly pale throat, malar stripe, and
eye surround and supercilium. **JUVENILE**

JUVENILE

Similar to adult female, but with pale feather margins on back,
faint pale wing bars, and streaked underparts. **VOICE** Song is a
couple of quacking gurgles followed by a thin, upslurred whistle; call is a rattling *krrr'k*. **STATUS AND HABITAT** Common and
widespread in farmland and open habitats. Resident in south of
range but a migrant summer visitor (present mainly Apr–Aug)
to northern and interior regions. Range and population expanded greatly during 19th century: Benefited from forest clearance
and creation of farmland. **OBSERVATION TIPS** Hard to miss.

FEMALE

BRONZED COWBIRD
Molothrus aeneus
L 8.75–9 in
Plump, thick-billed cowbird. Relative head size changes according
to whether generous nape feathers are raised and ruffled or not. All
adult birds have beady red eyes. Nest
parasite of other songbirds. Sexes are
dissimilar. **ADULT MALE** Has black plumage overall, with
bronze sheen to hood and back and blue sheen to wings and
tail. **ADULT FEMALE** Has dark brown plumage overall, darkest on wings and tail. **JUVENILE** Similar to female, but iris is
dark. **VOICE** Song is a series of weird gulping gurgles and upslurred squeaks; call is a harsh *tchak*. **STATUS AND HABITAT**
A mainly Central American species with a toehold in southern
states; locally common summer visitor (mainly May–Aug) to
farmland; winters mainly in Central America. **OBSERVATION
TIPS** Fairly easy to see in southern Texas.

FEMALE

MALE

BREWER'S BLACKBIRD

FEMALE

BROWN-HEADED COWBIRD

MALE

BRONZED COWBIRD

MALE

FEMALE

Icteridae

COMMON GRACKLE *Quiscalus quiscula* L 12–12.5 in

Eastern North America's commonest grackle, separated from black-birds by its long bill and long, graduated tail, which male holds keeled in cross-section. Male performs elaborate displays, including tail-fanning and body-arching. All adult birds have a pale iris. Male is larger than female and sexes are separable by plumage differences. Subspecies variation exists. **ADULT MALE** Looks all black in poor light. "Bronzed" ssp. has blue head and bronze sheen to body. "Purple" ssp. has blue hood and chest and purple sheen to body. Florida ssp. has green sheen to back. **ADULT FEMALE** Similar to respective male,

FEMALE

but duller overall and with less noticeable sheen. **JUVENILE** Recalls adult female, but plumage is uniform brown, darkest on wings and tail; iris is dark. **VOICE** Song is harsh and grating; call is a sharp *tchuk*. **STATUS AND HABITAT** Common in open and lightly wooded habitats, including farmland and gardens. Occurs year round in southeastern U.S. ("Purple" ssp.); "Bronzed" ssp. occurs north and west of Appalachians as a summer visitor (mainly May–Sep) with birds moving south and east in fall. Florida ssp. is resident in Florida. **OBSERVATION TIPS** Easy to see.

BOAT-TAILED GRACKLE *Quiscalus major* L 14–17 in

Distinctive, mainly coastal bird. Easy to recognize, within range, by male's long, paddle-shaped tail and extroverted behavior. Feeds mainly on the ground, probing for food with its pointed bill. Eye is pale in Atlantic coast birds, but darker and brownish in Florida and Gulf coast birds. Sexes are dissimilar and male is noticeably larger than female. **ADULT MALE** Has black plumage; in good light a bluish sheen is visible on the head, grading to greenish on the body. **ADULT FEMALE** Has reddish brown plumage overall, darkest on wings and tail. Tail is relatively shorter than in male. **JUVENILE** Similar to adult female, but duller. **VOICE** Song consists of a mixture of strange dry rattles, hisses, and grating chatters; call is a soft *tchak*. **STATUS AND HABITAT** Locally common resident of coastal wetlands; mostly sedentary, but harsh winter weather forces some northern birds to move south. **OBSERVATION TIPS** Easy to see within range and in suitable habitats.

GREAT-TAILED GRACKLE
Quiscalus mexicanus L 15–18 in

Large and raucous, slim-bodied grackle with a long, daggerlike bill. Forms flocks outside breeding season. All birds have relatively long, narrow wings and all adults have a pale iris. Male is larger than female and has a bizarrely long, diamond-shaped tail (appreciably longer than female's tail). Sexes are separable on plumage differences too. **ADULT MALE** Has blackish

FEMALE

plumage overall, but in good light note the bluish violet sheen on much of the body. **ADULT FEMALE** Has brown plumage overall, darkest on wings and tail, and warmest and palest on throat, chest, and supercilium. **JUVENILE** Similar to adult female, but with streaking on underparts, and dark eye. **VOICE** Song is a strange mix of slurred whistles and electrical static-type sounds, usually ending in a staccato, mechanical rattle; call is a soft *tchut*. **STATUS AND HABITAT** Formerly primarily a Mexican species that is now very common in southern U.S., favoring open habitats from farmland to parks and gardens; year-round resident in most parts but range extends north in summer. **OBSERVATION TIPS** Noisy and conspicuous, hence hard to miss.

COMMON GRACKLE

MALE, "BRONZED"

MALE, "PURPLE"

FEMALE

BOAT-TAILED GRACKLE

MALE

MALE

GREAT-TAILED GRACKLE

MALE

Icteridae

MALE, 1ST-SPRING

ORCHARD ORIOLE

Icterus spurius L 7.25–7.5 in
Eastern North America's smallest oriole; has a slender, pointed and slightly downcurved bill. Sexes are dissimilar. **ADULT MALE** Has a black hood, chest, and back, and brick-red underparts and "shoulders." Wings are black, with a white wing bar and white edges to flight feathers. Rump is brick-red and tail is black. **ADULT AND IMMATURE FEMALE** Have mostly yellow plumage, grading to olive-yellow on back. Dark wings have two white wing bars and white edges to flight feathers. Rump is yellow and tail is grayish. **IMMATURE MALE** Has a black face and throat, but otherwise mostly yellow plumage, grading to olive-yellow on back. Dark wings have two white wing bars and white edges to flight feathers. **VOICE** Song is a jaunty series of fluty whistles; call is a harsh chatter. **STATUS AND HABITAT** Locally common summer visitor (mainly May–Aug) to open wooded habitats, including orchards, parks, and waterside woodlands. Winters mainly in Central America. **OBSERVATION TIPS** Fairly easy to see in suitable habitats.

BALTIMORE ORIOLE *Icterus galbula* L 8.5–8.75 in

Colorful woodland bird. Bill is slender, pointed, and gray. Sexes are dissimilar. **ADULT MALE** Has black hood and back, and orange "shoulders" and underparts. Dark wings have white wing bar and white edges to flight feathers. Rump is orange and tail is orange overall with dark base and

FEMALE

midline. **ADULT FEMALE** Similar, but hood and back are variably mottled dark olive-brown, and "shoulder" stripe is white; rump and tail are dull orange-buff. **IMMATURE** Recalls adult female, but male is richer orange on breast and undertail coverts; female is much paler overall, especially on belly. **VOICE** Song is a whistling *chew-di-chewdi-chew-chew-che*, uttered as though bird is losing enthusiasm; call is a rattle. **STATUS AND HABITAT** Common summer visitor (mainly May–Aug) to deciduous woodlands. Winters mainly in Central and South America; a few linger in southeastern U.S. **OBSERVATION TIPS** Easy to see in suitable wooded habitats.

HOODED ORIOLE *Icterus cucullatus* L 8–8.25 in

Slim-bodied, colorful oriole with a proportionately long tail. Bill is slender and downcurved. Sexes are dissimilar. **ADULT MALE** Has mostly orange body plumage, with a black face and throat, and black back. Wings are black with two white wing bars and white edges to flight feathers. Tail is dark and rump is orange. In winter, pale feathers can be seen on back. **ADULT AND IMMATURE FEMALES** Have mostly dull yellow face and underparts, palest on flanks. Crown, nape, and back are olive-gray and dark wings have two white wing bars and white edges to flight feathers. Rump and tail are olive-gray. **IMMATURE MALE** Recalls female, but by first spring has acquired incomplete version of adult's black face and throat. **VOICE** Song is a rapid series of chattering, warbling phrases; call is a harsh *tchet* or *tchew*. **STATUS AND HABITAT** Locally common summer visitor (mainly Apr–Aug) to open woodland, often near water and sometimes in suburban areas; winters in Mexico. **OBSERVATION TIPS** Usually easy to see and sometimes quite bold, within its limited range.

ORCHARD ORIOLE

FEMALE

MALE

FEMALE

BALTIMORE ORIOLE

MALE

FEMALE

HOODED ORIOLE

MALE

Fringillidae

RED CROSSBILL *Loxia curvirostra* L 6–6.25 in

Plump-bodied finch whose bill has cross-tipped mandibles (feature shared only with White-winged); used to extract seeds from between scales of conifer cones. Precise size and shape of bill varies subtly across region and several forms (possibly even species) occur, each adapted to feed on different conifer species. Forms nomadic flocks outside breeding season. Sexes are dissimilar. **ADULT MALE** Has mostly deep red plumage overall, darkest and brownest on wings and tail. Note, some birds show indistinct pale wing bars (cf. White-winged). **ADULT FEMALE** Has dull yellow-green plumage

FEMALE

overall, darkest and brownest on wings and tail. **JUVENILE** Brown and heavily streaked, paler below than above. First-year male recalls adult female, but plumage is yellow-orange. First-year female is similar to adult female. **VOICE** Song begins with, and includes, several flight call-like *kip-kip* notes, and often ends in a buzzing trill. Experts can discern differences in calls among separate populations. **STATUS AND HABITAT** Locally common resident of mature coniferous forests. Irruptive and wandering behavior make precise occurrence hard to predict. **OBSERVATION TIPS** Listen for its distinctive call.

WHITE-WINGED CROSSBILL
Loxia leucoptera L 6.5–6.75 in

Cross-tipped mandibles and bold white wing bars make for easy recognition (wing bars are much more striking than on variant Red Crossbill). Forms roving flocks outside breeding season. Sexes are dissimilar. **ADULT MALE** Has bright pinkish red plumage overall, palest and grayest on belly and flanks. Dark wings have two broad white wing bars; tail is blackish. **ADULT FEMALE** Has streaked, dull olive-yellow plumage overall, but dark wings show similar pattern to male. **JUVENILE** Brownish and heavily streaked, paler below than above; wing bars are less distinct than on adult. First-year male recalls adult male but red elements of plumage are bright pinkish yellow. First-year female is similar to adult female. **VOICE** Song is a series of vibrating trills and whistles; flight call is a sharp *chip-chip*. **STATUS AND HABITAT** Fairly common resident of northern coniferous forests, especially favoring larch and spruce. Occurrence is hard to predict: wanders in search of ripe cones. **OBSERVATION TIPS** Feeding flocks can be hard to find.

PINE GROSBEAK *Pinicola enucleator* L 9–9.25 in

Plump-bodied finch with a stout, stubby bill. Sometimes forms small flocks outside breeding season, but often seen in ones and twos. Feeds on buds, seeds, and fruits. Typically, indifferent to observers allowing great views. In all birds, eye is emphasized by dark eyeline and subtle pale, elongate "eyelids." Sexes are dissimilar. **ADULT MALE** Has pinkish red plumage overall with varying amounts of gray on flanks and belly. Tail is dark and blackish wings have two strik-

FEMALE

ing white wing bars. **ADULT FEMALE** Shares male's dark tail and blackish wings with two white wing bars, but plumage is otherwise mostly grayish with varying amounts of olive-yellow on head, back, and rump. **JUVENILE** Brown overall, with pale wing bars. First-year birds are similar to adult female. **VOICE** Song comprises far-carrying, whistled phrases, such as *p'wee-wee, p'wee-wee, p'wee-wee...*; call is a whistled *piew*. **STATUS AND HABITAT** Local in coniferous forests; wanders and partly migratory outside breeding season. **OBSERVATION TIPS** Usually found in small numbers.

CROSSBILLS and GROSBEAKS

JUVENILE

MALE

RED CROSSBILL

MALE, MOLTING

JUVENILE

WHITE-WINGED CROSSBILL

FEMALE

MALE

PINE GROSBEAK

MALE

Fringillidae

PINE SISKIN *Carduelis pinus* L 5–5.25 in

Small finch with a slender, dainty bill. Feeds primarily on seeds; those of birch, alder, and spruce are favored. Forms roving flocks in winter and visits bird feeders. Sexes are dissimilar. **ADULT MALE** Brown overall and heavily streaked above, its whitish underparts also heavily streaked; some birds have yellow-washed underparts. Wings have two wing bars, upper one narrow and white, lower one broad and tinged yellow; edges of flight feathers are variably yellow (obvious in flight and when perched). **ADULT FEMALE** Similar to plain-colored male; yellow elements of wing feathering are much less intense than the brighter males. **JUVENILE** Similar to adult female, but plumage is washed buff-yellow overall. **VOICE** Song is a mix of chattering trills and wheezy whistles; call is a buzzing *zhreee*. **STATUS AND HABITAT** Common in coniferous and deciduous forests; found year-round in parts of range, but northern breeders move south for winter and wander, often visiting parks and gardens. **OBSERVATION TIPS** Attract it to your garden using seed feeders.

COMMON REDPOLL *Carduelis flammea* L 5–5.25 in

Compact, well-marked little finch. Pointed bill has curved culmen (Hoary's bill is stubby and culmen is straight). Feeds mainly on seeds, especially in winter, notably those of alder and birch. Forms roving flocks outside breeding season. Sexes are dissimilar. **ADULT MALE** Has heavily streaked gray-brown upperparts, the wings with two white wing bars and white edges to flight feathers. Head is streaked gray with a red forecrown ("poll") and black face. Underparts are whitish overall, but heavily streaked on flanks. Breeding male has breast and flanks flushed pinkish red; this character is usually lost in winter although flanks are often flushed buff. **ADULT FEMALE** Similar to seasonal male, but always lacks red flush on breast. **JUVENILE** Buffy brown, heavily streaked and lacks adult's red forecrown (acquired by fall). **VOICE** Song comprises rattling twitters and vibrating trills; call is a rattling *ji'ji'ji....* **STATUS AND HABITAT** Common breeder in northern forests; present year-round in parts of range, but northern breeders move south in fall and winter range extends to northern U.S. **OBSERVATION TIPS** Locate flocks by call.

HOARY REDPOLL *Carduelis hornemanni* L 5–5.5 in

Similar to Common Redpoll, but much paler, with a smaller, stubbier bill, and white, unstreaked (or nearly so) rump. Underparts are much less streaked than Common Redpoll counterparts. Forms flocks outside breeding season and sometimes mixes with Common. Sexes are dissimilar. **ADULT MALE** Has buffy white upperparts with streaking on back and nape. Head has pale gray face, red forecrown, and limited black at base of bill and on throat. Underparts are white, with faint dark streaks on flanks; in breeding season, breast is flushed pale pink, but this character is usually absent in winter. **ADULT FEMALE** Similar to winter adult male, but with subtly more noticeable streaking on flanks. **JUVENILE** Similar to adult female, but more heavily streaked on flanks and with buff wash to face and flanks. **VOICE** Song and calls are similar to Common Redpoll. **STATUS AND HABITAT** Breeds in tundra scrub; wanders south in fall and winter range extends across Canada. **OBSERVATION TIPS** Visit the high Arctic in summer or search for individuals among Common Redpoll flocks in winter.

FEMALE

ADULT

MALE

PINE SISKIN

COMMON REDPOLL

ADULT

ADULT

FEMALE

MALE

MALE

HOARY REDPOLL

Fringillidae

AMERICAN GOLDFINCH *Carduelis tristis* L 5–5.25 in

Familiar bird of weedy fields. Forms flocks outside breeding season and often feeds on thistle seeds. Breeding male is stunning. Sexes are dissimilar. **ADULT BREEDING MALE** Has largely bright yellow plumage with contrasting black cap and forehead; mostly black wings have a faint yellow wing bar. Rump and undertail coverts are white and contrast with black tail. **ADULT NONBREEDING MALE** Recalls breeding male, but yellow elements of plumage are yellow-buff above (brightest on face), grading to grayish white on belly; black on crown and forehead usually absent. Wing bar on greater coverts is more apparent and pale lesser coverts (bright yellow in breeding male) are whitish and form a second wing bar. **ADULT FEMALE** Similar to winter male, but brighter yellow overall in summer (with white upper wing bar, buff lower one) and grayer overall in winter (when both wing bars are buff). **JUVENILE** Recalls nonbreeding female but duller. **VOICE** Song is a series of chattering whistles and squeaks; calls include a tinkling whistle. **STATUS AND HABITAT** Common in open woodland and forest edge; widespread resident, but a summer visitor to north. **OBSERVATION TIPS** Easy to see.

FEMALE, BREEDING

PURPLE FINCH *Carpodacus purpureus* L 5.75–6 in

Plump, relatively large-headed finch. Culmen of conical bill is only very slightly curved. Forms small flocks outside breeding season. Sexes are dissimilar. **ADULT MALE** Has mostly reddish pink head and breast, color grading into reddish brown wash and indistinct streaks on flanks; underparts are otherwise whitish in eastern birds, but grubby gray in western birds, all with unstreaked undertail coverts. Back is streaked pinkish brown and dark wings have two pinkish buff wing bars and buffy edges to flight feathers. **ADULT FEMALE** Has mostly streaked gray-brown upperparts; contrast between pale supercilium, submustachial stripe, and throat, and darker ear coverts and malar stripe is greater in eastern birds than western ones. Underparts are whitish with dark streaks (except on undertail coverts), markings more distinct in eastern birds than western ones. **JUVENILE** Similar to adult female. **VOICE** Song is a burst of rich, warbling notes; call is a sharp *pik*. **STATUS AND HABITAT** Common in coniferous forests. Partly resident, but northern breeders move south and east in fall, wintering in southeastern U.S. **OBSERVATION TIPS** Easy to see.

HOUSE FINCH *Carpodacus mexicanus* L 5.75–6 in

Aptly-named: often found near dwellings and visits garden bird feeders. Could be confused with Purple Finch, but note its stubby bill with curved culmen (conical and straightish in Purple), male's brown cheeks and streaked flanks, and female's rather plain face. Sexes are dissimilar. **ADULT MALE** Typically has bright red breast, rump, forehead, and supercilium; center of crown, nape, and back are brown and dark wing has two white wing bars and pale edges to flight feathers. Belly and rest of underparts are mostly white, with clear demarcation from red breast, and bold streaks on flanks. Some birds have an orange tone to breast. **ADULT FEMALE** Has gray-brown plumage, streaked above and below, with two pale wing bars and pale edges to flight feathers. **JUVENILE** Similar to adult female. **VOICE** Song is a series of rich, chattering phrases; call is a shrill *whee'ert*. **STATUS AND HABITAT** Formerly found only in west, now widespread throughout in lightly wooded habitats, parks, and gardens. **OBSERVATION TIPS** Hard to miss.

FEMALE

ADULT, NONBREEDING

AMERICAN GOLDFINCH

MALE, BREEDING

PURPLE FINCH

MALE

FEMALE

MALE

HOUSE FINCH

MALE

Fringillidae and Passeridae

EVENING GROSBEAK
Coccothraustes vespertinus L 8–8.25 in
Plump-bodied finch with a large head and massive, conical bill. Unobtrusive when breeding, but forms noisy flocks in winter. Sexes are dissimilar.
ADULT MALE Unmistakable. Has a bright yellow forehead, supercilium, and
flanks. Lower back is bright yellow, grading through golden yellow to dull
brown on neck and crown. Underparts are golden yellow, flushed bright yellow on flanks. Tail is black and mostly black wings have white secondaries
and tertials; these appear as striking panel when perched and in flight. Bill is
grayish. **ADULT FEMALE** Plumage is mostly gray-buff with hint of yellow wash
on underparts. Mostly black tail has a white tip and mostly black wings have white bases to inner primaries and edges to tertials. Bill is grayish. **JUVENILE** Recalls respective-sex adult in terms of patterns;
female coloration is like adult female while in male yellow elements of adult plumage are buffy brown.
VOICE Song is presumed to be a series of *pee-irp* call notes. **STATUS AND HABITAT** Widespread and common in mixed and coniferous forests. Mostly resident although movements south occur in winter. More
significant irruptive movements south of usual range occur in some winters. **OBSERVATION TIPS** Visits
feeders within range.

HOUSE SPARROW *Passer domesticus* L 6–6.25 in
Introduced from Old World, but now familiar across North America,
mainly because of its affinity for people. Seldom seen far from houses
and farms. Frequently dust-bathes. Often tame where it is fed regularly. Sexes
are dissimilar. **ADULT MALE** Has a gray crown, cheeks, and rump. Nape, sides
of crown, back, and wings are chestnut-brown, underparts are pale gray, and
throat and breast are black. Bill is dark and legs are reddish. In winter, chestnut and black elements of plumage are less intense (due to pale feather fringes)

FEMALE

and bill is paler.
ADULT FEMALE Has
mainly brown upperparts, including crown;
back is streaked with buff. Underparts are
pale gray and note the pale buff supercilium
behind eye. **JUVENILE** Similar to adult female,
but plumage pattern is less distinct. **VOICE**
Utters a range of chirping calls; in combination, these comprise the song. **STATUS AND
HABITAT** Has flourished since its introduc-
tion to North America, first to New York City
in mid-19th century; now common and widespread in town parks, gardens, and farms.
It is faring better here than in many parts of
its native Europe. **OBSERVATION TIPS** Hard
to miss.

EURASIAN TREE SPARROW *Passer montanus* L 6–6.25 in
Well-marked bird that sometimes occurs alongside House Sparrow within its
restricted introduced range. Sometimes forms flocks outside breeding season.
Sexes are similar. **ADULT** Has streaked brown back and wings, with white wing
bars. Cap is chestnut and note the striking black patch on otherwise whitish
cheeks and side of head. Has a black bib; underparts are otherwise grayish
white. **JUVENILE** Similar, but facial markings are duller, darker, and less distinct. **VOICE** Utters chirps similar to a House Sparrow's, but also a sharp *tiktik* in flight. **STATUS AND HABITAT** Introduced from Europe in 19th century
and now an established resident, mainly in Illinois and Missouri; favors farms
and parks. **OBSERVATION TIPS** Hard to miss.

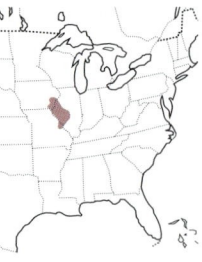

FEMALE

EVENING GROSBEAK

MALE

HOUSE SPARROW

MALE, WINTER

MALE, SUMMER

EURASIAN TREE SPARROW

ADULT

ADULT

BARNACLE GOOSE *Branta leucopsis* L 27–28 in

Striking black, gray, and white goose. Adult has white face, black nape and neck, and whitish underparts; back is gray overall, but submarginal black feather margins create barred effect. Breeds in Greenland, usually winters in Europe, but occasionally turns up in northeast in winter; also widely kept in captivity and regularly escapes.

ADULTS

BARNACLE GOOSE

ADULTS

GRAYLAG GOOSE

GRAYLAG GOOSE *Anser anser* L 34–35 in

Ancestor of domesticated goose, often seen in its ancestral wild-type plumage, but also as pure white. Wild-type bird has gray-brown plumage overall with white stern and pale panels on wing, seen in flight. Bill is stout and pink. Widespread in Eurasia, both wild and domesticated, and in North America widely kept in captivity from which it regularly escapes.

BAR-HEADED GOOSE *Anser indicus* L 30–31 in

Distinctive Asian goose that is widely kept in captivity and occasionally escapes. Adult has mainly gray body plumage with white stern. Neck is gray overall, but with dark nape and white stripe on side. White head is marked with two black bars. Bill is pinkish yellow and legs are orange-yellow.

ADULT

EGYPTIAN GOOSE
Alopochen aegyptiacus L 26–27 in

Distinctive African goose that is often kept in captivity and some-times escapes. Adult has buff plumage overall, grayest on breast (which has dark central spot) and palest on head and neck (eye is dark-masked). Wings have black flight feathers and white coverts, bill is pink and legs are red. Juvenile is paler overall than adult.

ADULT

COMMON SHELDUCK *Tadorna tadorna* L 25–26 in

Goose-sized duck. Common on coasts and wetlands in Europe and Asia. In North America, occasionally escapes from captivity. Adult has green-glossed head and neck (often looks black), black back and flight feathers, and otherwise white plumage, except for orange breast band and flush on undertail coverts. Legs are pink and bill is red, male with a large basal knob. Juvenile shows less plumage contrast than adult.

RUDDY SHELDUCK *Tadorna ferruginea* L 25–26 in

Attractive, goose-sized duck. Widespread Asian wetland species, often kept in captivity. Adult has most-ly orange-brown body plumage, with black flight feathers and white wing coverts, above and below. Neck is orange-buff grading to whitish on face; demarcation between neck and body plumage is clearly defined and marked with narrow black collar in male. Juvenile is paler overall than adult.

MANDARIN DUCK *Aix galericulata* L 16–18 in

Exotic duck that recalls Wood Duck (*see* p.28). Sadly, probably commoner in captivity today than in the wild, in its native China. Male has a striking orange mane with a broad, white supercilium, and orange "sails" near stern. Flanks are finely marked buff and separated from darker breast by vertical black and white lines. Female is similar to female Wood Duck, but has a white eyering, not large white eye surround, and is grayer overall, with more striking pale spots on flanks.

BARNACLE GOOSE — ADULT

GRAYLAG GOOSE — ADULT

BAR-HEADED GOOSE — ADULT

EGYPTIAN GOOSE — ADULT

COMMON SHELDUCK — MALE

MALE

RUDDY SHELDUCK — ADULTS

MANDARIN DUCK — MALE — FEMALE

BROWN BOOBY *Sula leucogaster* L 30–31 in

Large, tropical seabird that recalls immature Northern Gannet (*see* p.70) with its long, narrow wings, cigar-shaped body, and brown and white plumage; seen occasionally off Florida coast and Dry Tortugas. Adult has a white belly, undertail coverts, and underwing coverts, but otherwise dark brown plumage; legs and bill are yellowish. Juvenile is dark brown overall.

GREATER FLAMINGO *Phoenicopterus ruber* L 45–46 in

Unmistakable long-legged, long-necked wetland bird. Common in Caribbean, but status in U.S. is mostly that of an escapee, although genuinely wild birds do sometimes join feral birds in Florida. Adult has pinkish plumage and a banana-shaped, black-tipped pink bill; in flight, wings reveal black flight feathers and reddish pink coverts; the neck and reddish legs are held outstretched. Juvenile has similarly unmistakable shape, but very pale pink plumage.

APLOMADO FALCON *Falco femoralis* L 15–17 in

Impressive and beautifully marked falcon. Widespread and generally scarce in Central and South America; formerly widespread in southern U.S. and becoming re-established thanks to Peregrine Fund program. Male has white face and chest, dark breast band, and otherwise rufous underparts; upperparts are dark. Female has white elements of male's plumage replaced by speckled rufous. Visit Laguna Atascosa Wildlife Area near Brownsville, Texas, for a chance of seeing this species.

COMMON RINGED PLOVER *Charadrius hiaticula* L 7.5–7.75 in

A mainly Eurasian wader, very similar to Semipalmated Plover (*see* p.116). Breeds in Greenland and high Arctic Canada; rare vagrant to northeastern coasts. Adult has sandy brown upperparts and white underparts with a continuous black breast band and collar; has black and white markings on face, and white throat and nape. Dark-tipped orange bill is marginally longer than in Semipalmated; head has a pale supercilium (missing in adult Semipalmated) and its soft *tuu-eep* call is subtly different. Juveniles of two species are hard to separate.

ADULT

ADULT, SUMMER

NORTHERN LAPWING
Vanellus vanellus L 12–13 in

Spiky-crested wader that looks black and white at a distance. Rounded, black and white wings are striking in flight. Eurasian species, rare in northeast in fall and winter, favoring open grassland. Adult has dark green upperparts with sheen in good light; underparts are white, except for orange vent and black foreneck. In winter plumage, throat and foreneck are white, nape is flushed with buff, and back feathers have buffy fringes.

BLACK-HEADED GULL
Larus ridibundus L 16–16.5 in

Mainly Eurasian species that is a rare visitor to northeast and an occasional breeder. Found mainly on coasts, sometimes with Bonaparte's Gulls. Adult has white leading edge to wing and dark trailing edge to outer upper wing. Has a dark brown hood in summer, but dark smudges on otherwise white head plumage in winter. Bill and legs are red, duller in winter than summer. First-winter has bands of rufous and black on upper wings, dark tip to tail, and dark-tipped pink bill.

BROWN BOOBY

ADULT

GREATER FLAMINGO

ADULT

MALE

APLOMADO FALCON

COMMON RINGED PLOVER

ADULT, SUMMER

NORTHERN LAPWING

ADULT

BLACK-HEADED GULL

ADULT, WINTER

ROSS'S GULL *Rhodostethia rosea* L 13–14 in

Stunning Arctic gull. Breeds mainly in Siberia (sometimes Churchill, Manitoba) and winters mostly in Arctic seas. Adult has pale gray back and upper wing, gray underwings, and otherwise mostly white plumage, including wedge-shaped tail and trailing edge to wing; in summer, underparts are faintly flushed pink. Hood is defined by neat black collar; feature reduced or absent in winter birds, which have a dark ear spot. Juvenile recalls winter adult but has dark wing bar.

IVORY GULL *Pagophila eburnea* L 17–19 in

Beautiful Arctic gull. Breeds on Canadian high Arctic islands and Greenland, winters mainly in Arctic seas. Vagrants occur further south in winter. Adult has pure white plumage, with black legs and eye, and yellow-tipped blue bill. First-winter is similar, but with grubby black face markings and black spots on upperparts and wingtips. Feeds on carrion, and vagrants are sometimes attracted to tide-line cetacean corpses.

SOOTY TERN

ADULT

SOOTY TERN *Sterna fuscata* L 14–16 in

Striking, mainly tropical and oceanic tern that breeds on Dry Tortugas, Florida; vagrant on Gulf and Atlantic coasts. Adult has mostly white underparts, with subtly darker flight feathers, and mostly black upperparts, except for the white forehead. Note the deeply forked tail and long, dark bill. Juvenile is similar to adult, but black elements of plumage are sooty brown, as is forehead. Flight is buoyant and powerful, and feeds by picking fish from surface waters.

BRIDLED TERN *Sterna anaethetus* L 13–15 in

Another mainly tropical, oceanic tern that is occasionally seen off Gulf and Atlantic coasts. Similar to Sooty Tern, with mostly white underparts, except for contrastingly dark flight feathers, and sooty black upperparts, except for white forehead; note, however, that dark cap is separated from blackish back by white nape. Juvenile is similar, but black elements of plumage are brown. Flight and habits are similar to Sooty.

BROWN NODDY *Anous stolidus* L 14–16 in

Attractive tropical tern that breeds on Dry Tortugas, Florida and nests in bushes, not on ground like other terns; occurs as a vagrant on Gulf and Atlantic coasts. Adult has mostly sooty brown plumage, but with white cap and nape; juvenile is similar, but with darker cap and nape. Feeds by picking fish and other food from surface of sea, and flight is buoyant and graceful.

WHITE-CROWNED PIGEON *Patagioenas leucocephala* L 13–14 in

Distinctive, mainly Caribbean species that is an Everglades and Florida Keys specialty. Typically nests on isolated mangrove islands and feeds on fruits of tropical shrubs and trees in woodlands on mainland. Has dark plumage overall, with a striking white crown and white iris; in good light an iridescence can be seen on head and neck. Sometimes seen in flocks.

ADULT, WINTER

ROSS'S GULL

ADULT

IVORY GULL

ADULT, WINTER

ADULT

SOOTY TERN

ADULT

ADULT

BRIDLED TERN

BROWN NODDY

ADULT

ADULT

WHITE-CROWNED PIGEON

GREEN PARAKEET *Aratinga holochlora* L 13–14 in

A mainly Mexican species with established feral populations in Florida and Texas, derived from escapes from captivity. In flight, the relatively long tail is striking. Adult plumage is green overall and note the pale eye and pinkish bill; juvenile is similar but has a duller, darker eye.

RED-CROWNED PARROT *Amazona viridigenalis* L 12–13 in

Endangered Mexican native, but a popular cagebird. Feral populations now thrive, locally, in Texas and Florida. Adult has green plumage overall, with black tips to primaries, red flash on secondaries, and red forecrown and bluish hindcrown; extent of red is greatest in male.

MONK PARAKEET *Myiopsitta monachus* L 11–12 in

Distinctive South American species with well-established and possibly increasing feral populations in several areas. Looks long-tailed in flight, and when perched it is recognized by its pale face and underparts, green-capped appearance to rear of head, and otherwise greenish upperparts except for the blue flight feathers.

NOTE: Many parrot family members—from Budgerigars to Macaws—are kept captive as pets. Inevitably, birds escape to freedom and feral populations become established from time to time, a few of which persist. The trade in captive-bred birds fuels, and to a degree, masks, the vile trade in wild-caught birds.

RUFOUS HUMMINGBIRD
Selasphorus rufus L 3.5–3.75 in

Colorful hummingbird that breeds in West (outside range of this book). Winters mainly in Mexico, but in small numbers on U.S. Gulf Coast. Adult male is mainly rufous with variable green feathering; note pale chest band and shining orange-red gorget seen at certain angles; in most light, throat looks dark. Adult female has green upperparts and mainly pale underparts, with rufous on flanks and spots on throat (central red spot seen at certain angles). Juvenile resembles adult female; male soon acquires adult characters. Call is a sharp *tiktik*.

IVORY-BILLED WOODPECKER
Campephilus principalis L 19–20 in

Huge and iconic woodpecker that once lived in forests of southern U.S.; sadly, now almost certainly extinct thanks to habitat loss and degradation. Similar to Pileated Woodpecker (*see* p.202) but with a pale bill, striking white secondaries, and a white line on the side of the back. (Note: A digitally manipulated photograph of a Pileated Woodpecker is shown here to give an impression of what an Ivory-billed would look like.)

GREEN JAY *Cyanocorax yncas* L 10–11 in

Mainly Mexican species that occurs in southern Texas. Has rich green back and wings, grading to blue on nape, above eye, and on cheeks; face is otherwise black, except for white patch in front of eye. From above, tail is blue-green with yellow outer feathers; from below, appears mainly yellow. Underparts are otherwise mostly pale green. Juvenile is duller than adult. Calls include bell-like tones and insectlike, chattering notes.

SPOT-BREASTED ORIOLE *Icterus pectoralis* L 9–10 in

Colorful Mexican oriole, introduced to Florida and now established in gardens there. Adult has mostly orange-yellow plumage, but with black throat, black spots on breast, and black tail and back with white patch at base of primaries and tertials; note also the orange-yellow "shoulder." Juvenile is similar, but black elements of plumage are paler, particularly on the back.

GREEN PARAKEET
ADULT

RED-CROWNED PARROT
ADULT

MONK PARAKEET
ADULT

GREEN JAY
ADULT

SPOT-BREASTED ORIOLE
ADULT

GENERAL BIRDING INFO

Alderfer, Jonathan, and Jon L. Dunn. (eds). 2006. *Complete Birds of North America*. National Geographic Books.

Alderfer, Jonathan, and Jon L. Dunn. 2007. *Birding Essentials*. National Geographic Books.

American Birding Association. 2002. *ABA Checklist: Birds of the Continental United States and Canada*, 6th ed. American Birding Association.

American Ornithologists' Union (AOU). 1998. *Check-list of North American Birds*, 7th ed.

Barrow, M.V. 1998. *A Passion for Birds: American Ornithology After Audubon*. Princeton University Press.

Baughman, Mel (ed). 2003. *Reference Atlas to the Birds of North America*. National Geographic Books.

Dunn, Jon L., and Jonathan Alderfer (eds). 2006. *Field Guide to the Birds of North America*, 5th ed. National Geographic Books.

Ehrlich, Paul R., Dobkin, David S., and Wheye, Darryl. 1988. *The Birder's Handbook*. Simon & Schuster/Fireside.

Elphick, Chris, John B. Dunning, Jr., and David Allen Sibley. 2001. *The Sibley Guide to Bird Life and Behavior*. Alfred A. Knopf.

Gill, Frank B. 2007. *Ornithology*, 3rd ed. W.H. Freeman.

Kaufman, Kenn. 1996. *Lives of North American Birds*. Houghton Mifflin Company.

Kerlinger, Paul. 1995. *How Birds Migrate*. Stackpole Books.

Poole, A., and F. Gill (eds). 1992–2002. *The Birds of North America*. The Academy of Natural Sciences and The American Ornithologists' Union.

Pyle, Peter, with Steve N.G. Howell, David F. DeSante, Robert P. Yunick, and Mary Gustafason. 1997. *Identification Guide to North American Birds, Part I*. Slate Creek Press.

Sibley, David A. 2000. *The Sibley Guide to Birds*. Alfred A. Knopf.

Sibley, David A. 2002. *Sibley's Birding Basics*. Alfred A. Knopf.

WEB RESOURCES

American Birding Association
www.americanbirding.org

American Ornithologists' Union
www.aou.org

Birding on the Net
www.birdingonthe.net

Brian E. Small – Bird and Nature Photography
www.briansmallphoto.com

Cornell Laboratory of Ornithology
www.birds.cornell.edu

eBird
www.ebird.org

The Birds of North America Online
www.bna.birds.cornell.edu/bna

All photographs taken by **Brian E. Small** with the exception of the following:

Nature Photographers Ltd.
Mark Bolton 67(tr), 162(t & b), 315(upper m), 327(lower mr); Laurie Campbell 93(bl); Kevin Carlson 95(lm), 179(tr); Andrew Cleave 61(m inset), 62(b), 170(t), 171(tr), 327(tr & upper mr); Michael Gore 326; Michael Harris 327(bl); Barry Hughes 53(bl); Ernie Janes 53(tl), 95(mr), 115(tl), 132(b); David Osborn 37(b), 69(ml), 71(b and b inset), 73(mr & mr inset), 77(tr), 82(b), 85(bl), 87(ml), 103(bl), 115(b & b inset), 128(upper & lower m), 129(b), 161(m), 164(b), 165(br and upper bl), 166(b), 327(lower m); Bill Paton 53(tr), 176, 183(br); Richard Revels 157(upper ml), 163(lower tl), 168(t), 169(tr), 171(upper bl); Peter Roberts 146(b), 158(t); Paul Sterry 8(l), 11, 12(t & b), 13(t & b), 14(b), 15(b), 16(m), 18(b), 19(t), 21(t), 22(b), 23(Mute Swan × 4), 24(b & b inset), 26, 27(m), 27(upper ml, upper mr, & bl), 30, 31(t & t inset), 32(b), 33(t & upper m), 34(t & b), 36(upper m), 37(t), 40(m), 41(m & m inset), 44(m), 45(m & m inset), 47(t & t inset, m & m inset, & b inset), 48(m & b), 49(m, b, & b inset), 51(upper & lower m, & b), 52, 53(m & m inset), 57(tl, tr, ml, & mr), 58(Yellow-billed Loon × 2), 59(all pictures), 61(t & t inset, & m), 62(t), 63(t), 65(tl, ml, tr, & bl), 67(b), 70(all pictures), 71(t & t insets), 73(ml & bl), 77(tr inset, m, & b), 78(t), 79(tl & tr), 81(tr), 83(tl), 84(t & b), 85(tl), 104(t), 105(tr), 109(tl), 110(t), 118(t), 123(b), 125(b), 129(b inset), 130(t & b), 131(Purple Sandpiper × 3, upper bl), 132(t), 133(upper ml & mr), 135(lower tr), 137(t & bl), 139(ml & b), 140, 141(tl, lower mr, bl, & br), 145(m), 146(t), 147(m & m inset), 149(t, b, & b inset), 150(all Little Gull pictures), 151(bl), 153(tr), 155(tr, mr, bl, & br), 156, 157(tl, tr, upper mr, lower ml, & br), 158(b), 159(t, upper ml & mr, bl, & br), 161(t inset), 163(Arctic Tern × 2), 169(tl, bl, & br), 170(m & b), 171(tl, ml, mr, bl, & br), 172, 175(t & t inset, & bl), 180(b), 181(tr), 182, 193(upper ml), 195(ml & mr), 213(b), 223(bl), 227(bl), 247(t center), 250(t), 251(tl & tr), 253(tr, bl, & br), 267(bl), 274, 296, 297(ml), 298, 299(ml & mr), 320, 321(ml, mr, bl, & br), 322(t & b), 323(all pictures), 324(t & b), 325(tr, mr, bl, & br), 327(tl & ml); Roger Tidman 32(t), 46(t), 57(m center), 58(b), 63(bl & br), 67(tl), 92(t & b), 93(tr, upper br, & lower br), 99(m center), 102(b), 105(m), 117(m & b), 147(bl & br), 148(t & b),
160(t), 164(t), 165(t), 169(mr), 183(bl), 184, 226(t & lower m), 227(tl inset).

Individual photographers
Ron Austing 265(br); Glenn Bartley 195(br); ©J. Culbertson/VIREO 90(tr), 329(br); Mike Danzenbaker 28(b), 36(t), 38(t), 42(t, m, & b), 44(t & b), 51(t inset), 65(mr & br), 66, 89(m inset), 110(m), 112, 114(b), 116(t & b), 128(t), 134(m & b), 136(t), 139(tl inset), 142(t), 144(t), 151(lower ml), 154(m inset & b), 168(b), 206(b), 229(tl), 263(Magnolia Warbler, imm.), 269(bl); Joe Fuhrman 89(t inset); Phil Jeffrey 265(tl); Kevin Karlson 22(t), 23(tl), 31(m & m inset), 40(t & b), 43(t), 79(ml), 83(b inset), 88(b), 94(t), 95(bl), 99(bl), 114(t), 122(b), 128(b), 130(m), 138(t), 142(m & b), 150(t), 152(b), 155(lower mr), 162(b), 185(tr), 205(tr), 213(t inset), 220(t), 222, 224(b), 226(upper m), 239(t), 257(Orange-crowned Warbler, imm.), 259(br), 266(t), 267(tl), 272(t & b), 276(b), 281(bl), 286(b), 287(br), 292, 295(b), 307(bl); Russ Kerr 33(b inset), 36(lower m), 86(t), 94(m), 163(Forster's Tern r inset), 180(t), 183(t inset), 319(bl); Greg Lasley 89(tl), 97(t center), 137(m), 201(tl inset), 229(ml), 291(tl); Peter LaTourrette 124, 129(t inset), 136(b), 280(br); Wayne Lynch 105(br), 187(tr), 188, 189(tr); Garth McElroy 127(br), 163(tl), 200, 201(tl & bl), 233(t), 239(bl), 246(t), 260(b), 315(lower ml & lower mr), 319(ml & mr); Debbie McKenzie 281(br); ©Philip D. Moylan/VIREO 209(ml); Robert Royse 55(tl); William Schmoker 69(tr); ©Robert Shantz/VIREO 172(b); Lloyd Spitalnik 120(t), 144(b), 145(b), 163(tl), 257(Tennessee Warbler, imm.), 258(t & b), 263(Cape May Warbler, female, imm.), 264(b), 271(ml), 293(lower ml), 306; Bob Steele 23(tr), 24(b), 25(upper mr & lower mr, & br), 51(t inset), 68, 74, 95(tr), 102, 120(b), 121(ml & br), 122(t), 131(Stilt Sandpiper juv.), 143(br), 149(t inset), 153(upper ml), 177(br), 181(tl, bl, & br), 212, 226(b), 227(br), 228(b), 241(t inset), 242(t), 247(ml), 252(t), 259(bl), 266(b), 270, 291(ml & bl); Brian Sullivan 38(b), 78(b), 126(b), 228(t), 267(Prairie Warbler, imm.); Brian Wheeler 90(tl), 94(b), 95(br), 96(t & b), 97(tl, ml, bl, & br), 98(t), 99(Red-tailed Hawk × 5 & lower ml), 100, 101(ml, m center, & mr), 325(ml); Christopher Wood 27(tr), 55(ml); Jim Zipp 48(t), 134(t), 179(b), 261(bl).

Abbreviations: t = top, m = middle, b = bottom, l = left, r = right.